Growing Up in Armyville

Studies in Childhood and Family in Canada Series

A broad-ranging series that publishes scholarship from various disciplines, approaches and perspectives relevant to the concepts and relations of childhood and family in Canada. Our interests also include, but are not limited to, inter-disciplinary approaches and theoretical investigations of gender, race, sexuality, geography, language and culture within these categories of experience, historical and contemporary.

Series Editor:
Cynthia Comacchio
History Department
Wilfrid Laurier University

Growing Up in Armyville

Canada's Military Families during the Afghanistan Mission

Deborah Harrison
Patrizia Albanese

WILFRID LAURIER
UNIVERSITY PRESS

Wilfrid Laurier University Press acknowledges the support of the Canada Council for the Arts for our publishing program. We acknowledge the financial support of the Government of Canada through the Canada Book Fund for our publishing activities. This work was supported by the Research Support Fund.

Library and Archives Canada Cataloguing in Publication

Harrison, Deborah, 1949–, author
   Growing up in Armyville : Canada's military families during the Afghanistan mission / Deborah Harrison and Patrizia Albanese.

(Studies in childhood and family in Canada)
Includes bibliographical references and index.
Issued in print and electronic formats.
ISBN 978-1-77112-234-4 (paperback).—ISBN 978-1-77112-257-3 (pdf).—ISBN 978-1-77112-258-0 (epub)

   1. Children of military personnel—Canada. 2. High school students—Canada. 3. Families of military personnel—Canada. 4. Afghan War, 2001– —Social aspects—Canada. I. Albanese, Patrizia, author II. Title. III. Series: Studies in childhood and family in Canada

UB405.C3H37 2016   355.1ʼ20971   C2016-903696-0
                                                 C2016-903697-9

Cover design by Blakeley Words+Pictures. Interior design by Daiva Villa, Chris Rowat design.

This book is printed on FSC® certified paper and is certified Ecologo. It contains post-consumer fibre, is processed chlorine free, and is manufactured using biogas energy.

Printed in Canada

Every reasonable effort has been made to acquire permission for copyright material used in this text, and to acknowledge all such indebtedness accurately. Any errors and omissions called to the publisher's attention will be corrected in future printings.

*This book is dedicated to
Canadian Armed Forces veterans
and to their children.*

Contents

Acknowledgements

This book was long in the making, and it was made possible by many persons' work and goodwill. Our research was funded by the Social Sciences and Humanities Research Council of Canada Standard Research Grants Program (#410-2008-0176), after chance conversations with Kathleen Kufeldt, Karen Davis, and Lissa Paul had put the project into motion. Marilyn Ball, then superintendent of the Armyville School District, and David McTimoney, then acting principal of Armyville High School, agreed to a partnership between the Armyville School District and our team.

Mary Mesheau, a former administrator in the Armyville School District, contributed to the planning of both phases of data collection, gave us feedback on drafts of publications (including this one), and always provided good counsel. Karen Robson designed the survey we administered to Armyville High School students in 2008. Working at a Statistics Canada Regional Data Centre in Toronto together with her research assistant, Chris Sanders (now an assistant professor), Karen analyzed the survey data, ran statistical comparisons to national data, and disseminated some of the survey findings. Christine Newburn-Cook oversaw the data entry of the 1,066 completed surveys. From afar in Alberta, she was a supportive team member until her unexpected sudden death in 2011. Lucie Laliberté introduced Deborah to military family research after Deborah had read about the efforts of the Organization of Spouses of Military Members (OSOMM)— the organization Lucie had co-founded—in the *Globe and Mail*. Deborah and Lucie worked together on three large projects, beginning in 1990. Both Lucie and Rachel Berman contributed immensely to this project's interview phase, including publications. Danielle Kwan-Lafond, herself once a military adolescent, assisted us with our literature and bibliography tasks, did her own analysis of some of the interview data, and was the first author of one of our papers. Riley Veldhuizen carried out the lion's share of our interviews and deserves most of the credit for their superb quality. Peggy Blackwell, of Blackwell Court Reporting, organized and executed our interview transcription flawlessly. Shanyn Small, an Armyville school psychologist, accompanied Deborah to a Service Children's Support Network conference in Oxford, England, in 2012, and made her own presentation; she also helped with some of the writing of this book.

As acting principal of Armyville High School, David McTimoney offered his endorsement in 2007. Between 2008 and 2014, when David was an official member of our team, his contributions to our efforts were extraordinary, and frequently courageous. It was mostly as a result of David's steadfast support that we were able to navigate successfully through our data collection at Armyville High School, our collaboration with Canadian Forces Base Armyville, our wrap-up symposium in 2011, and the implementation of the symposium's policy recommendations.

Jennifer Phillips, our site coordinator, effortlessly managed every piece of what we did. She organized the administration of our survey—including the hiring and training of 47 research assistants—and every logistical aspect of what we carried out next. Jennifer's kitchen, complete with flip chart, was the site of many exuberant planning meetings. Like Danielle, Jennifer had grown up in a military family, and she took ownership of our project with pride.

Marilyn Ball, superintendent of Armyville School District from 2001 to 2010, saw the value of our project from its beginning and lent her support to it until its end, several years after she had retired. We benefited, too, from our associations with Greg Lubimiv, the executive director of the Phoenix Centre for Children and Families in Pembroke, Ontario; Joy O'Neill, founder and chair of the Service Children's Support Network in the UK; and Family Enrichment and Counselling Services of Fredericton.

We owe special thanks to everyone who worked at Armyville High School (or in the district office) while we were carrying out our research: especially Principal Sharon Crabb, Catherine Blaney, Cathy Buck, Carol Clark-Caterini, Ed Griffin, Jean MacIntyre, Gary Nason, and Suzanne Reid. We also appreciate the support we received from personnel at CFB Armyville: Colonel (Ret.) Ken Chadder, Colonel (Ret.) Michael Pearson, and the executive director of the CFB Armyville Military Family Resource Centre, Beth Corey.

Thank you to the people at Wilfrid Laurier University Press, with whom we worked very productively over the last several years: Ryan Chynces, Brian Henderson, Blaire Comachio, Lisa Quinn, Rob Kohlmeier, and Clare Hitchens. We are grateful for the careful copy editing carried out by Margaret Crammond, and for the constructive feedback from the three reviewers who anonymously assessed our manuscript. The publication of this book was assisted by a grant provided by the Office of the Dean of Arts, Ryerson University.

Each of the following individuals helped us in a significant way during our project: Dwight Ball, David Charters, Linn Clark, Claire Corriveau, Angie Deveau, Bryant Eaton, Maureen FitzGerald, Laura Hache, Mary Hill, Ann Koller, Hugh Lautard, Caryn Levine, David Lewis, Tracy McDonald, Marg Malone, Susan McDaniel, Marilyn Merritt-Gray, Doug Miles, Nancy Nason-Clark, Judee Onyskiw, Mike Ornstein, Larry Richardson, Bea Sainz, Heather Sears, Steve Turner, and the late Fred Arensberg.

On a more personal note, Patrizia is grateful for having had Slobodan Drakulic, her late husband, passionate intellectual, partner, and mentor, in her life. She thanks her parents, Cosimo and Rosa, for their ever-present support; Mark Waterhouse for his love, patience, and encouragement; and Pokie for reminding her to take breaks, cuddle, and go for walks. Deborah thanks her friends who made her laugh and constantly asked how the book was "coming," especially Maureen FitzGerald and Frances Harding. Deborah also thanks her husband, Walter Schenkel, who was always present and supportive, and who sacrificed over and over again, to enable her to spend time on this project. Walter always listened, and provided wise feedback.

Most of all, we are indebted to the 1,066 Armyville High School students who filled out our survey, and to the 61 Armyville High School interview participants who changed our world view by sharing their lives with us.

Introduction

It was 2006, and 800 soldiers from the Canadian Armed Forces (CAF) base in "Armyville," Canada, were scheduled to deploy to Kandahar, Afghanistan, early in 2007. More than 40 staff members and over 1,600 students in the Armyville School District (ASD) had a close relative serving in the CAF. In response to feedback from teachers who had warned them that the Afghanistan deployment would be "different," Marilyn, the Superintendent of the ASD, and Ed, the ASD's Learning Specialist for Student Services, began the process of implementing an action plan.

The Afghanistan deployment indeed promised to be different. Larger numbers of students' parents would be participating, and, unlike most previous recent Canadian international military involvements, this deployment's purpose would be combat. There would be a higher likelihood of deaths.

As a cornerstone of their support strategy, the Student Services staff prepared a deployment and information binder, based on the results of international academic research. The contents of the binder tried to answer the question, What impact will the Afghanistan deployment be likely to have on students and staff in the ASD? Marilyn assembled an emergency response team, consisting of the Learning Specialist for Student Services, two school psychologists, plus other Armyville community professionals (such as clergy, retired teachers, and counsellors) who had volunteered to help. This emergency response team worked in partnership with the Deployment Coordinator and a social worker at the CFB (Canadian Forces Base) Armyville Military Family Resource Centre (MFRC). Training sessions on the binder were organized for each of several categories of district employees: guidance counsellors, administrators, the teachers in each school, and district office staff. A portion of the binder was copied and distributed to all military and civilian parents in the ASD.

Around the same time, Marilyn spoke to her counterparts in three other Canadian communities that had been affected by deployments to Afghanistan. None of them were engaged in any similar preparations but, based on her experience, Marilyn's counterpart in another military town provided Marilyn with insight into the impact of an Afghanistan combat death on the members of a military community—especially what to expect from the media. Parents who had recently been relocated to Armyville (by the CAF) from the other town were invited by the ASD to participate in a focus group on this topic.

When the first major incident occurred in Afghanistan involving multiple casualties, the emergency response team was both prepared and able to support the affected principals and the students who attended their schools.

In the meantime, Deborah, this book's first author, had completed two large research projects on CAF spouses (one on spouses' routine unpaid work for the CAF, which had produced the book *No Life Like It* [Harrison & Laliberté, 1994], the other on the CAF's response to spouses whose CAF partners have abused them, which had produced the book *The First Casualty* [Harrison et al., 2002]). Deborah, located at the University of New Brunswick (UNB) in Fredericton, was, along with Lucie Laliberté (a lawyer and the wife of a retired CAF member), ready to shift her attention to CAF adolescents; Deborah and Lucie both realized that research on adolescents could shed light on the intergenerational aspects of the impact of military life stressors (especially deployments) on the civilian members of military families. At the time (2005), no major civilian-driven research had been carried out on children growing up in CAF families.

The Afghanistan mission represented the first occasion since the Boer War that Canadian troops would participate in a counterinsurgency, and the first time since the Korean War that Canadian military members would sustain a significant number of casualties. While by 2012 Canada's intervention in Afghanistan was destined to wind down (even if the impact of injuries and casualties on families would not), the level of international instability has recently escalated, as evidenced by the rise of ISIS (the Islamic State in Iraq and Syria), the continued deployment of Canadian troops and advisors to locations such as Syria and Iraq (Foreign Affairs, Trade and Development Canada, 2014a, 2014b), and the crisis of the Syrian refugees (Ditmars, 2015; Foreign Affairs, Trade and Development Canada, 2015; United Nations High Commissioner for Refugees, 2015). We hear from the media daily about the pros and cons of the deployment of troops to volatile areas. But we hear almost nothing about the impact of dangerous deployments on the members of military families, especially children. As a result, Canadians who are not members of the military community rarely think about how deployments affect members of military families, and they know even less. In our view, Canadians need to learn about the impact of combat deployments on families, so that they can take into account the human costs of military tours when they contemplate lending their support to—or withholding their support from—each new commitment their government proposes to make to an international mission.

Accordingly, Deborah and Lucie brought together a multidisciplinary collaborative team to conduct research on how CAF adolescents were experiencing parental deployments during the post-9/11 Afghanistan era of the beginning of the twenty-first century.

Schools are crucial aspects of military adolescents' lives. They comprise the main way that geographically mobile military youth manage to forge meaningful connections in a community into which they have newly moved. Schools also often assume heightened importance in the lives of youth whose parents are participating in an overseas deployment. It was therefore almost inevitable that Deborah and Lucie's embryonic team would seek to partner with a school board. A colleague introduced Deborah to Mary, a former administrator in the ASD, who was serving as an elementary-school principal during the few years leading up to her retirement. Deborah described the proposed project to Mary over a lunch meeting, and Mary agreed to join the team. Mary in turn introduced Deborah to Marilyn, the then superintendent of the ASD, who agreed to lend ASD's official partnership to the team's work. During the process of preparing them to respond to the Afghanistan mission, Marilyn had become aware that her staff knew too little about what the ASD students were experiencing at home. Marilyn entered the ASD into a partnership with our team because she believed that reliable Canadian research data could lead to an improved, evidence-based ASD response.

Our team's application for Social Sciences and Humanities Research Council funding (2007) met with success. In the spring of 2007, Mary introduced Deborah to David, who was then the young, energetic acting principal of Armyville High School (AHS). David was immediately enthusiastic about the project. His acting principalship ended in the spring of 2008, at which time he became Coordinator of Professional Development in the nearby district office and an official member of our team. In 2010, upon Marilyn's retirement, David became superintendent of the ASD.

Before beginning this project, we knew that military adolescents are profoundly affected by parental deployments. Research literature, produced mainly in the United States, had provided insights into how they are affected—at home, at school, with their friends, and in their extracurricular activities. We knew nothing, however, about the unique ways in which deployments might affect Armyville CAF adolescents; nor did we know how these youth perceived the quality of deployment support that at the time was provided by Armyville High School. This book was written to furnish some answers to these questions, to describe our research process, and to document our partnership with the Armyville School District.

Our partnership with the ASD was an example of collaborative action research (CAR) (Abraham & Purkayastha, 2012; Byers & Harrison, 2004; Small, 1995; Weiner, 2004), a research strategy that is multidisciplinary, collaborative, and action- (and/or policy-) oriented. In a CAR project, the university-based members of the research team collaborate, from the project's beginnings, with the community-based eventual "users" of the research results. The hope of all members of the research team is that the results will exercise impacts on policy and practice. The school-district-affiliated members of our specific team hoped that our research would generate information that could lead to improved school support to students from CAF families who were living through deployments.

All the members of our team were interested in how CAF adolescents have experienced recent deployments, with special emphasis on the Afghanistan mission. Despite this relatively specific focus, the first event of our project was a broad mental health and family functioning quantitative survey, based on the [Canadian] National Longitudinal Survey of Children and Youth (NLSCY), that we administered to all the students at AHS (civilian and CAF alike) during Period One of a school day in October 2008.[1] Some details regarding this survey can be found in chapter 3. Shortly before the survey was administered, David organized a meeting with the CFB Armyville base commander, at which the ASD and CFB Armyville expressed their joint support for the project and their intention to cooperate, post-data-collection, on the policy implications of the results. On the morning of the survey, David met the busload of 47 research assistants at the door of the school, and made sure that each navigated quickly to his/her designated classroom. Several months later, when a few of the survey findings proved to be disturbing, David initiated a productive dialogue among Marilyn, the team, and an AHS guidance counsellor.

After the survey, we conducted interviews on the impact of deployments and other military life stressors on the lives of CAF adolescents. To this end, and as we will describe in chapter 3, Jennifer (our site coordinator) constructed an interview sample of 61 out of the 450 "CAF adolescents" who had volunteered on the day of the survey by filling out information sheets that had been attached to their survey booklets. We conducted most of the interviews during the winter of 2009–2010 at the school, during class time. David found a suitable room in an out-of-the-way location and introduced Jennifer and Deborah to the school librarian, whose territory adjoined this room. During the interview phase, both the librarian and the AHS office staff notified Jennifer ahead of time of any school events that would affect the interview schedule, such as exams, assemblies, photo days, and professional development days.

The project's final major event was a two-day symposium at an Armyville hotel in the spring of 2011, which included most research team members, AHS and ASD representatives, and a representative from CFB Armyville. The purpose of the symposium, which, along with its follow-up, will be described in chapter 7, was to discuss study findings, make policy recommendations to the ASD, and consider strategies for implementation. In consultation with Deborah, David drew up a list of ASD employees who would be invited and issued the invitations. Through David (in his new capacity as superintendent), the ASD made both financial and in-kind contributions. As part of the follow-up to the symposium, David organized two meetings related to the symposium recommendations—one with the new CFB Armyville base commander and one with all the principals in the school district.

In the fall of 2012, Deborah was invited to present some of the team's findings at the national conference of the United Kingdom's Service Children's Support Network (SCSN), at the University of Oxford. The SCSN works with military and civilian educational and social services professionals to provide knowledge-based support to military children and their families. An important part of its mission is educating the relevant civilian professionals about the impact of military life upon children. No equivalent organization to the SCSN exists elsewhere in the world.[2]

The SCSN chair encouraged Deborah to bring along a service provider from the ASD, who would make her own presentation about how the ASD currently supports CAF children and about the improvements in this support that had occurred following our research. Deborah invited Shanyn (a school psychologist and member of the emergency response team described above) to accompany her to England. Shanyn made a presentation to a large audience of school personnel from London and Oxfordshire, which was followed by a lively discussion.

You can see that our school-district-affiliated team members bought in to the research project to an enormous extent and contributed to every phase of its work. Mary introduced Deborah to Marilyn and David; Marilyn agreed to the partnership between the team and the ASD; Shanyn made an international contribution to our dissemination phase; David lent his mentorship and efforts to all stages of the project; and David, Marilyn, Shanyn, and Mary contributed to the writing of this book.

Since the ASD and CFB Armyville have always cooperated closely, the ASD's willingness to enter into a partnership with university researchers was admirable, because the partnership risked straining the district's relationship with the local representatives of a "closed community" that has been historically suspicious of research undertaken and controlled by civilians. As it turned out, CFB Armyville co-operated with both our data collection and the post-symposium follow-up.

As an example of a collaborative action research team, the members of our project worked quite smoothly together, and some of us have wondered, in retrospect, why. The literature on CAR notes that CAR research projects do not typically unfold quickly, uneventfully, or easily. Academic and community partners approach the enterprise with different desires and expectations. Participants on the community side are most interested in the potential policy and action outcomes, and in the beneficial social change that will occur after the research is done. While the academic participants are also interested in these tangible outcomes, it is publications that they mostly focus on. If too few members of the academic side of the team are interested in the social benefits of the project, the partnership may end up floundering. A second difference relates to the process of the research. Academic researchers are willing to put up with a less inherently enjoyable research process than are their community counterparts, because they are paid to devote some of their work hours to research activities, and they have been socialized, to some extent, to believe that the publications will comprise a big enough reward. Community members of a research team, on the other hand, receive no economic benefits from participating in a university-driven research project, and they contribute their time and energy exclusively as volunteers (although unanticipated positive professional spinoffs may accrue to them). They may therefore be less motivated than their academic colleagues to work over a long period under circumstances that can be time consuming and challenging (Byers & Harrison, 2004). CAR literature emphasizes the importance of effective team building and shared decision making, as ways of attempting to make the research process rewarding for everyone involved.

One reason our particular venture worked was that every team member recognized the need for a civilian-driven research project on military adolescents and the Afghanistan mission, and they hoped that important insights, policy changes, and modifications to the ASD school curricula would emerge from its results. The timing of our project was also auspicious. Our survey and interviews took place during some of the CAF's most dangerous deployments to Afghanistan, a period when the CAF's involvement in this mission was prominent in the consciousness of all members of the Canadian public, including the members of our team. For both the above reasons, every team member understood that, if our research were carried out, its results would be useful and would make an important international contribution.

The Afghanistan mission was a uniquely challenging stressor for the civilian members of CAF families. We ask the reader to keep this fact in view as we begin the book with two background chapters. Chapter 1 situates the involvement of the CAF in Afghanistan in the broader context of Canada's international military involvements since World War II. Chapter 2 provides an introduction to the concept of "stressor," and how stressors are part of the lives of Canadian adolescents, including adolescents from CAF families. The chapter also discusses the stressors that are experienced most frequently by the members of CAF families. Chapter 3 introduces readers to the town of Armyville, to the processes we followed when we undertook our research, and to our general findings on the mental well-being of Armyville adolescents. Chapters 4, 5, and 6 zero in on how Armyville CAF adolescents have experienced recent deployments, especially to Afghanistan, throughout the three stages of a typical deployment cycle: pre-deployment (chapter 4), deployment (chapter 5), and post-deployment (chapter 6). Chapter 7 focuses on the action phases of our research project: our two-day symposium with ASD personnel in 2011, the recommendations that emerged from the symposium, and how the recommendations were followed up by the ASD from 2011 until 2015. We hope that these chapters will illuminate some of the essence of CAF adolescents' experiences of deployments during a challenging historical period.

1

Real Changes for Real People: Canadian Military Involvements since the Second World War

Many yearn for a return—indeed in some cases to a virtually exclusive focus—on classical international peacekeeping. Peacekeeping is a wonderful concept. A Canadian invention and frequently necessary. But it covers only a limited portion of the security challenges we face in today's international environment.... United Nations–mandated peace missions increasingly rely on the robust use of force to protect civilians.... That's the reality of our world for the foreseeable future and if Canada wants to contribute to global security, we will have to participate in UN peace enforcement missions, not just traditional peacekeeping.

—Prime Minister Stephen Harper, speech to the
Conference of Defence Associations, 2008.[1]

Classical or traditional peacekeeping may have been "a Canadian invention" and "a wonderful concept," but it is far from what Canada has been doing since 2001. Canadian soldiers' involvement in delivering what Harper referred to as "a robust use of force" in Afghanistan marked a sharp departure from Canada's traditional and idealized role as a middle-power peacekeeper. While changes to the Forces' role began about a decade before this, the Afghanistan mission was longer, more demanding, and more dangerous than what had come before it, resulting in a very different set of experiences for Canadian soldiers and their families.

On top of the more than 40,000 soldiers who fought in Afghanistan—the longest active military engagement in Canadian history (Government of Canada, 2014)—the over 2,000 who were injured in combat, and the 158 who lost their lives, tens of thousands more family members of soldiers and other military personnel were profoundly affected by what happened during that mission. Even without the Afghanistan mission, the military organization had comprised a "greedy institution" that required exclusive and undivided loyalty from members and their families (Coser, 1974; Segal, 1986). The heightened exposure to danger that characterized the Afghanistan mission upped the ante by making significantly more demands. Canadian soldiers and their families were expected to remain committed and consumed, amid enormous changes that were occurring in the nature and danger of the missions they participated in.

Additionally, a report of the Standing Senate Committee on National Security and Defence (Kenny et al., 2008) and a battery of Canadian journalists repeatedly drew attention to what Harper intentionally did *not* include in his speeches and public addresses. According to these sources, the Harper government was attempting to keep the Canadian public unaware of the heightened level of violence that surrounded Canada's involvement in Afghanistan (Akin, 2007; Bell, 2013; Brewster, 2011; Chivers, 2009; Kenny et al., 2008; Manley et al., 2008; TorStar News Service, 2010). The report of the Independent Panel on Canada's Future Role in Afghanistan (Manley et al., 2008, p. 20) blamed both the Liberal and Conservative administrations, stating: "To put things bluntly, governments from the start of Canada's Afghan involvement have failed to communicate with Canadians with balance and candour about the reasons for Canadian involvement, or about the risks, difficulties and expected results of that involvement."

Media outlets, on the other hand, named and blamed the Harper government. For example, CTV News reported that in his first Quebec appearance following the death of two Quebec-based soldiers, then Prime Minister Harper almost completely refrained from commenting on the mission (Akin, 2007). He instead thanked military members for defending our values and way of life, and refused to answer reporters' questions (Akin, 2007).

Other media outlets pointed out that the government's policy of releasing the names of injured soldiers only once a year (on December 31) obscured the intensity of fighting faced by Canadian soldiers, masked the nature of the life-altering injuries, and provided Canadians with "a mental buffer against the numbing realities of war" (TorStar, 2010, para. 4). In 2013, the *National Post* reported on a declassified memo that had been sent to the prime minister by the Privy Council Office during the height of the Afghanistan mission, downplaying statistics that revealed Canadian troops to be suffering significantly higher casualty rates than their allies (Bell, 2013).

More deaths, more injuries, and more invisible wounds, such as post-traumatic stress disorder, with little acknowledgement of the impact of these on soldiers and their families, made the Afghanistan mission an overwhelmingly challenging set of Canadian deployments for those who experienced them.

Canadians knew little about the Afghanistan mission as it was unfolding. They knew even less about how the mission was experienced by the members of military families. This chapter will provide an overview of the shifting nature of Canada's role as a peacekeeper, and will conclude with a discussion of the special challenges faced by the CAF during the Afghanistan mission.

A Brief History of Postwar Canadian Forces Missions

Between the end of World War II and the end of the twentieth century, Canada participated in over 34 United Nations peacekeeping and peace-observing missions (Bouldin, 2003). As a result, it came to see itself and to be seen by others as a peacekeeping nation. Indeed, Canadians constructed a series of beliefs that amounted to "a national consensus, that peacekeeping [is] a special Canadian talent" (Granatstein, 2012, p. 47). These beliefs shaped the Canadian national identity for many years.

Shortly after September 11, 2001, there were only 269 Canadian peacekeepers among the 40,000 in the service of the UN (Janigan, 2003, p. 33); both supporters and critics of Canadian militarism agree that, at the very least, by 2001 Canadian peacekeeping had changed (Pellerin in Janigan, 2003, p. 33). In fact, the CAF were now very much in the business of war (Fremeth, 2010, p. 53; Murray & McCoy, 2010).

An important characteristic of the Canadian military—one that has changed little and is true of all militaries—is its ability, as a greedy institution, to demand loyalty and service at all costs (Coser, 1974; Segal, 1986). *Greedy institutions* have been characterized by Coser (1974) and others (Segal, 1986; Sullivan, 2014; Vuga & Juvan, 2013) as institutions requiring exclusive and undivided loyalty and devotion from their members; and, inevitably, also from the members' families (Segal, 1986; Vuga & Juvan, 2013).

Canada, the Reluctant Peacekeeper

Canada's military involvement in the immediate postwar period was slow and light. Canada was a peace observer in Palestine in 1948. Canada sent a few officers to the UN Military Observer Group in India and Pakistan to oversee the dispute over Kashmir in 1949, and to the UN Truce Supervisory Organization to try to prevent war between Israel and its Arab neighbours in 1953. Canada was also involved in overseeing the conflict in Indochina, starting in 1954.

After observing the peace with the UN through the 1940s and 1950s, Canada's "true peacekeeping" is alleged to have begun in 1956, as part of the Suez crisis (Bouldin, 2003, p. 265). And what a celebrated start it was, as then Prime Minister Lester Pearson won the Nobel Peace Prize for Canada's role. This positive start set the stage for how Canadians would shape their national identity and form their perception of themselves vis-à-vis the rest of world for the following several decades (Abram, 2012). It helped construct a domestic vision of Canada as a custodian of global civility (Härting & Kamboureli, 2009). It also affected how soldiers and their families/partners understood the emerging role of Canadian soldier as peacekeeper (Segal, Segal, & Eyre, 1992).

Following the Suez crisis of 1956, John Diefenbaker's Conservative government, elected in 1957, believed that peacekeeping mattered. Canada became involved in Lebanon in 1958, Congo in 1960, and Cyprus in 1964.[2] The Canadian Secretary of State for External Affairs, Paul Martin (Sr.), won international respect for Canada's efforts in Cyprus, as Canadian soldiers worked to prevent two NATO members, Greece and Turkey, from fracturing the alliance. Despite these promising beginnings, Canada was reluctant to get involved in UN missions, and early postwar governments "lurched from one military controversy to another" (Granatstein, 2012; Kasurak, 2013, p. 75). Challenges were rampant, and organizational restructuring was a common occurrence (Kasurak, 2013).

Unification and Reorganization of the Forces

The CAF in the postwar period were plagued by many challenges. Two problems identified early on were (1) the Forces' fragmented management and control structure and (2) their rising costs of maintenance and organization (Gosselin, 2009). Throughout World War I and II (Kasurak, 2013), but increasingly in the late 1940s and 1950s (Gosselin, 2009), it was recognized that the Forces needed to be reorganized and restructured. In 1964 the Pearson Liberal government tabled a White Paper on Defence that proposed an integrated administrative structure for the CAF under a single Chief of Defence Staff (CDS).[3] Until this point, there had been 11 subordinate service commands.[4] The Minister of National Defence at the time, Paul Hellyer, strongly supported the idea of an integrated structure. The proposed unification would merge the (three) traditional services and introduce a common rank structure and uniform. The government promised that cost savings would free up funds to replace aging equipment.

The act came into effect in February 1968, and more reorganization took place in the decades that followed.[5] In the CAF's view, the Forces languished and operational capabilities diminished; in civilians' view, the promised financial savings never materialized (Gosselin, 2009; Kasurak, 2013). All the while, CAF members on the ground "soldiered on," with the members of their families always, usually invisibly, making their work possible (Enloe, 1983; Harrison & Laliberté, 1994; Wertsch, 1991).

In a classic piece, Segal (1986) analyzed military families as the intersection of two greedy institutions—the military and the family—that demand commitment, loyalty, time, and a great amount of energy. Members of the armed forces and their families struggle with the risk of injury or death, geographic mobility, and family separations, while at the same time the lifestyle significantly constrains the behaviour of spouses and children (Segal, 1986). When they compared the two greedy institutions, Vuga and Juvan (2013) found that the majority of military families accept the concept of loyalty to the military almost as much as service members do. They noted that a high level of family loyalty to the military makes the balancing of work and family demands easier for military members. This is fortunate, because during recent times the demands for loyalty and hard work on the part of soldiers and their families have increased. This process began during the 1970s and 1980s, when, at the height of the Cold War, Canada developed a reputation as a relatively important middle power. And it reached a crescendo during the decades following.

Cold War Middle Power and Multilateralist—At Least for a While
According to Murray and McCoy (2010), the logical interventionist strategy of a middle power is peacekeeping. Peacekeeping is considered to be a logical strategy of middle powers because peacekeeping exempts middle powers from intentions of domination. Middle powers are expected to concern themselves with the right of state sovereignty/independence, the equality of states, national security, and a non-interventionist approach aimed at upholding the principle of coexistence (Murray & McCoy, 2010). Furthermore, while a strong ally with the United States during the Cold War—the "war without battles" (Kasurak, 2013)—Canada nonetheless feared American manifest destiny; it therefore sought to balance the small perceived threat from the United States with the larger perceived threat posed by the Soviet Union. Canada's focus on peacekeeping allowed it to focus on diplomacy, conflict resolution, and the bridging of the East-West divide (Keating 1993, in Murray & McCoy, 2010, p. 174; Murray & McCoy, 2010). As a result, throughout the Cold War Canada's involvement in international organizations and its multilateralist policies came to define what it meant to be Canadian on the international stage (Murray & McCoy, 2010, pp. 174–175). It was generally agreed that Canada did not have the resources to play a more robust military role (Granatstein, 2012; Hartfiel, 2010; Murray & McCoy, 2010).

Regarding military spending, the views of civil authorities are perhaps best encapsulated by Desmond Morton's response to a question put by Defence Minister Douglas Young (1996–1997): "How much is enough?" "As little as possible" (Kasurak, 2013, p. 284).[6]

The multilateral approach inherent in peacekeeping allowed Canadian foreign policy and the CAF to remain limited in scope compared to larger, more powerful states (Murray & McCoy, 2010). Canada also historically relied on its geographic isolation, relatively small population, and coalitions, mainly with Britain and the United States, to keep its military involvements limited. By supporting multilateral agreements and forsaking expansionist goals, Canada would not have to enter into the arms race or rely solely on its own military resources for protection (Murray & McCoy, 2010).

Apart from peacekeeping, Canada's defence planning—connected to its participation in the North Atlantic Treaty Organization (NATO) during the Cold War—was primarily "commitment-based" or "threat-based" (Bland & Maloney, 2004; Hartfiel, 2010; also see Kasurak, 2013). While complex in their own way, NATO-related decisions regarding doctrine and force structure were relatively clear, and were made in relation to perceptions of Soviet doctrine and structure. Western militaries were tailored for a particular kind of war against the Soviet Union, with defence planning being primarily threat-based and involving a fixation on particular enemies (Hartfiel, 2010, p. 327). With the end of the Cold War, this strategy and force structure became obsolete. At the same time, in the early 1990s many NATO member states were hit by economic downturns and responded by slashing defence budgets. Between 1993 and 1999 Canadian defence spending was cut by 30 percent; the acquisition of new equipment was delayed or cancelled; and personnel in the CAF were reduced from 75,000 to 50,000 (Hartfiel, 2010). One of the major strategic assumptions of the 1994 White Paper on Defence was that the CAF would do less with less in the coming years (Department of National Defence Canada, 1994, p. 21). As it turns out, the "doing less" part never happened.

As cuts to Canadian military spending were occurring, an upsurge in intrastate conflicts was resulting from the termination of superpower support to, and control of, various regimes around the world. The rising number of conflicts and the end of a Cold War deadlock on the United Nations Security Council produced a dramatic increase in UN peacekeeping operations throughout the 1990s. Between 1990 and 2002, the number of uniformed personnel deployed on UN peacekeeping missions increased by over 400 percent—from 27,000 deployed to 138,000 (Hartfiel, 2010). Demand on the CAF increased steadily throughout the 1990s, especially as a result of Canada's participation in the 1990 Gulf War, and in missions in Cambodia, Somalia, Rwanda, Bosnia, and Haiti (Hartfiel, 2010). These changes inevitably entailed consequences for individual military members' subjective understanding of what they were doing and why (Battistelli, 1997). They also affected the lives of members' families. The military organization's demands for loyalty were unrelenting as their demands on their members increased.

In the decade following the end of the Cold War, Canada participated in about 70 international missions (Hartfiel, 2010). In contrast, it had participated in about 25 during the previous 40 years (Hartfiel, 2010). The operational tempo throughout the 1990s was estimated to be higher than in any period since the Korean War (Canada, Parliament, Senate, Standing Committee on National Security and Defence 2002a in Hartfiel, 2010, p. 328). The CAF were unable to operate overseas in hostile environments without significant allied support (Hartfiel, 2010, p. 330). And yet, the 1992–1996 Force Reduction Program had seen almost 14,000 members of the CAF leave the Forces. Hartfiel (2010) noted that the legacy of these cuts was visible in the CAF's distorted demographic profile, which showed a shortage of personnel in the middle ranks. A 2006 report from the Office of the Auditor General revealed that, after 1997, CAF members with fewer than eight years of service were numerous; however, the number of members with 9 to 14 years of service was insufficient to replace the members with 15 or more years of service whose retirement dates were looming (Hartfiel, 2010). The strain of this high operational tempo on members of the CAF was inevitable. In 2004, the Chief of Defence Staff declared an operational pause, citing the need to rest, retrain, and refit equipment (Harfiel, 2010, p. 331).

The years between the release of the White Paper on Defence in 1994 and the 2005 Canada International Policy Statement[7] were years of crisis in the Forces (Hartfiel, 2010). The Forces' operational tempo increased significantly, despite the defence budget being cut by a quarter. As Hartfiel (2010, p. 324) noted, defence policy decisions were made "on the fly," and military officers felt that their concerns were not being heard. According to one officer, the CAF found itself "literally living day to day.... The day-to-day challenges were such that nobody thought beyond next week.... We gave up on strategic planning.... We had a failure of strategic leadership" (Hartfiel, 2010, p. 324). An army colonel noted, "We did not have a clear understanding of what we were about, and what we were going to do, and the Forces were ill-prepared," adding that "the failure in Somalia... was... attributable to the fact we did not articulate national interests and specific objectives for the Force" (Hartfiel, 2010, p. 334). Lack of preparedness was a feature of the Canadian military for many years, owing to the Forces' implicit assumption that they would always carry out their work within multilateral coalitions; furthermore, Canadians were rarely politically enthusiastic about supporting lengthy overseas missions (Kasurak, 2013).

Since the Second World War, and especially following the end of the Cold War, Canadian military deployments have changed and struggled under the weight of a transformed international political landscape. Canada played a relatively minor but respected role during World War II (Murray & McCoy, 2010). Following the war, Canada acted as a middle power in international relations by playing a key role as a peacekeeper; more recently, Canada became "a robust practitioner of counterinsurgency" in Afghanistan (Murray & McCoy, 2010, p. 172)—a role that many believe the Forces were unprepared to assume.

From Peacekeeper to Peace Builder: The Changing Nature of Canadian Overseas Deployments

The international political scene has changed dramatically in the 20-plus years since the end of the Cold War. Since then we have seen a rise in intrastate conflict and in the number of non-state actors in those conflicts. Even before September 11, 2001, things had begun to shift. Under the Liberal governments of the 1990s and the early twenty-first century, Canadian foreign policy began to move away from middle-powermanship and toward a new period of "peace building" (Murray & McCoy, 2010, p. 176). On a micro level, this shift has affected how soldiers have seen, understood, and experienced their role within the military (Battistelli, 1997), which has in turn transformed the experiences of their families (Vuga & Juvan, 2013). Significant transitions have occurred in Canadian military practice as a result of the need to adapt to changing forms of warfare and to a changing international political climate.

Many have argued that Canada has supported American imperial objectives since the 1980s and has been pulled closer to the United States through its support of the "War on Terror" (Albo, 2007). The consensus seems to be that in the wake of September 11, 2001, Canada became a security partner to the United States (Murray & McCoy, 2010, p. 177). Albo (2007) notes that while the Chrétien Liberals kept Canada out of the Iraq War, they contributed to making Canada one of the top participants in the US War on Terror. The bilateral Smart Border Declaration and Action Plan (2001) and the tripartite North American Security and Prosperity Partnership (signed March 2005) further integrated Canada into American geopolitical strategies (Albo, 2007).

Research by Middlemiss and Stairs (2002) suggests that the move to integrate the Canadian Armed Forces with those of the United States long preceded September 11, 2001. For example, Colonel Alain Pellerin, executive director of Conference of Defence Associations,[8] was quoted in a 2003 *Maclean's* article as saying, "Saying we are a peacekeeping nation is a rewriting of our history" (Janigan, 2003, p. 33). According to Pellerin, profound changes had begun with Canada's role in the Balkans (1991–2001), where since 1992 tasks performed by the CAF had included complex military operations beyond traditional peacekeeping (Janigan, 2003). Fighting had become an even greater focus following September 11, 2001.

Supporters and critics of Canadian military involvement on a global stage agree that a significant transition has taken place in the way that Canada employs its military. In general, Canada has carried out its "peace building" by becoming a robust practitioner of counterinsurgency (Murray & McCoy, 2010, p. 171). Peace building involves an enhanced conception of interventionism, including a greater use of force to dismantle what our allies define as a failed government. Peace building also commits Canadian troops to missions of indefinite length (Murray & McCoy, 2010, p. 173).

For Canada, a major change came with our involvement in Afghanistan (see Jefferess, 2009). The mission in Afghanistan represented a strong shift away from middle-powermanship—militarism without the expectation of enforcement—toward a new policy of counterinsurgency and "terrorism prevention" (Murray & McCoy, 2010, p. 177). Unlike the missions in Bosnia and Kosovo, military objectives in Afghanistan involved combat-intensive ground operations and counterinsurgency (Murray & McCoy, 2010, p. 172). In the words of an anonymous active senior Canadian military source, the CAF in Afghanistan developed into a "killing machine" (Murray & McCoy, 2010, p. 179). If this is correct, a significant shift would have occurred in military members' understanding of what they were doing and why they were doing it (see Battistelli, 1997). Their families would have been left to struggle under a spectre of heightened risk.

Canada's Afghanistan Missions

In late 2001, the United States launched an invasion of Afghanistan. Not long after, on October 8, 2001, Canada announced that it would contribute air, land, and sea forces to Operation Enduring Freedom (Government of Canada, 2015). Canada's immediate involvement in this "war on terror" officially marked its departure from its traditional peacekeeping role (Jefferess, 2009).

The CAF deployed to Kabul in August 2003, under the mandate of Operation Athena, to take part in the International Security Assistance Force mission. Their official mandate was to maintain security in Kabul and the surrounding areas (Government of Canada, 2015). This second mission to Afghanistan, between 2003 and 2005, shifted the focus from policing Kabul to offensive operations in the hills. Despite this shift, Canada continued to officially represent itself as a peacekeeper (see Chrétien, 2007; Jefferess, 2009).[9] This was exemplified in a 2003 address to Canadian soldiers in Kabul by then Prime Minister Jean Chrétien: "By bringing peace and stability to Kabul and Afghanistan you do much to bring peace and security to the region. And ultimately we all benefit" (as cited in Jefferess, 2009, p. 709).

Between 2003 and 2005, the mission focused on overseeing the 2004 elections and maintaining security around Kabul. Throughout this period, the Canadian mission in Afghanistan resembled a peacekeeping mission; it involved monitoring and enforcing peace, rather than engaging in combat (Murray & McCoy, 2010). Until this point, there were also relatively few casualties. But in 2005 things started to change. As reporter John Geddes (2006, p. 26) noted at the time, "Bill Graham, Martin's defence minister, embarked on what some called a 'pre-body-bag' speaking tour last fall [i.e., fall 2005], trying to brace the public for the inevitable casualties."

In February 2005, General Rick Hillier was named Chief of the Defence Staff, a development that transformed the rhetoric of Canada's role in Afghanistan. Hillier openly declared that the job of Canadian soldiers was "to kill people," and that their primary aim was to protect Canada's national interests (Jefferess, 2009, p. 710). By August 2005, Canada assumed leadership of the Kandahar Provincial Reconstruction Team (KPRT). With 2,500 soldiers, Canada took command of a military mission to secure this rural province, which was the size of Nova Scotia (Government of Canada, 2015). In July 2006, the newly elected Conservative government reaffirmed this commitment by removing Canadian troops from Kabul and deploying a battle group to Kandahar province (Jefferess, 2009). Despite debates, the establishment of an independent panel (resulting in the "Manley Report"—see Government of Canada, 2015), and numerous other reports, in February 2008 the Canadian Parliament voted to extend the combat mission in Kandahar until 2011 (Government of Canada, 2015).

At this point, the Canadian mission entered a new phase. Command of southern Afghanistan changed in July 2006 from Operation Enduring Freedom to a mission under NATO control. In Kandahar, Canada became involved in Operation Archer (Government of Canada, 2015). With this shift, the United States expected increased combat capability from the CAF, despite the latter's endemic limitations in personnel, equipment, and general preparedness to assume this new role. Although the new combat role for Canadian troops materialized in Kandahar in 2006, the extent of the Canadian public's awareness of the nature and scope of this change was unclear. Considerable confusion may have existed in the public mind, given that, as late as 2005, Canadian troops had participated in a traditional peacekeeping mission in Kabul (Boucher, 2010). Canada was at war, yet political leaders appeared to be downplaying the fact that Canadian peacekeepers now saw regular combat and had been given orders to shoot at the enemy (Geddes, 2006; Jefferess, 2009).

What had become obvious to insiders, if not to the rest of Canada, was that the operations in Afghanistan marked the first significant armed conflict involving Canadian troops since the Korean War, and it marked the first time since the Boer War (at the turn of the twentieth century) that Canadian troops had fought in a counterinsurgency. Canadian troops were posted to the most dangerous region of Afghanistan, a decision which resulted in the death of 158 Canadian soldiers and at least 2,071 physical injuries—a figure that does not include operational stress injuries such as post-traumatic stress disorder (Daigle, 2013). Both Liberal and Conservative governments, under the leadership of Jean Chrétien, Paul Martin, and Stephen Harper, supported the operations, and to date, Afghanistan has been the largest recipient of Canadian bilateral aid (Holland and Kirkey, 2010, p. 167). Aside from that, the cost to Canadian taxpayers is believed to have exceeded $11 billion. Millions more will be needed for years to come to assist Afghanistan war veterans and their families as they continue to cope with the physical and emotional aftermath of a fraught and unprecedented combat situation.[10] For the most part, both military and civilian health services have been ill-prepared and plagued with inadequate resources to tackle the new problems (Brown & Hollis, 2013; Daigle, 2013; Sudom, Zamorski, & Garber, 2012).[11] All the while, Canadians have received little information about the plight of Afghanistan veterans and their families.

Despite escalating casualties in Kandahar, members of Harper's cabinet were forbidden to use the word *war*, as politicians downplayed the military losses in public speeches (Stein & Lang, 2007, cited in Boucher, 2010). An analysis of almost 140 official statements by prime ministers, ministers of national defence, and ministers of foreign affairs made between September 2001 and 2009 found that Canadian casualties were acknowledged on only 17 occasions (Boucher, 2010). Relatedly, Canadian governments elected between 2001 and 2011 (led by Jean Chrétien, Paul Martin, and Stephen Harper) downplayed Canada's military actions in Afghanistan (Boucher, 2010). In order to garner public support, the Canadian press followed the US media's lead in casting Afghan women as victims in need of rescuing by our "knights of civilization" (Jiwani, 2009, p. 728).

The downplaying of military actions, and especially of casualties, in Afghanistan was intended to create and maintain public support for the war (Boucher, 2010; Fletcher & Hove, 2012). As Chivers (2009) has noted, public support for a war is always weakened by loss of life. As a result, appropriate media coverage of the conflict, and of the soldiers who waged it, was considered vital to the interests of those who wished to promote the view that Canada was "winning." Boucher's 2010 study initially found that mounting casualties among Canadian troops had little effect on public attitudes toward the mission in Afghanistan (Boucher, 2010; Fletcher & Hove, 2012). When Boucher disaggregated the data by regions of Canada, however, he found that public opinion in Alberta consistently supported the intervention, regardless of casualties; those in Quebec opposed the mission, regardless of casualties; and those in Ontario and the Atlantic provinces withdrew their support for the war as the casualties increased (Boucher, 2010). In their study of the "Highway of Heroes,"[12] Fletcher and Hove (2012, p. 34) learned that images of flag-draped coffins did not always lead to decreased support for war. Their analysis reveals a complex blend of attitudes and responses among Canadians that they attributed to a distinctive combination of sadness and pride, tempered by support for Canada's mythical traditional peacekeeping role (see also Managhan, 2012).

On April 25, 2006, amid the growing movement of people on overpasses along the Highway of Heroes, the Harper government announced a ban on media coverage of the repatriation of dead soldiers in coffins at the Trenton, Ontario, base (Fletcher and Hove, 2012). This ban came immediately following the deaths of four soldiers, killed in a roadside bombing, and three additional casualties the month before. As Chivers (2009) noted in her journal article "Hiding Private Ryan," there is a tactical aspect to refusing to publicize battlefield mortality.[13] The Canadian news media reported that this blackout was permanent policy, and that the government was responding to the fear that the increasing frequency of casualties might weaken public support for the mission in Afghanistan (Akin, 2007; Bell, 2013; Brewster, 2011; Chivers, 2009; Fletcher & Hove, 2012; TorStar News Services, 2010). At first, the prime minister defended the media ban as being respectful of the privacy of the soldiers' families, but not long after the widely publicized funeral of Nichola Goddard, the first female military casualty, in May 2006, he reversed it (Fletcher & Hove, 2012).

Again, under some pressure, but mostly in response to what our allies were doing, in July 2011 Canada officially ended its combat mission in Kandahar province and began a new engagement based in Kabul with a focus on four priorities: (1) investing in Afghan children and youth through development programming in education and health; (2) advancing security, the rule of law, and human rights (through the provision of CAF trainers, support personnel, and Canadian police to help train Afghan National Security Forces); (3) promoting regional diplomacy; and (4) delivering humanitarian assistance (Government of Canada, 2013).

In 2011, Operation Attention, Canada's component of the NATO Training Mission–Afghanistan (NTM-A), was put in place to deliver training and professional development services to the national security forces of Afghanistan, especially the Afghan National Army (ANA) and the Afghan National Police (ANP) (Government of Canada, 2011). In the spring of 2012, then Prime Minister Harper issued a statement confirming that Canada's military mission in Afghanistan "[would] come to a firm and final end once the training mission concluded on March 31, 2014" (Government of Canada, 2013). Canadian soldiers would yet again be expected to shift their understanding of what they were doing and why, and to accept their new role without question, perhaps partly because those whose performance is limited to a single all-encompassing role in a greedy institution become dependent on that role (Coser, 1974; Vuga and Juvan, 2013).

Real Changes for Real People

The CAF were ill-prepared for the operations they carried out in Afghanistan and, as a result, they not only risked members' lives but were mocked by other national armies and allies. For example, in the former Yugoslavia, British officers called Canadian troops the "Can'tbats" rather than their unit names, "Canbat 1" and "Canbat 2" (Granatstein, 2012, p. 50). Changing foreign policy objectives also compromised the effectiveness of the CAF's organizational culture (Murray & McCoy, 2010, p. 172). Hartfiel (2010, p. 334) refers to this to "Canada's commitment-capability gap." More seriously, despite having sustained proportionately fewer casualties than the UK forces, the CAF sustained a large number of casualties in combat and from improvised explosive devices (IEDs) (see tables 1.1 and 1.2).

Between the beginning of 2006 and the beginning of 2010, Canada's military contribution in Kandahar cost the lives of 131 members of forces (see Murray & McCoy, 2010, p. 179; and see tables 1.1 and 1.2 for exact numbers) (Boucher, 2010, p. 237). Indeed, the Afghanistan missions were the deadliest in which Canada has taken part since the Korean War (Boucher, 2010, p. 237). As of January 2011, Canadian deployments to Afghanistan had resulted in 615 battle injuries and 1,244 non-battle injuries among the approximately 30,000 deployed Canadian soldiers (Besemann, 2011). The injuries of 147 of these soldiers had been considered to be debilitating enough to preclude further military service (Besemann, 2011).

Table 1.1 Combat Deaths by Nation By Year

	2006		2007		2008		2009		2010		Total	
	Deployed	Deaths	Deployed	Deaths	Deployed	Deaths	Deployed	Deaths	Deployed	Deaths	Deployed	Deaths
US	51,870	98 0.19%	58,181	117 0.20%	81,013	155 0.19%	13,3247	316 0.25%	326,047	500 0.15%	650,358	1186 0.18%
Can	4,307	36 0.84%	5,568	30 0.54%	6,054	32 0.53%	7,462	32 0.43%	3,571	15 0.42%	26,962	145 0.54%
UK	6,200	39 0.63%	7,700	42 0.55%	8,300	51 0.61%	9,500	108 1.14%	9,500	102 1.07%	41,200	342 0.83%

Note: Adapted from "Temporal changes in combat casualties from Afghanistan by nationality: 2006–2010," by A. J. Schoenfeld, J. H. Nelson, R. Burks, and P. J. Belmont, Jr., 2013, *Military Medicine*, 178(4), p. 391.

Table 1.2 IED Deaths by Nation By Year

	2006		2007		2008		2009		2010		Total	
	Deployed	IED Deaths	Deployed	IED Deaths	Deployed	IED Deaths	Deployed	IED Deaths	Deployed	IED Deaths	Deployed	IED Deaths
US	Same	30	Same	33	Same	83	Same	144	Same	262	Same	552
Can	Same	17	Same	23	Same	19	Same	27	Same	14	Same	100
UK	Same	3	Same	13	Same	34	Same	76	Same	56	Same	182

Note: Adapted from "Temporal changes in combat casualties from Afghanistan by nationality: 2006–2010," by A. J. Schoenfeld, J. H. Nelson, R. Burks, and P. J. Belmont, Jr., 2013, *Military Medicine*, 178(4), p. 391.

CAF injury statistics are difficult to determine with accuracy because the Department of National Defence does not release the names of wounded members or the nature of their wounds unless directly asked about a particular member (Chivers, 2009). However, the inevitable increase in acquired disability[14] has been due to Canada's increasingly violent role in the conflict (Chivers, 2009). Additionally, while instances of PTSD increased with each Afghanistan deployment, Canadian press attention to the injury was "remarkably sparse" (Chivers, 2009, p. 336).

Although no one can predict the future with certainty, Canada's role in international conflicts has changed over the past five decades. At the same time, the demands on soldiers and their families have remained high and largely invisible. It is likely that Canada's new combat role has escaped the notice of most Canadians (Chivers, 2009, p. 322). The public invisibility of what Canadian military families have sacrificed has been surpassed only by the paucity of physical and mental health services that have been available to assist them (Daigle, 2013).

We will end this chapter by returning to the "greedy institutions" metaphor. Vuga and Juvan (2013) have noted that some families provide loyalty to the greedy military institution almost as willingly as service members themselves. Other families struggle under what they consider to be the unbearable weight of the demands placed upon them by the military lifestyle (Daigle, 2013). Families' support for the military way of life plays a crucial role in the performance and effectiveness of military members, their units, and the whole military organization. How does this process unfold, and what does it cost the family members who are part of it? One important piece of the answer to this question is the story of how military adolescents experience dangerous parental deployments. It is to this story that we will shortly turn.

2

Growing Up in a Military Family

At first sight, military families strongly resemble other families: their members care for one another, support each other economically, and raise children. However, they do so under circumstances that are different from those that affect most other families (Crum-Cianflone, Fairbank, Marmar, & Schlenger, 2014). While virtually every Canadian family[1] experiences a range of *stressors* that affect the everyday lives of its members, military families experience more stressors than their share.

A *stressor* has recently been defined as "a condition of threat, challenge, demand, or structural constraint that, by the . . . fact of [its] occurrence or existence, call[s] into question the operating integrity of the organism" (Wheaton & Montazer, 2010, p. 173). The most common family stressors include financial stress related to high cost of living and un(der)employment/economic precariousness, low socioeconomic status, disrupted family structure, cumulative major life events, and interpersonal conflict (Cassidy, Lawrence, Vierbuchen, & Konold, 2013; Chappel, Suldo, & Ogg, 2014; Emmen et al., 2013).

Family researchers have made a distinction between normative and non-normative life transitions that is relevant to the concept of stressor. Normative life transitions occur as family members transition from one stage of life into another. These transitions include the moves that children make from elementary school to high school. For the most part, normative life transitions have limited negative long-term effects on the individuals and families living through them. In contrast, non-normative life transitions comprise unexpected major life events, such as job loss, death, divorce, and interpersonal conflict (Chappel et al., 2014). The duration of a transition is a significant aspect of the extent to which it is experienced as a stressor, and of the seriousness of the stressor it represents. A job loss result-ing in a subsequent move to a new home or community, involving a change in school for the children, is typically identified as an acute stressor, but a transition to a condition of poverty is considered to be a chronic stressor.

What may be a normative transition for other families, like moving to a new neighbourhood and changing schools, is non-normative for military families, because military moves happen frequently, and for the most part are outside of the families' control. With the frequent relocations that are connected to the military member's postings (more on this below), mili-tary families face the additional challenges of spousal un(and/or under) employment; living in temporary or impermanent housing; lacking con-tinuity of child care, health care, and education; separation from extended family; and the family instability that accompanies the frequent long sepa-rations related to training and deployments (Black, 1993; Daigle, 2013; Dur-sun & Sudom, 2009; Park, 2011; Snyder, 2013; Sudom, 2010). Deployments also constitute major acute life stressors for military family members.

Following a general discussion of adolescent stressors, this chapter will introduce common stressors that affect adolescents who grow up in mili-tary families. It will also discuss Military Family Resource Centres and schools as potential sources of extrafamilial support.

Stressors in the Lives of Adolescents
Adolescence has long been recognized as a period of change, stress, and turmoil (see Hall, 1904). The major stressors experienced by adolescents are related to self-image, physical changes, peer and family conflicts, academic challenges, school transitions, and establishing and maintaining romantic relationships (Seiffge-Krenke, 2004).

Eighty-four percent of the stressors affecting youth are challenges that involve social relationships with parents, teachers, peers, and romantic partners (Seiffge-Krenke, 2004). Young people develop varied mechanisms for coping with these stressors. For example, they turn to others, especially their peers, for support (Werner & Smith, 1992). Friendship networks have also been found to affect health-related behaviors, including participation in sports, engaging in various forms of exercise, and the consumption of fast food—all affecting body weight, self-esteem, and psychological well-being (Ali, Amialchuk, & Heiland, 2011; Fitzgerald, Fitzgerald, & Aherne, 2012; Kenny, Gallagher, Alvarez-Salvat, & Silsby, 2002).

Relative to boys, girls use higher levels of support-seeking coping (Gay-lord-Harden, Taylor, Campbell, Kesselring, & Grant, 2009); girls also use avoidant coping (i.e., they attempt to avoid dealing with their stressors) (Sanchez, Lambert, & Colley-Stickland, 2013; Seiffge-Krenke, 2004). In contrast, boys tend to use distraction coping: diverting their attention away from a stressor and towards thoughts or behaviours that are unrelated to it, and/or externalizing (Gaylord-Harden et al., 2009; Sanchez et al., 2013; Seiffge-Krenke, 2004). Externalizing symptoms include aggression and rule breaking, as opposed to internalizing symptoms, which include depression, anxiety, loneliness, and withdrawal (Card et al., 2011). Interestingly, one study of male youth living in a low-income urban neighbourhood found that, because they were socialized differently, some African American boys used avoidance coping strategies instead of externalizing strategies; these boys, who were perceived to be passive and vulnerable, were sometimes victimized by their peers (Sanchez et al., 2013).

Adolescents who agree to undergo treatment for their problems often benefit from it (Seiffge-Krenke, 2004). That said, many young people dealing with stressors are reluctant to seek professional help. Among possible forms of support, peer-support group counselling has been found to be economical and effective (Seiffge-Krenke, 2004). The peer-support approach encourages adolescents to assume an active role in dealing with their problems. The egalitarian structure of communication that is characteristic of peer support also enables adolescents to feel at ease (Seiffge-Krenke, 2004, p. 379).

Family relocations, for both positive (e.g., job promotions) and negative reasons (e.g., job losses or marital dissolution), happen frequently. Census data reveal that over 40 percent of the Canadian population changes residence within a five-year period (Allen, 2008). Early researchers found that mobile employees and their spouses tended to be more satisfied with their lives, families, and marriages than were stable employees and their spouses; however, moving, even for job promotion, often created problems for children and adolescents (Brett, 1982). When it occurs, family relocation turns out to be a significant stressor in the lives of the affected children and adolescents.

Research has been carried out on the timing and number of children's and adolescents' school transitions. Crockett, Petersen, Graber, Schulenberg, and Ebata (1989) compared three groups of adolescents: those making a single school transition before Grade 6, those making a single transition prior to Grade 7, and those making double transitions before Grades 6 and 7. Those who had experienced both early and repeat transitions scored lower, both on course grades and self-image. Gender differences were found to be small; however, the differences that emerged pointed to girls struggling more than boys (Crockett et al., 1989). Similarly, Simpson and Fowler (1994) found that children who moved three or more times were 2.3 times more likely to experience emotional/behavioural problems, 2.2 times more likely to receive psychological help, 1.7 times more likely to repeat a grade, and

1.9 times more likely to be suspended or expelled from school, compared with children who had never moved.[2] Dobson, Henthorne, and Lynas (2000) and Leckie (2008) found a similar negative association between mobility and school attainment in the United Kingdom.

More recent research is mixed. After they had carried out a meta-analysis of 22 published research studies, Jelleyman and Spencer (2008) summarized that the following personal and social problems are typically associated with residential mobility: behavioural and emotional problems among young people, teen pregnancy, adolescent depression, and reduced continuity of health-care use. In contrast, Hango (2006) found that while family relocations have short-term negative effects on children (e.g., poorer school outcomes and loss of social relationships), many family moves improve the child's neighbourhood and family environment. It is possible, then, that, over the long term, residential mobility has a beneficial impact on school attainment.

What about peer friendships? Relocation to a new community in early adolescence has been found to produce a period of diminished access to close friends (Vernberg, Greenhoot, & Biggs, 2006). However, according to the same researchers, most relocating adolescents have as many friends as their residentially stable peers by the end of their first school year at the new place (Vernberg et al., 2006). These mixed results show that the impact of family relocations is hard to assess.

Stressors originating from outside the home impact upon individual family members in unique ways (Repetti, Wang, & Saxbe, 2009). In general, factors that cause stress within families also lead to adverse outcomes in young people (Chappel et al., 2014). Additionally, stressors and families' ability to cope with them may have a lasting effect on the children in these families (Chappel et al., 2014; Lytle et al., 2011; Valdez, Chavez, & Woulfe, 2013; Watkins, Pittman, & Walsh, 2013). Children's and youth's individual perceptions of the stressors also contribute to the stressors' impacts (Chappel et al., 2014).

All adolescents face both normative and non-normative stressors as they transition into adulthood. Their peers, through their presence or absence, are a source of both stress and social support, depending on the circumstances. Things get complicated for young people when they lose social ties as a result of family relocations. At the same time, many young people are resilient, especially when supported by their peers, schools, and families.

Stressors in the Lives of Military Families

Sixty-eight percent of Canadian Regular Forces members and 37 percent of Canadian Reserve Force members are married (Department of National Defence, as cited in Vanier Institute of the Family, 2012). As a result, most

Regular Forces members live in nuclear families that numbered 57,352 in 2012. The same year, over 64,200 Canadian children under the age of 18 had a parent in the military (Department of National Defence, as cited in Vanier Institute of the Family, 2012).

A recent Canadian military ombudsman's report noted that three key stressors shape the lives of military members and their families: geographic relocations, frequent separations due to training and deployments, and living under a blanket of risk (Daigle, 2013; also see Sudom, 2010). The blanket of risk that Daigle refers to is closely connected to the notion of unlimited liability: the fact that military members lack the right to workplace safety that is enjoyed by many civilians in Western nations. Unlike other workers, military members do not have the right to refuse to do something that would put their lives at risk. Instead, they are contractually obliged to embrace risk as part of their job to further the objectives of a mission (Coleman, 2013). As many have noted, this places significant stress on families, especially when members are in training or on a deployment (Basham, 2009; Huebner, Mancini, Wilcox, Grass, & Grass, 2007; Mmari, Bradshaw, & Sudhinaraset, 2010; Park, 2011; Sudom, 2010; Williams, 2013).

Geographical Mobility and Relocations
The geographic relocations experienced by CAF families occur at the discretion of, and reflecting the operational needs of, the CAF. For the most part, the Forces decide when, where, and for what length of time families will move, leaving little control in the hands of families (Daigle, 2013).[3] According to a recent CAF study, 76 percent of Canadian military spouses have relocated at least once due to their partner's military posting (Sudom, 2010).

CAF families relocate three times more frequently than civilian families (Daigle, 2013). Most families live on or near a military base located in one of 30 communities across nine provinces and territories (CFB Summerside in PEI was closed in 1989). A significant minority of these families deal with the Canadian Forces Housing Agency (CFHA), which manages military housing on behalf of the Department of National Defence (DND). The CFHA is responsible for the allocation and maintenance of approximately 12,500 homes (Permanent Married Quarters or PMQs) in those 30 locations across the country. Since most of the PMQs were built between 1945 and 1960, the present quality of this housing is very poor.[4] As a result, about 80 percent of CAF families currently live off base in civilian communities, encouraged by the CAF to purchase their homes (Canadian Forces Military Family Services, 2013). However, since families have little control over the timing of their relocations, some find themselves purchasing homes in locations and at times when housing prices are high, and selling homes when the market is low.

To assist with this financial challenge, the Department of National Defence introduced the Home Equity Assistance Program, which provides financial assistance to CAF families who are selling their principal residence. In principle, families who incur a loss when selling are entitled to be reimbursed for up to 80 percent of the difference between the original purchase price and the sale price, to a maximum of $15,000. Unfortunately, families who try to access the assistance frequently find stringent conditions that make them ineligible for the support (Daigle, 2013).

Economic stressors are common in CAF families.[5] While relocations often provide career advancement opportunities for the military member, his or her non-serving spouse typically fails to find and sustain adequate employment (Daigle, 2013; Dunn, Urban, & Wang, 2011; Dursun & Sudom, 2009; Urban, Wang, & Dunn, 2011). In 2009, as noted by Dursun and Sudom (2009), only 46 percent of military spouses were employed full-time (see also Ambert, 2011; Daigle, 2013; Urban et al., 2011).

Using data from the 2006 long-form census, Dunn et al. (2011) analyzed employment incomes of female CAF spouses, compared to female spouses of federal and provincial police personnel, federal public servants, and other civilians. They found that CAF spouses had lower average employment incomes than spouses of federal and provincial police personnel, federal public servants, and other civilians.[6] Spouses of non-commissioned members had lower average employment incomes than spouses of officers (Dunn et al., 2011). Spouses with professional training and experience were especially challenged. The smaller communities in which many military bases are located offer few professional opportunities. Spouses with professional accreditations, who lose these accreditations as a result of moves, never recover from these losses economically—or psychologically (Daigle, 2013).

The relentless upheaval of military life is a disruptive force in military families that affects many aspects of daily life, including sustained access to family health-care services. CAF families have access to and are dependent on the same provincial health-care services as other Canadians (no special health-care provisions exist for them), yet often have needs that are unique to themselves, such as needing access to mental health services that can support them through the stresses of military life.

Like many other Canadians, the civilian members of military families struggle to find family doctors, especially in underserviced rural areas. Owing to their frequent relocations, they experience the additional challenge of maintaining continuity of care. They often find themselves on waiting lists, waiting for their medical files to be transferred, and/or using walk-in clinics or emergency rooms, instead of benefiting from an ongoing relationship with a health practitioner. Some travel back to the location of a previous posting, often across provincial borders, to consult former physicians for chronic physical or mental health conditions (Daigle, 2013). Military families with a child with autism spectrum disorder (ASD) are especially stressed, due to challenges associated with both the military life-style and having a child with special needs (Davis & Finke, 2015; Farrell, Bowen, & Swick, 2014; Lewis-Fleming, 2014).

Military family relocations are accompanied by physical separations from extended families and other support networks, resulting in increased isolation (Basham, 2009; Black, 1993). As a result, military families often rely on other military families for support (Daigle, 2013).

Spouses who find employment require child care if they have young children. However, young CAF families continually find themselves being placed at the bottom of waiting lists for child care as they move in and out of diverse communities. Some bases have Military Family Resource Centres (MFRCs) that offer a range of services including child care, casual care, and drop-in services, with flexible hours to accommodate the chang-ing care needs of military families with young children. However, spaces are limited and/or not available at all MFRCs across the country, and MFRCs are not resourced to provide child care to military spouses who work full-time (Daigle, 2013).

Parents with school-aged children face other challenges. For example, due to provincial variations in the age of entry into kindergarten, some military children are set back (or forward) a year compared to their civil-ian peers because of their interprovincial moves (Daigle, 2013). Being pushed forward or held back for these kinds of reasons has been shown to have negative effects on self-esteem, adaptation, and behaviour (Aronson & Perkins 2013; Astor, De Pedro, Gilreath, Esqueda, & Benbenishty, 2013; Daigle, 2013; Williams, 2013). With each move, children also experience significant losses in their social networks. For adolescents, creating new social networks can be especially daunting. Focus groups with adolescents growing up in military families in the United States found that the most stressful aspect of moving was having to leave behind their friends and develop new relationships at each new location (Mmari et al., 2010).

It is common knowledge among military families and service provid-ers that children who were high achievers and well behaved in one loca-tion can become the opposite in the next one. Many military families are consequently worried about the long-term impact of military life on their children (Daigle, 2013). As a dissenting voice, one US study found that parental perceptions of the relocations' impact on their children's school performance became more positive over time; the parents also believed that their children experienced fewer behavioural problems as the number of relocations they experienced grew (Weber & Weber, 2005). This result suggests that adolescents growing up in military families may grow accustomed to the moves and develop coping strategies that create resilience.

Frequent Separations
A second life condition shared by most CAF families is frequent separations, because most serving members of the Forces are called upon to be away from their families for long periods (up to 15 months at a time) for training and/or deployments (Ambert, 2011; Daigle, 2013). As is the case with relocations, military families have little say in when, where, how often, and for how long the member will be away (Daigle, 2013). The parent who remains at home, as well as some of the children, are then expected to take on the family roles and duties that are usually performed by the military member (Basham, 2009; Harrison & Laliberté, 1994; Kwan-Lafond, Harrison, & Albanese, 2011).

In the not-so-distant past, most military families were composed of a military father and a stay-at-home mother. Today, 13 percent of military spouses are male (DND, as cited in Vanier Institute of the Family, 2012); although not enumerated, some of those—a small proportion—are likely to be in same-sex unions; some female spouses are in same-sex unions with a female military member; and women comprise about 12 percent of the Regular Forces in the CAF (Basham, 2009; Gouliquer & Poulin, 2005; Poulin & Gouliquer, 2012; Poulin, Gouliquer, & Moore, 2009; Snyder, 2013).[7] In some couples, whether heterosexual or same-sex, both partners are members of the military (for more on dual-military marriages, see Lietz, Stromwall, & Carlson, 2013; Taber, 2013). About 20 percent of Regular Forces members are married to another Regular Force member, while 80 percent of Regular Force members are married to civilians (Sudom, 2010). Hence, military families are more diverse today than they were 30 years ago; however, a woman is still much more likely than a man to be the parent who remains at home while her military partner is away in training or combat.

Many separations occur as part of a military member's regular training. And while these separations are usually less dangerous than deployments, they often involve little advance warning or predictability (Daigle, 2013). Actual deployments almost always augment the duration of the separation; more significantly, the heightened risk that accompanies them adds stress to family members' lives (Basham, 2009; Daigle, 2013).

Living under a Blanket of Risk

CAF families live under considerable risk, given the type of training military members undergo, the combat operations they engage in, the types of environments that they are assigned to, and the working condition of unlimited liability (Basham, 2009; Daigle, 2013). Families often fear the injury, illness, or death of their loved one.

As noted in the previous chapter, the level of risk associated with deployments has been greatly elevated during the last 20 years. CAF families have therefore been at increased risk of experiencing the anxiety and stress that accompany dangerous deployments (Basham, 2009; Dursun & Sudom, 2009). Combat injuries during deployments are common, and they significantly affect the lives of family members—straining interpersonal relationships, disrupting day-to-day activities, undermining parenting functions that support children's well-being, and disconnecting families from military resources (Cozza, Holmes, & Ost, 2013).

Deployments

Seventy percent of Canadian military spouses have experienced the deployment of their military partners at least once, and 17 percent have experienced deployment more than five times within their union (Sudom, 2010). Away-from-home military assignments occur for reasons related to peacekeeping, aid-to-the-civil-power operations (e.g., after floods and other natural disasters), training courses, exercises, peace building, and combat (cf. Harrison & Laliberté, 1994, p. 49). As we will discuss in chapter 4, a deployment involves a cycle of events with distinct features, sets of experiences, and effects in each of at least three periods: pre-deployment, deployment, and post-deployment (Gewirtz, Polusny, Erber, & Forgatch, 2011; Johnson & Ling, 2013; Lester & Flake, 2013; Swenson & Wolff, 2011). Daigle (2013) notes that a six- or nine-month deployment commonly turns into a year- or year-and-a-half-long commitment and set of experiences for all involved (also see Johnson & Ling, 2013). An overseas deployment typically involves an intensive training period beforehand, which takes place at a distant location away from families. But the worrying and adjustments begin from the moment that the family is informed of the deployment (De Burgh, White, Fear, & Iversen, 2011; Gewirtz et al., 2011).

Research on parenting and temporary parental absence suggests that mothers' resources, relationships, health, and day-to-day challenges influence how children cope with and adjust to their parents' absences (Andres & Moelker, 2011; Gabany & Shellenbarger, 2010; Lara-Cinisomo et al., 2012). Research on deployments and parent-child relationships that was carried out in the 1990s focused on how mothers' parenting effectiveness during fathers' deployments was undermined by their own stress (e.g., Kelley, 1994; Medway, Davis, Cafferty, Chappell, & O'Hearn, 1995). Stress levels have only intensified since then, as the nature and risk level of deployments connected to the post-9/11 period of the "War on Terror" have been augmented (Dursun & Sudom, 2009). Stress levels of female spouses of deployed members appear to increase after initial deployments, but then decrease after about two deployments—suggesting an element of resiliency that builds up as spouses acclimate to a deployment lifestyle (Van Winkle & Lipari, 2015). The same researchers found that stress levels increase again after several deployments—a result that suggests limitations to resiliency over time (Van Winkle & Lipari, 2015).

The new forms of electronic communication—such as real-time video calls, which are now available to families while a spouse or parent is deployed (Daigle, 2013; Paley, Lester, & Mogil, 2013)—have simultaneously alleviated and intensified family anxiety. The advantage of this technology is that deployed members, their spouses, and their children can see each other and communicate regularly. The disadvantage is that these new technologies enable family members to visualize the deployment risks more vividly, sometimes at the exact moment that they are occurring. For better or worse, the new technologies also keep deployed military members closer to the day-to-day preoccupations of home, including being more in tune with the negative impact of their absence on the family—for example, a child's poor performance at school (Daigle, 2013).

Adolescents who have experienced a large number of family deployments over the past 10 years and have moved frequently have been found to be more likely to have been victimized by their peers and/or to have carried weapons (Gilreath, Astor, Cederbaum, Atuel, & Benbenishty, 2013). A recent California survey found that adolescents who had experienced a higher number of parental deployments were more likely to be using substances (alcohol, tobacco, and marijuana) (Gilreath, Cederbaum, et al., 2013).[8] According to another recent study, more depressive symptoms, lower academic performance, and lower persistence were experienced by youth who belonged to military families that reported higher levels of cumulative risk (an accumulation of stressors related to having a family member in active military duty). However, youth in the same study who reported high levels of family support and the presence of informal networks were less depressed and performed better academically than their peers from families that had experienced the same level of cumulative risk (Lucier-Greer, Arnold, Mancini, Ford & Bryant, 2015).

The impact of parental deployment on adolescents is unique for several reasons. First, coping with a deployment complicates an adolescent's urgent growing-up task of developing a sense of his/her own identity (Fitzsimons & Krause-Parello, 2009; Mmari, Roche, Sudhinaraset, & Blum, 2009). Second, adolescents are frequently required to become caregivers for younger siblings and/or undeployed parents during a deployment, and to have their own needs to be cared for put on the back burner (Mmari et al., 2009). Third, unlike their younger siblings, adolescents possess the ability to empathize with other family members' perspectives on a deployment and to anticipate future developments during the mission as they will potentially unfold (Mmari et al., 2009). Finally, adolescents are more exposed to the news media than their younger siblings, and more adept at understanding the messages that the media communicate (Mmari et al., 2009).

PARENTAL UNAVAILABILITY AND PARENTIFICATION DURING DEPLOYMENTS

Given that deployment—and then reintegration—involves an array of family stressors, including separation, transitions, role changes, relationship challenges, and mental health difficulties, deployments often have a detrimental impact on parent–child relationships (Andres & Moelker, 2011; Gewirtz et al., 2011). One frequent by-product of the stress experienced by the parent remaining at home during a deployment has been labelled *parental emotional unavailability* (Hooper, 2007; Lum & Phares, 2005; Maccoby, 1992). Steinberg and Davila (2008, p. 352) have characterized parental emotional availability as "parents who demonstrate warmth, consistency, understanding, support, and positive communication and conflict styles with their child and their partner." Conversely, Hooper (2007) has defined parental emotional neglect as "[the failure] to provide the necessary attention to the child's need for affection and emotional support... [and] to provide needed psychological care, and [an inability] to foster an appropriate attachment relationship and environment for the child to develop." Research on the impact of parental unavailability on adolescent children suggests that adolescents whose parents are unresponsive, neglectful, coercive, harsh, or inconsistent may have trouble dealing with negative life events and stressors, and thus be more vulnerable to depression (Avison, 1999; Verdeli et al., 2011). When a parent becomes unable to focus on the child's experience due to his/her own (i.e., the parent's) reactivity to stressful situations, the child may become overwhelmed by the parent's emotions (Saltzman, Pynoos, Lester, Layne, & Beardslee, 2013).

Parental emotional unavailability is frequently accompanied in families by the *parentification* of older children and adolescents (Hooper, 2007). Parentification can be defined as a family interactional pattern in which children or adolescents are assigned roles and responsibilities that are typically considered the responsibility of adults but which parents have relinquished

(Barnett & Parker, 1998; Broszormenyi-Nagy & Spark, 1973; Hooper, Moore, & Smith, 2014). Parentified children are often expected to fulfill caretaking roles, which include the care of siblings and providing comfort, advice, or protection to family members (Earley & Cushway, 2002).

Some researchers have distinguished among different types of parentification: for example, using the term *instrumental parentification* to refer to children taking on an unreasonable number of instrumental tasks, such as household chores and food preparation; and *emotional parentification* to refer to children catering to the emotional needs of a parent or siblings, and/or acting as the family peacemakers. The work undertaken by parentified children can be seen as an attempt on their part to restore equilibrium to a family that has been partly or wholly destabilized by a situation of parental unavailability (Hooper, 2007).

Parentification has, at times, been contrasted with the notion of children as *young carers*—a seemingly less problematic outcome of parental unavailability (Charles, Stainton, & Marshall, 2008). As one commentator has put it, "While it is true that all parentified children are young carers of a sort, not all young carers are parentified" (Charles, Stainton, & Marshall, 2012, p. 8). When true parentification is present, the parent-to-child support that would be expected in a healthy parent-child relationship is absent. The distinction seems to be a matter of degree, as a young carer is defined as anyone under the age of 18 who—beyond what would be normally culturally expected—is a primary caregiver in the family due to parental illness, disability, or addiction (Charles et al., 2012).

Parentification has already been observed as occurring during parental deployments (Daigle, 2013; Harrison & Albanese, 2012; West, Mercer, & Altheimer, 1993). Parentification sometimes has desirable outcomes, such as youth becoming more resourceful (Ungar, Theron, & Didkowsky, 2011); parentification also has adverse effects, including emotional distress, problem behaviour, and interpersonal struggles (Earley & Cushway, 2002). We will explore parentification further in chapters 5 and 6.

POST-DEPLOYMENT

Despite feelings of elation for all involved when the military member is home from a deployment, the reintegration process is a struggle for most families (Daigle, 2013; Dekel & Monson, 2010; Lester & Flake, 2013; Mmari et al., 2010; Pittman, Kerpelman, & McFadyen, 2004). During the post-deployment period of the deployment cycle, military members must reintegrate into homes whose internal rhythms have changed, and where both children and spouses have taken on new roles (Lester & Flake, 2013; Mmari et al., 2010; Theiss & Knobloch, 2014).

It takes families between one month and over a year to return to their pre-deployment rhythm; some military members' relationships with children and spouses are never completely restored (Daigle, 2013). By the time an equilibrium is reached—if it is reached—it is not uncommon for the military member to get news that (s)he is being redeployed. As we will explore in chapter 6, some members' ability to meet the demands of partnership and parenting can be permanently compromised as a result of physical and emotional injuries sustained in combat.

Operational Stress Injuries and Post-traumatic Stress Disorder

One result of the recent heightened operational tempo in the CAF is *operational stress*. Operational stress is "intense and unrelenting stress experienced in a theatre of operations or on exercises, common to all participants" that results from long separation from family and friends, long hours and heightened work pace, adjustment to living in a different community setting, change in culture, climate, diet, and so on (Kohler, 2012, p. 6; Veterans Affairs Canada, 2015). An operational stress injury (OSI) can be defined as "any persistent psychological and biological difficulty that can be attributed to functions carried out by a Canadian Forces member as part of an operation" (Kohler, 2012, p. 8; Veterans Affairs Canada, 2015). The term OSI is now used in the CAF to describe a range of disorders that result in a diminished ability to cope—one of the more commonly known and possibly most debilitating of these is post-traumatic stress disorder (PTSD).

PTSD is a psychological injury frequently sustained in combat. Military-related post-traumatic stress disorder is caused by trauma suffered as a result of a war experience (Dekel, 2007). A diagnosis of PTSD is appropriate, according to the American Psychiatric Association's *Diagnostic and Statistical Manual of Mental Disorders* (2000), if two conditions have been met: (1) experiencing or witnessing an actual or threatened death or serious injury; and (2) responding to this trauma with intense fear, helplessness, or horror (cited in Gifford, Hutchinson, & Gibson, 2011).

A difficulty accompanying PTSD that greatly affects CAF members and the members of their families is the severe stigma attached to reporting mental health problems within military (especially army) cultures, and the social isolation that this situation creates (Baker & Norris, 2011; Chapin, 2011; Harrison, Albanese, & Berman, 2014). In the CAF ombudsman's first report on the topic (*Systemic Treatment of CF Members with PTSD*), military members with PTSD were described as "stigmatized, ostracized, and shunned by their peers and the chain of command" as a result of being labelled as "fakers" (Marin, 2001, pp. vi–vii). In an effort to change the culture in the CAF surrounding PTSD, this report recommended that regular and mandatory training about PTSD be organized for every CAF member and unit. A follow-up report by the ombudsman's office in late 2002 noted that this recommendation had not been implemented (Marin, 2002). The 2003 ombudsman's report, *Off the Rails: Crazy Train Float Mocks Operational Stress Injury Sufferers*, again noted "the gap between the commitment of senior leadership and the lack of progress at the unit level in changing the culture and stigma associated with operational stress injuries (OSIs) [including PTSD]" (Marin, 2003, p. 1). The ombudsman's 2008 follow-up report, *A Long Road to Recovery*, similarly made reference to the "persistently negative" attitudes of the peers and superiors of members suffering from PTSD and other OSIs (Daigle, 2012, p. 8). Finally, the ombudsman's 2012 follow-up report, *Fortitude Under Fatigue*, noted that, while the organizational climate had improved for PTSD sufferers, the latter continued to be "denigrated or openly ostracized" by leaders at the subunit and unit levels (Daigle, 2012, pp. 58–60). The 2012 report also noted the emotional toll exacted by this situation—and by the whole experience of PTSD— from afflicted CAF members and from their spouses and children (Daigle, 2012, p. 61). We will explore PTSD in more detail in chapter 6.

Family Violence

A stressor that is under-researched and under-reported in most families, especially in military families, is family or intimate partner violence. Military communities are just one of the many Canadian social contexts in which intimate partner violence, if it occurs, is notably difficult for the survivor to deal with, especially if the survivor is an economically dependent female partner. Other particularly problematic Canadian social contexts for intimate partner violence are rural communities, Aboriginal communities, and situations where one or more partners has a disability or is an immigrant who can speak neither English nor French (Cripps & McGlade, 2008; Doherty & Hornosty, 2004; Harrison et al., 2002, 2004, 2006; Miedema & Wachholz, 1998; Roeher Institute, 1995; Wuest & Merritt-Gray, 2008). As a result of the geographical-mobility stressor of military life, an intimate partner violence survivor who is liaised with a military member (hereafter referred to in this section as a "civilian spouse") is likely to be both economically dependent on the person who is abusing him/her and far away from extended family and long-time friends (Harrison et al., 2002; Harrison, 2004, 2006). A civilian spouse who lives in a PMQ additionally loses the right to continue living there if her/his relationship dissolves (Harrison et al., 2002; Harrison, 2004, 2006). Both of these considerations augment the stress that already overwhelms a civilian spouse who contemplates reporting family violence and/or co-operating with a police charge after it has been laid (Harrison et al., 2002).

Since 1995, it has been official CAF policy to intervene aggressively in known instances of family violence and to require supervisors at all lev-els to pass instances that come to their attention up the chain of com-mand (Department of National Defence Canada, 1995; Harrison et al., 2002; Zamorski & Wiens-Kincaid, 2013). However, two recent qualitative Canadian studies, based partly on interviews and focus groups with CAF supervisors and service providers, found that older supervisors continue to minimize and avoid taking action on the violence perpetrated by members who are deployable and who generally perform their military duties well (Harrison et al., 2002; Harrison, 2004, 2006; Sudom & Dursun, 2006).

Comparative US research has found the rate of intimate partner violence to be higher in military than in civilian families (Cronin, 1995; Griffin & Morgan, 1988; Heyman & Neidig, 1999; Rentz et al., 2006; Travis, Collins, McCarthy, Rabenhorst, & Milner, 2014). Two recent surveys of civilian spouses commissioned by the Department of National Defence attempted to discover the rate of intimate partner violence in CAF families. However, the response rate to both surveys was less than 25 percent, and the results were inconclusive (Sudom, 2010; Sudom & Dursun, 2006). It is generally acknowledged that the rate of alcohol abuse is relatively high among mil-itary members who abuse their partners (Fear et al., 2007; Zamorski & Wiens-Kincaid, 2013); that the aggressive, control-oriented, and patriar-chal nature of the military occupational environment often spills over into the home (Harrison et al., 2002; Sudom, 2009); and that associations have been found within military member populations between recent lengthy deployments and the probability of aggression against intimate partners (McCarroll et al., 2000; Sudom, 2009).

At CFB Petawawa, the number of family violence incidents that were reported to military police by families living on the base was 3.75 times higher during the period January 2007 to December 2008 than it had been between January 2005 and December 2006; that is, the number of reported incidents increased from 16 during the first time frame to 59 during the second. The biggest spike (January–March 2007) coincided with the return of a large army deployment from Afghanistan (Department of National Defence Canada Military Police Criminal Intelligence Program, 2009).

Family Support Provided by the CAF

On April 12, 1991, the Department of National Defence inaugurated its first national Military Family Support Program (MFSP), largely in response to a 1980s movement of CAF spouses who desired greater input into deci-sion making on issues affecting their daily lives; by 1985 these spouses had established the national Organization of Spouses of Military Members

(OSOMM) (Douglas, 2003; Harrison & Laliberté, 1994, 1997). By March 1993, 38 domestic bases and stations (plus the two then-operating bases in Germany) had received DND funding for multiservice military family resource centres (MFRCs) that would respond to family needs as defined by each local base community and be governed by boards made up of 51 percent (or more) civilian spouses. Over the years, the services provided by MFRCs have become increasingly coordinated and standardized at the national level (Douglas, 2003), despite the fact that variations continue to exist among bases with respect to specific programs (Daigle, 2013, p. 28). MFRCs are non-profit organizations incorporated under provincial laws (Harrison et al., 2002). According to the 2015 Military Family Services website, the services provided by MFRCs across the country fall into the following categories: children and youth (e.g., parent education, activities for children and youth, respite child care), education and training (e.g., for CAF spouses wishing to upgrade their vocational skills), employment assistance (e.g., on-base job opportunities for spouses), geographical mobility support, deployment support, and short-term family crisis support. MFRCs are significantly underutilized by the civilian members of CAF families (Daigle, 2012, p. 26; Douglas, 2003; Harrison et al., 2002). They are also underfunded. Between 2007 and 2012 the MFRCs received little or no increase in operating funds (Daigle, 2012). As a result, MFRCs have increasingly relied on outside funding in order to continue to offer a range of services to military families. For example, since its creation in 2013, the Bell True Patriot Love Fund has provided 32 grants of $5,000 to $25,000 across Canada to programs delivered through MFRCs and related charities that work to improve access to mental health care in military communities across the country (Bell Canada, 2015).

Advantages and disadvantages are associated with MFRCs as sources of support for members of CAF families. On the advantage side, MFRC staff are in a position to know more about the impact of military life stressors than are civilian organizations such as schools. During a deployment, many MFRCs are also equipped to provide video conferencing links between deployed CAF members and the members of their families. On the disadvantage side, MFRCs are an arm of the CAF and, as such, their overriding goal is the operational readiness and retention of CAF members (Douglas, 2003; Harrison et al., 2002). Many CAF spouses do not use the support and counselling services of MFRCs because of their concerns around possible breaches of confidentiality vis-à-vis the CAF chain of command (Daigle, 2012, p. 45; Harrison et al., 2002).

Resilience

Resilience has been defined as "the ability to adapt and cope successfully, despite threatening or challenging situations" (Agaibi & Wilson, 2005, p. 198). Military life, with all its hardships, offers many opportunities for the development of resilience; after all, the military offers a strong sense of belonging to a community that has a shared mission and values (Rossetto, 2015). Children of military members may build their self-confidence by taking on new responsibilities in the family during separations and deployments, and frequent moves may offer opportunities for adventure and personal growth. Resilience, however, is not a personal trait, but rather a product of the relationships between children and the people and resources around them (Lester & Flake, 2013). Hence, having strong social supports is key (Easterbrooks, Ginsburg, & Lerner, 2013; Skomorovsky, 2014). Most of the research referred to in this chapter made reference to the benefits of enhanced social supports and resources for military children and their families. For example, research has found that youth with better social connections to their parents, their peers, their schools, and their neighborhoods are more adept at coping with military life stressors (Chandra, Martin, Hawkins, & Richardson, 2010; Mmari et al., 2010).

Role of Schools

Schools can and do play a key role in how young people experience and cope with life in a military family (Aronson & Perkins, 2013; Astor et al., 2013; Bradshaw, Sudhinaraset, Mmari, & Blum, 2010; Milburn & Lightfoot, 2013). A growing body of research has highlighted the need for educators to recognize the unique circumstances surrounding military students, particularly when their parents are deployed (De Pedro, Astor, Gilreath, Benbenishty, & Berkowitz, 2015; Mmari et al., 2010; Williams, 2013). Especially in civilian communities and schools, military children and their families tend to be essentially invisible, with most schools failing to routinely assess the military (or non-military) status of new students' parents (Kudler & Porter, 2013).

Numerous challenges have been identified as being experienced by military children attending school. Frequent school transitions often result in students being required to repeat classes, missing critical topics (such as fractions, multiplication, and cursive writing), and/or being unable to complete all the graduation requirements in time. Students' military status also poses a challenge to their involvement in extracurricular activities, as some coaches hesitate to put military students on teams for fear of losing a starting player to a military-related move (Bradshaw et al., 2010). Any of these problems are likely to have a negative effect on the adolescent's self-esteem, attitudes toward school, and/or academic motivation.

The way school staff interact with military students can either buffer or exacerbate the stress that students experience. Focus-group research with adolescents, parents, and school personnel in schools on military bases has found that schools are ill-equipped to support students while their parents are deployed (Mmari et al., 2009). School staff have also reported great difficulty in finding the "right things" to do and say to military students regarding their parents' service or deployment (Bradshaw et al., 2010).

When they recently explored the role of school climate in the mental health outcomes of military-connected adolescents, Kris Tunac De Pedro and his colleagues identified a favourable school climate, from the standpoint of an adolescent, as consisting of the following dimensions: meaningful participation, relationships with caring adults, school connectedness, high expectations from school adults, and feeling safe (De Pedro et al., 2015).[9] In upcoming chapters we will learn more about school climate and military-connected adolescents.

Conclusion

This chapter has explored the three key stressors that shape the lives of military members and their families: geographic relocations, frequent separations, and living under a blanket of risk. As a result of geographic relocations, civilian spouses of military members struggle with financial challenges, underemployment, problems with access to health care for themselves and their children, separation from their extended families, and disruptions to their children's school progress and friendships. Lengthy and high-risk deployments create additional stresses for spouses, as we will soon see.

Deployments are also stressful for the spouses' adolescent children. Civilian adolescents already face self-esteem issues, academic and relationship challenges, their first romantic partnerships, and, in some cases, geographical and school transitions. Military adolescents struggle with this long list of common adolescent stressors; in addition, they are expected to surmount the obstacles placed in their way by each of the three major military life stressors discussed in this chapter. Additional stressors such as family violence, physical combat injuries, or operational stress injuries may also be part of their lives.

The impact of parental deployments on adolescents is unique for several reasons. Perhaps the most important reason is that military adolescents have a heightened understanding of the dangers of a volatile deployment, relative to their younger siblings; furthermore, they are often required to become family caregivers at a time when their own developmental needs are strong.

The next chapter will introduce us to the site of our study—Armyville, Canada—and describe how our research proceeded.

3

Growing Up in Armyville

Although its fast-food strip looks like any other fast-food strip, Armyville is an enjoyable summer's day drive. Normal driving speed—it is true—is a crawl. But what you see from the main road is spacious, well-ordered, and green. The buildings, sparse in number, are far from the road. Distant from each other, but easy to see, are the hospital, the high school, the school district offices, the ample playing fields, and some attractively well-spaced PMQs. For the entirety of Canada's time in Afghanistan, a large and prominent "Support the Troops" sign was displayed on the lawn outside the school. Many yellow ribbons were in view.

Armyville was a small, stable, closely knit, and economically marginal community—population 250—until the early 1950s, at which time it transformed almost overnight into the site of an enormous army base. Armyville became a company town in 1956, to the extent of having its existing town council eliminated and replaced by a new management structure that was dominated by CAF personnel. Many members of Armyville's old families relocated elsewhere, because their homes had been expropriated by the CAF (Lewis, 1996). The town changed completely.

As of the 2011 census, there were almost 9,000 people residing in Armyville, up from about 8,400 in 2006 (Statistics Canada, 2014a). Just over 2,500 of these 9,000 were under the age of 20, making the mean age of this population—29.5—significantly younger than the mean age of the population of the capital city of the province (38.7 years) and the mean age of the population of the entire province (43.7 years). The 2011 census also revealed that there were approximately 2,500 families living in the community: just over 1,600 were married couples with children living at home; just over 500 were common-law couples with children living at home; and almost 300 families consisted of lone parents with children (Statistics Canada, 2014a).

Today Armyville is largely a single-industry town. One or more members of the majority of Armyville's present families are either current or past CAF members or are current or past civilian employees of the base, and Armyville is mainly organized around the CAF presence (Chapman, 1981; Lewis, 1996). The magnitude of the base's presence is evident in the municipal government's website list of the community's major employers: the Canadian Armed Forces base (1,500 civilian employees and 5,000 military); the local schools and school district offices (500 employees); the local hospital (250 employees); two large chain grocery stores and a distribution centre (414 employees); the township and other governing/civil services (260); other major retailers (167); restaurant chains (220); and major banks (51). A good proportion of the civilians who work in Armyville live in outlying rural areas.

The 2006 census revealed that the labour force participation rate in Armyville was higher than in the province as a whole (76.7% compared to 63.7% for the province), likely attributable to the base. The census also found that, among those who worked full-year, full-time, average earnings were $37,875—significantly higher than the provincial average. However, the gender gap in income was greater in this community than in the province: men working full-time, full-year, earned $51,435, compared to women who on average earned $15,689. At the provincial level, men earned, on average, $26,692, compared to $17,352 among women. The largest employer in Armyville—disproportionately hiring men in its well-paying jobs—is the base (Statistics Canada, 2006).[1]

Armyville is a 20-minute drive from one of the largest cities in the province. Armyville High School (AHS) was the largest school within its school district when we carried out our research, and it remains one of the largest schools in the province. Its staff serve more than 1,270 students from Grades 9 to 12. The school building was constructed in 1965, with additions made in 1976. Sixty-five percent of AHS's student population is bused in, and just over 60 percent of the school's students are members of current military families. Adolescents from military families make up an even larger majority of the students if past, as well as present, parental affiliations with the CAF are counted.

The school and the base enjoy a close relationship. Many school events are held at the base, to take advantage of the latter's substantial facilities. Reciprocally, military recruiters are welcomed to the school at least once each year and, indeed, many adolescents from both military and civilian families, especially males, join the army upon graduation.

Methodological Excursus One: Our Survey[2]

The first phase of our project was a quantitative survey that we adminis-tered to most of the students attending AHS (1066 out of a total of circa 1200) on October 7, 2008. Using measures from the (Canadian) National Longitudinal Survey of Children and Youth (NLSCY), we compared the well-being, family functioning, attitudes toward school, and peer relation-ships of adolescents from CAF families with those of (1) their civilian peers at the same school, and (2) their peers in Cycle 7 (2006–2007) of the NLSCY.

The NLSCY is a national study that began in 1994 to collect informa-tion on Canadian children's development and well-being. The NLSCY followed its initial cohort of over 22,000 children (0–11 years) every two years until Cycle 8, the last cycle, which was collected between Septem-ber 2008 and July 2009[3] (Statistics Canada, 1997, 2014b). The NLSCY sample was selected in such a way that children from military families were excluded.[4]

All AHS students had been informed of our survey and invited to par-ticipate. An information package had been sent to parents and students that had included a supportive letter from the principal, along with a "dis-sent" form, which the parent (or student aged 16 or over) had been asked to complete and return to the school if s/he did not want (his/her child) to participate. Youth for whom the school had received no dissent form, who were present on the day of the survey, and who signed a consent form indi-cating that they (or, if applicable, their parents) had read and understood the information that had been sent home, completed the survey. Several students who had come to school intending to fill out the survey did not do so, by virtue of admitting to the research assistant that they had not shown the information package to their parents.

In addition to NLSCY measures, our survey included selected measures from (a) the Children of Alcoholics Screening Test (CAST) (Clair & Gen-est, 1992; Jones, 1983; Lease & Yanico, 1995) and (b) the Juvenile Victim-ization Questionnaire (JVQ) (Finkelhor, Hamby, Ormrod, & Turner, 2005; Hamby, Finkelhor, Ormrod, & Turner, 2004), in order to address specific stressors associated with military life that are not included in the NLSCY. Finally, the survey included questions that were designed to elicit each par-ticipant's "CAF status." The final question of the CAF status section of the questionnaire asked participants if either their mother or father had ever served on an overseas deployment.[5]

We defined a "CAF adolescent" as someone who had at least one par-ent or step-parent who either (a) was a current regular or reservist CAF member or (b) took his/her release from the regular or reserve CAF during the previous five years *and* had been a member for at least four years prior to release. In our view, a CAF adolescent's parent or step-parent needed to have been a member of the CAF long enough to have experienced the impact of CAF membership upon family life. We considered four years to have been long enough. If the parent was a former CAF member, we believed that s/he needed to have been released during the five years before our survey so that his/her CAF experience was recent and could be remembered by the adolescent offspring we interviewed. Adolescents with parents who met these criteria (as well, of course, as adolescents with parents who were still serving) were counted as CAF adolescents. A "civilian" youth had no parents or step-parents who had ever belonged to the CAF. Fifty-two adolescents fell into neither category (e.g., they had parents who had been CAF members for two years 20 years ago) and were excluded from our quantitative analyses. Fifty percent (481) of the participants who answered the survey questions about CAF status were CAF adolescents. Forty-five percent (436) were civilian youth.[6]

NLSCY measures, as modified for a survey format, were appropriate for our research because they enabled CAF adolescents to be compared with their civilian Canadian peers on a range of health and social indicators. Our national comparison group was the CAF AHS students' age-appropriate peers who had participated in the NLSCY during Cycle 7 (2006–2007).

The survey data entry was organized and supervised by the late Christine Newburn-Cook of the University of Alberta. Once this had been done, other team members, led by Karen Robson, were able to perform various statistical analyses on the survey data set, both on its own and together with the Statistics Canada NLSCY Cycle 7 data.[7] Karen, with doctoral student (now assistant professor) Chris Sanders, took the lead in looking at various social and psychological indicators,[8] with two major comparisons in mind:

- Were there any significant differences in these social and psychological indicators between CAF youth and civilian youth in Armyville?
- Were there any significant differences between the AHS survey sample and the NLSCY national sample?

For reasons that will be discussed below, Karen and Chris also examined the potential role of gender in shaping social and psychological outcomes. A third major survey data analysis question was therefore asked:

- Were there any significant differences between CAF adolescent males and females on the indicators that were considered in this analysis?

Statistical tests were performed, to compare group differences and to build models that highlighted the personal characteristics that appeared to have the most impact on the social and psychological outcomes we observed among the youth. Karen and Chris conducted simple (bivariate) comparisons as part of their preliminary analysis before they began controlling for other potentially false (spurious) relationships in the data. The bivariate analyses provided rough approximations (e.g., they did not include controls for family structure and age) and helped Karen and Chris to decide where to focus their later analyses.

Karen and Chris then conducted more complex analyses, in order to avoid assigning too much importance to the fact of being an Armyville resident or a member of a CAF family. To do that, they controlled for (in other words, took into account the effects of) age and family structure. Age and family structure typically play large roles in determining the well-being of young people. For example, a meta-analysis of 122 studies of family structure and child well-being in OECD countries found a disadvantage associated with being raised by a sole parent as compared with being raised in a two-biological-parent family (Chapple, 2009). Age, measured in years, was a straightforward control variable that Karen and Chris used to improve model fit. They then created "family structure"—the second control variable—using the following categories: biological two-parent family, stepfamily, single-parent family, and other.

Contrary to the research team's expectation, Karen and Chris found that the mental well-being of CAF adolescents attending AHS was no worse than that of their civilian school peers. In fact, the CAF youth at AHS seemed to be doing better than their civilian peers on a few measures that were marginally related to mental well-being. When the effects of age, gender, and family structure were taken into consideration,

- CAF youth generally exhibited a more positive attitude towards school;
- CAF youth were less likely to skip school;
- CAF youth had slightly higher educational ambitions;
- CAF youth were less likely to have friends with bad habits.

However, both groups of youth were equally affected by depression, low self-esteem, and suicide ideation.

School Engagement

Although *school engagement* has been defined and operationalized in various ways, it generally refers to the extent to which children are connected and committed to school and are motivated to learn and achieve. For the purpose of our research, our working definition of school engagement included the survey measures "school attitude," "attachment to school," "skipping school," and "talking to teachers." We were especially interested in learning whether the frequent moves and parental deployments that are characteristic of CAF families affected school engagement among CAF adolescents.

Our survey revealed that 380 CAF students out of 419 (or 90.6%) who answered the question on residential mobility noted that they had moved more than once in their lifetime. This compared to 230 civilian students out of 359 (or 64%) who had moved more than once in their lifetime. Needless to say, this difference between the two groups was significant. Consistent with some of the research presented in chapter 2 (Aronson & Perkins 2013; Astor et al., 2013; Daigle, 2013; Mmari et al., 2010; Williams, 2013), our survey also revealed evidence that residential mobility had produced some negative school engagement outcomes (Robson, Albanese, Harrison, & Sanders, 2013).

Students, both CAF and civilian, who had experienced more than one move in their lifetime scored differently—and more poorly—on the school engagement outcome measures, compared to those who had not moved and those who had moved once (Robson et al., 2013; see table 3.1). Compared to those who had not moved, students who had moved once in the last three years scored more poorly on the measures of school attachment, school attitude, and talking to teachers.[9] This is consistent with literature cited in chapter 2, which noted that the timing and number of moves negatively affect school attachment and experiences among civilian children and children in military families (Aronson & Perkins, 2013; Astor et al.,

Table 3.1   Number of Moves and School Engagement Outcomes for AHS Students

Moves over last three years	School attachment	School attitude	Skipping	Talking to teachers	N
None	3.175	3.227	1.255	3.188	256
Once	3.134	3.188	1.300	2.794	173
More than once	3.123	3.162	1.441	3.033	483
F	1.01	1.35	4.22**	3.70*	

Note: A version of this table appeared in "School engagement among youth in Canadian Forces families: A comparative analysis," by K. Robson, P. Albanese, D. Harrison, and C. Sanders, 2013, *Alberta Journal of Educational Research, 59*(3), pp. 363–381.
$^*p < 0.05$ $^{**}p < 0.01$ $^{***}p < 0.001$

Table 3.2   Parental Deployment and School Engagement Outcomes, for CAF Youth Only

Parent deployed	School attachment	School attitude	Skipping	Talking to teachers	N
Yes	3.284	3.342	1.142	3.283	279
No	3.153	3.212	1.262	2.826	156
T	5.309***	5.682***	4.304***	3.207**	

Note: A version of this table appeared in "School engagement among youth in Canadian Forces families: A comparative analysis," by K. Robson, P. Albanese, D. Harrison, and C. Sanders, 2013, *Alberta Journal of Educational Research, 59*(3), pp. 363–381.
* $p < 0.05$ ** $p < 0.01$ *** $p < 0.001$

2013; Crockett, et al., 1989; Daigle, 2013; Mmari et al., 2010; Simpson & Fowler, 1994; Williams, 2013).

Interestingly, Karen and Chris found that CAF youth who had experienced a parental deployment were more attached to their school, had a more positive attitude toward school, talked to their teachers more often, and skipped school less frequently than their CAF peers (Robson et al., 2013; see table 3.2).[10] This may reflect a readiness on the part of CAF adolescents to benefit from extrafamilial support during a deployment (see Chandra et al., 2010; De Pedro et al., 2015). We will return to the implications of this particular finding when we discuss the impact of deployments on CAF adolescents—and the support that children of deployed parents receive from their school and community—in chapter 5.

Young Women in Armyville

Given recent international research findings on gender and self-esteem (Bacchini & Magliulo, 2003; Cambron & Acitelli, 2009; Gentile et al., 2009; Moksnes & Espnes, 2013, 2014), we expected that AHS girls from CAF families would score lower on measures of self-esteem compared to AHS boys from CAF families. Karen and Chris's analysis found that CAF females scored virtually identically to their male peers on the items pertaining to school engagement and personal and family relationships (after accounting for age and family structure). However, consistent with the international research (Bacchini & Magliulo, 2003; Cambron & Acitelli, 2009; Gentile et al., 2009; Moksnes & Espnes, 2013, 2014), Karen and Chris also found that females—civilian and CAF—scored lower on self-esteem measures than their male peers either at AHS or in the NLSCY comparison group (see table 3.3). Hence, their preliminary analysis found that being female in Armyville (civilian or CAF) negatively affected young women's self-esteem. They also found that there was no significant difference between the self-esteem scores of the CAF females and the scores of their civilian female peers.

Table 3.3   Multivariate Analyses of Well-being Measures by CAF Status, Gender, and Other Variables

	Depression	Low self-esteem	Suicide ideation
	Unstandardized OLS regression coefficients	Unstandardized logistic regression coefficients	Unstandardized logistic regression coefficients
Armyville sample	0.278*	0.516**	1.187***
Female	0.144**	0.329*	0.500+
Armyville sample – female	–0.069	0.228	–0.645
Age	—	–0.005	0.0911+
CAF	–0.070	0.137	–0.193
CAF – female	0.221	–0.460	–0.855*
Stepfamily	0.043	0.188	–0.111
Single-parent family	0.139	–0.086	–0.046
Other living arrangements	0.423	–0.196	–1.123
Stepfamily – female	0.353*	0.000	1.194*
Single-parent family – female	0.025	0.769**	0.665
Other living arrangements – female	–0.340	0.679	2.392*
Constant	0.294	–1.539	–2.613
N	922	7184	7184
	R^2 = 0.087		

Note: The numbers in the first two rows ("Armyville sample" and "Female") are all statistically significant, and therefore reflect higher scores than the NLSCY national average on depression, low self-esteem, and suicide ideation. Numbers without asterisks are not statistically significant and therefore can be interpreted as having no effect. A version of this table appeared in "The impact of shared location on the mental health of military and civilian adolescents in a community affected by frequent deployments: A research note," by D. Harrison, K. Robson, P. Albanese, C. Sanders, and C. Newburn-Cook, 2011, *Armed Forces and Society*, 37(3), pp. 550–560.
***$p < 0.001$ **$p < 0.01$ *$p < 0.05$ +$p < 0.10$

Our Sample Compared to the Rest of Canada

After analyzing the survey data we had collected, Karen and Chris carried out ordinary least squares (OLS) and logistical regression analyses of the pooled data set, which also included the relevant age-comparative cohort from Cycle 7 of the NLSCY.[11] After controlling for age, CAF status, and gender, they found some somewhat disturbing comparative results pertaining to adolescents living in Armyville. For example:

1. All AHS students, CAF and civilian alike, were significantly more likely than their national peers to be depressed, to suffer from low self-esteem, and to have thought of committing suicide (see table 3.3).

2. Membership in the AHS sample had mixed effects on school engage-
    ment: while civilian and CAF AHS students were significantly less
    likely to skip school, they were also less likely to participate in school
    activities than other students in Canada.
3. All AHS students, CAF and civilian alike, had poor relationships
    with their mothers, and (to a slight extent) were more likely to have
    friends with bad habits (e.g., substance abuse, suspensions from
    school), relative to their peers in the national sample.
4. All AHS students, CAF and civilian alike, were more likely to have
    experienced the death of someone close to them.

The results from Karen and Chris's preliminary analyses were surprising. Contrary to what the team had expected, they found no evidence that
CAF youth experienced disadvantage on the indicators they examined,
compared to their civilian peers at AHS. However, Karen and Chris had
also not expected to find that the whole AHS sample itself, both CAF and
civilian students, would score significantly worse on mental well-being
measures than the national sample from the NLSCY.

Interpreting These Survey Findings
While our team had expected to find differences between AHS CAF youth
and youth in the national sample, we had not anticipated the similarities
we would find between AHS CAF youth and the civilian youth at the
same school.

Our failure to accurately predict the similarity between the two sub-
groups of AHS students can be traced to an erroneous assumption we
made. In retrospect, we realize that when we designed the survey, we made
assumptions that would have been more appropriate for a school population in a large urban centre, in which the students from military families
comprised a numerically marginal minority. In a large urban context, the
presence of adolescents from military families would have had relatively
little impact on the lives of the adolescents from civilian families who
attended school with them and made up the "majority culture." Armyville,
in contrast, is a small community, separated from the nearest urban centre
by close to 20 kilometres of highway driving, with no public transportation linking the two locations. Armyville is also a single-industry town, in
which a large proportion of the population sustains some past or present
connection to the adjoining base.

More than 2,000 soldiers from the Armyville base deployed to Afghanistan between 2002 and 2014, and a significant proportion of these returned
suffering from physical injuries and/or post-traumatic stress disorder

(PTSD). From the literature (see especially Cozza et al., 2010; Davidson & Mellor, 2001; Gibbs, Clinton-Sherrod, & Johnson, 2012; Samper, Taft, King, & King, 2004; Sayer et al., 2010; Taft, Street, Marshall, & Dowdall, 2007; Taft, Vogt, Marshall, Panuzio, & Niles, 2007; Teten et al., 2010), and as we will explore in chapter 6, we know that combat injuries exercise a negative impact on family dynamics. Hence, it is possible that the relatively isolated nature of Armyville and its integrated military/civilian culture mean that spillover negative effects of the Afghanistan mission and Afghanistan casualties have accrued to all Armyville area adolescents, as opposed to simply the adolescent children of CAF families. If so, not only would the error of our expectations be accounted for, but also the fact that all the youth in the AHS sample—military and civilian alike—scored more poorly on mental health measures than their age peers in the national sample. Interestingly, in 2011, three years after we had carried out our survey, data collected as part of the California Health Kids Survey (CHKS) of California students in Grades 7, 9, and 11 (n = 14,299) revealed that the military-connected students (defined as having a parent or sibling in the military) scored higher on depression and suicide ideation[12] than their civilian peers. However, since only 13.5 percent of the students sampled were military-connected, it is possible that relatively few of them lived in geographically isolated single-industry army communities such as Armyville, and that relatively few of the civilian peers of these military-connected students had been significantly affected by Iraq and Afghanistan (Cederbaum et al., 2014).[13]

We will return to this spillover theme in the conclusion.

Methodological Excursus Two: Our Interviews

The second phase of our project was our interview study of the impact of deployments and other military life stressors on CAF adolescents' lives. To this end, we conducted semi-structured, two-hour interviews with 61 of the CAF adolescents during the fall/winter of 2009–2010. We recruited these 61 participants by inviting the adolescents in each classroom who had participated in the survey to volunteer by filling out the contact information sheets attached to their surveys. From the pool of 450 volunteers, we constructed a quota sample,[14] consisting of 15 CAF adolescents from each grade (16 from Grade 9), with gender proportions reflecting our volunteer pool demographics, and an attempt to include youth with parents representing all ranks, and both regular and reservist status. We interviewed 35 girls and 26 boys who, among them, had 69 parents who were current or recently retired CAF members. Only 16 (23%) of these parents were other than current regular members, and all of these 16 parents were recently retired regular members, retired regular members who now worked as reservists, or regular members who had been medically released. None of them had ever been career reservists. Seven (10%) of the 69 parents were present or former commissioned officers (captains, majors, or lieutenant-colonels); the remaining 62 (90%) were present or former non-commissioned members (warrant officer, sergeant, corporal, and private ranks). This ratio varied from the 20:80 ratio of officers to non-commissioned members that currently exists in the CAF (Treasury Board of Canada, 2007). All 69 parents were present or former army members, except for four who were from the air element or the navy. Since we carried out the interviews a year following the survey, the interviews were with students who, when interviewed, were in Grades 10, 11, 12, and recently graduated.

We conducted the majority of the interviews in a private room at AHS during the school day. We conducted the remainder during evenings and weekends in a conference room near the school. Almost all the interviews were done by Deborah, Jennifer (our site coordinator), or Riley, one of our research assistants. Each participant signed a consent form. The interviews covered a range of topics unique to military life and not covered in the survey, including relocations, deployments, deployment-related PTSD, family functioning, the participants' perceptions of the impact of military life stressors on their families and lives, their perceptions of how they and their families had been supported by the school and the local Military Family Resource Centre (MFRC), and their perceptions of their own resilience. Each participant who was interviewed during the school day was instructed to leave his/her class, attend the interview, and then return to class. Jennifer confirmed the student's participation in the interview with the school secretary, who then changed the student's attendance record to "absent *with* permission." The intent of this process was to safeguard students' privacy regarding their decision to participate in interviews during the school day.

Several counsellors in the area had agreed to provide pro bono counselling to participants who identified themselves as requiring it. At the conclusion of each interview, the interviewer raised the topic of counselling options and handed the participant an information sheet regarding sources of assistance. The interviewers had also been rigorously trained to respond in the events of participants requiring immediate counselling, or of disclosures of child abuse, family violence, or suicide ideation. After each interview, the interviewer completed a "contact sheet," on which she noted the participant's manner of participating in the interview, his/her state of mind, and whether counselling had been recommended and/or accepted.

Our interview schedule (see appendix 1) provided a general guide; however, we conducted the interviews in a relatively unstructured manner. We instructed our interviewers to develop excellent rapport and obtain rich description from participants. Given time limitations, the consequence of this strategy was that every participant did not answer every interview question. This is the reason for the "Not discussed" category in table 3.4.

All the interviews were tape-recorded. After they had been transcribed, we organized the responses to our open-ended questions thematically, via an inductive process of generating categories from data, which resembled (but was not synonymous with) grounded theory methodology (Charmaz, 2004; Strauss & Corbin, 1990). We developed initial open codes; in our second stage of coding, we further developed the open codes with the strongest evidence. In our (final) axial coding stage, we created links among the open codes. Our interview schedule was divided into the following sections: Geographical Transfers, Deployments, PTSD, School, the Military Family Resource Centre, Family Dynamics/Crises, and Gender. Unsurprisingly, the names of all of these sections except that of the Military Family Resource Centre represented our most prominent initial descriptive open codes. Once our descriptive open codes had been created, three team members worked independently, eventually merging their work in order to arrive at the set of "subcodes" within each open code that best reflected the interview data. In order to "expedite and expand data organization, storage and retrieval possibilities" (Lofland, 2006, p. 204), we used MS Word to assist in coding and filing our interview data.

Gender and Self-esteem in Armyville

We will discover in chapter 5 that the stress experienced by adolescents affected by deployments is accompanied by potential mental health implications—especially for girls. For this reason, gender and self-esteem is a subtheme of our study, one which will recur at several places during our discussions of how CAF adolescents experience deployments. We will begin exploring this subtheme here, as we report our main interview findings on gender and self-esteem and demonstrate that these findings parallel the gender differences in self-esteem that we had found after analyzing the results of our survey.

As you will recall, our survey of AHS students found that female students at AHS, both CAF and civilian, scored lower on self-esteem than male students, both at AHS and in the national (NLSCY) sample. This result was not surprising, given that, as we mentioned above, research has found adolescent girls to have lower self-esteem than adolescent boys (Bacchini & Magliulo, 2003; Cambron & Acitelli, 2009; Gentile et al., 2009;

Table 3.4   Rating One's Own Self-Esteem

How would you rate your own self-esteem?	Relatively high	% of total	Relatively low	% of total	Not discussed	Total interviewed
Boys	8	31%	1	4%	17	26
Girls	9	26%	10	29%	16	35

Golan, Hagay, & Tamir, 2014; Moksnes & Espnes, 2013). Our survey additionally found that *all* Armyville youth—CAF and civilians alike—are more likely than their national NLSCY peers to be depressed, to have low self-esteem, and to have been driven to thoughts of suicide.

Many of our interview participants were asked the question: "How would you rate your own self esteem?" From table 3.4, you can see that, among the 28 participants who answered this question, there was about an equal number of girls and boys who reported having high self-esteem. However, only one boy admitted to having relatively low self-esteem, as compared with 10 girls.

This finding is consistent with the gender differences in self-esteem that we had found in our survey results.

The participants' open-ended answers to this interview question provide further insight into this gender difference. We will begin with some of the responses from the boys. Sam,[15] a senior student who rated his self-esteem a 9 out of 10, explained:

> If someone says something, I don't care. I'm not going to change for anybody. I do what I want to do, and that's it. Like if a teacher doesn't like the way I write, then I really don't care. I've already told teachers it's too bad—that's how I write. 'Cause I get a lot of them—they think it's messy, and they're like, "Well do this." And I'm like, "I don't want to. I like to write like that, so I'm not going to change just for you."

Joe, another senior student, added,

> Definitely a nine. I just feel really comfortable around anybody. I don't give two shits what people think about me.... I try and keep myself well dressed and good looking. I always had a high respect for appearance.

Roger, another senior student, said,

> I would say roughly an eight. Because there is times I do question, you know, "Does that person like me?" or stuff like that. And I wonder

*what it is I'm doing that they're not liking about me. But then again,
if the person doesn't like me for who I am, and being who I am makes
me happy, then it's their opinion. I've no right to change that but, you
know, maybe I just shouldn't hang around them. Maybe I should just
hang around people more like me. Like, you know, be myself and whoever wants to, wants to. Whoever doesn't, doesn't.*

The one exception was Clive, a senior boy, who told us,

*I just take everyone else's problems, I blame them on myself. Like if she's
mad, then it must be my fault. I must have done something wrong,
even if I didn't. If someone else is sad, even if I wasn't there and they're
sad, I feel like it's my fault. And I say "Sorry" for everything.... That's
what I've lived with. 'Cause I'm used to keeping stuff inside and taking
everything on me, and being blamed for things.*

You can see from the above quotes that the boys mostly expressed confidence in who they were and an unwillingness to spend time worrying about
what other people thought of them. Roger described the strategy he had
adopted for extricating himself from friendships that failed to enable him to
feel good about himself. As the exception, Clive confessed to having low self-
esteem and to blaming himself for the problems of the people around him.
Since even the boys who attended AHS were found to score higher on the
survey measures of depression, self-esteem, and suicide ideation than their
national peers, Clive's comment should not be considered too surprising.

The comments from the girls contrasted sharply with those of most of
the boys just quoted. They did not reflect an imperviousness to the negative
feedback of others. We will begin with Louanne, a senior girl, who told us,

*I have low self-esteem. I've actually spoken to my psychiatrist about it. I
have had it, like, my whole life. I don't even know when it started.*

Simone, a senior girl, said,

*The most problems I have is, like, looks. Like, comparing to other girls
that are in the high school that are drop-dead gorgeous.... With looks I'm
not very confident. With my personality and how I am, I'm not afraid
to go up and talk to someone I don't know. Or dress a certain way—that
doesn't bother me. It's just the looks. That's all that bothers me.*

Paula, a senior girl, added,

*I know myself in comparison to my boyfriend or my guy friends. I don't
know. I feel more self-conscious, like there's prettier girls out in the
world... and there's thinner girls, and I'd like to look like them. And*

I'm always told I'm ridiculous, but I don't know. I could definitely agree with the statement that men have more confidence, I guess you could say, than women.

Jasmine, a senior girl, noted,

Like, if guys talk about you badly, it brings you right down. It's just like no guys like me.... It's like, "Oh great, I don't even have a chance with anyone."... Like, if they were talking about girls and how they're fat and stuff like that—or if they're gross.... Well, I think that about me, so it kinda makes me feel like they're saying that about me.

She added,

It's usually [that] magazines and the media and stuff bring you down.... And what girls say too. Like, I find the girls say stuff to you that brings you down.... I think I need depression pills. That's how I feel sometimes.

Marilee, a senior girl, shared insight on how having a disability had made matters worse for her:

It's because some boys through middle school and high school actually pick on the girls sometimes—and that really lowers self-esteem. I know it lowered mine back in middle school.... [It was] because I was different from people in my class. All it took was one kid to move in. And then he... made fun of me because of [my disability]. No one had bothered to say anything to my face about it. And it just started a thing throughout the whole school.

Shanda, a senior girl, described her dependence on other people's opinions:

I'm hard on myself because I don't like failure. I definitely take into consideration other people's opinion. Which can be a really bad thing.... Just what people think of how I play my sport, or how I dress, or why I'm so into schoolwork. It's hard to know that people disagree with the way that you are.

In contrast, Petra, a junior girl, spoke confidently about herself in relation to others. Her comment echoed that of Roger, one of the boys quoted above:

It's not that I have more confidence. It's just kind of like I've given up caring what people think about me. It doesn't bother me anymore. So it's like I don't care what they think about me. It doesn't matter if I'm bad at playing guitar, I'm still going to sit there and play it. Because if you don't care what other people think about you, it's almost like your self-esteem doesn't matter any more.

Similarly, Krista, a recently graduated young woman, said,

> *I see that this is happening, and this is what they're [the media] doing, and this is why this is there in that image. [But] even as a woman I don't feel objectified. I do have self-confidence issues from time to time, [but] I'm the kind of person that goes, "No, I don't look like that. That's okay, 'cause I'm still hot."... It feels a lot better than looking at an image of a woman and saying, "Why don't I look like her?"*

Mostly for reasons related to physical appearance, most of the girls just quoted confessed to having low self-esteem and to having feelings of shame around the physical image they presented to their peers, both boys and girls. Relatedly, Marilee attributed her low self-esteem to the fact that her peers had made fun of her disability. Shanda perhaps best exemplified how our female participants' perspective on their self-esteem contrasted with the perspective of their male peers when she commented, "It's hard to know that people disagree with the way you are."

After asking participants about their own self-esteem, we asked many of them to try to account for the gender differences in self-esteem that we had found in our survey results. Our question was, "The survey you filled out in 2008 showed that girls at AHS have lower self-esteem than boys. Do you have any thoughts on why this might be so?" A summary of their answers appears below in table 3.5.

Table 3.5   Thoughts on Why Girls Have Lower Self-Esteem Than Boys

The survey you filled out in 2008 showed that girls at AHS have lower self-esteem than boys. Do you have any thoughts on why this might be so? (both genders provided each of these answers except the last)	# Responses
Girls are conditioned to be more obsessed with their physical appearance and popularity.	27
Girls are upset more easily than boys.	15
Girls are victimized by other girls, who participate in bullying and spreading rumours, to bolster their own self-esteem.	12
Boys put girls down.	8
In Armyville, the army values young men more than young women.	6
Boys are less likely to be honest on surveys about having low self-esteem.	4
There is a sexual double standard (girls who "cheat" are considered sluts; boys who do this are admired). [Note : Only girls provided this answer.]	4

The most popular answer provided by all participants was "Girls are conditioned to be more obsessed with their physical appearance and popularity." This answer mirrors what the girls quoted above had told us during their interviews. The second most popular answer was "Girls are upset more easily than boys" followed by "Girls are victimized by other girls, who participate in bullying and spreading rumours, to bolster their own self-esteem." Several participants also chose each of "Boys put girls down and "In Armyville, the army values young men more than young women."

Both the boys and the girls provided insightful elaborations of these answers to the question. Sam echoed the negative comments that several of the girls (above) had voiced about themselves:

> I think it's more because we [boys] don't care what others say. And the girls are always like, "Well if they think that, well then I've got to change and do this." And the [boys], we don't care. "You say what you say, it doesn't mean it's true."... Most of [the girls], they want to look a certain way and all like the people on TV. And guys, they just want to do what they want to do. They want to play sports or whatever.... If someone says [a girl is] ugly, they might not necessarily be ugly, but maybe in that person's mind they are. But maybe to everybody else they're not. So then they start freaking out and trying to change how they look and all that, and they don't even need to. I've seen it a couple times.

As did Jasmine:

> If you read magazines and stuff like that, it's like this. And then we look at other people. You know, it just brings you right down. You're like, "Oh I feel really bad about myself."...I don't think guys have stuff to worry about, because [they] wake up, they put on something to wear, and then they go to school. Girls try to compete with other girls and try to look the best, or be the best. And like, yeah, you want to be the one who gets noticed, because it makes you feel better. But when you don't, you feel really bad.

As—interestingly—did Max, a junior boy who mirrored the girls' paranoia about their looks—but from a boy's perspective:

> I'm more likely to want to date a girl who likes me who is beautiful, than someone who's uglier.... Guys would be more shallow on that aspect of wanting to date good-looking girls.... It's like you get peer-pressured a lot. If you date a not-so-good-looking girl, you get to put up with everything that the guys are going to throw at you for it.... Making fun of you and your girlfriend is the main problem that it would be.

Max's comment suggests that girls are not being paranoid when they believe that they are valued by boys primarily for their appearance. For her part, Marilee focused on how boys treat girls:

> Sometimes [boys pick on girls] as a joke—like thinking you're imme-diately gonna pick up on it. But sometimes you don't, and they don't realize it, but it gets to you. And it will get to you and start eating away, and just make your self-esteem drop.

Louanne, however, blamed young women themselves:

> Girls are catty. They're rude to each other.... Guys don't care as much as girls do. How they look or what they're wearing. If their hair's sticking up.

Simone raised the same point as Louanne:

> Girls are a lot more catty. Everyone knows that. Girls get into more fights. They're more judgmental. You'll see a girl walking down the hall, and she's wearing a tutu or something. And then you know everyone's looking at her and making fun of her. Whereas guys, I think they just go with the flow more. They're not really making fun of them. It's more like play fighting or something.

In marked contrast, Janis, a senior girl, attributed girls' low self-esteem to the male-dominated army culture of Armyville:

> The guys, I find, are getting recruited a lot more. There's more pressure on them to sign up, because of the fact that a lot of the military already is male. They say they're not biased or anything, but I find that they're more willing to recruit males. They put more of an effort in recruit-ing them than females, which is really unfair.... Girls are having more issues, more stress, put on them. They have to do better in school, they have to try and get better marks and be involved in different school activities. They have to go to university and get a good degree, or else they're worth nothing.... Guys can join the military. As long as they play sports and stuff, they're valued.

Relatedly, Jocasta, an exceptional interview participant, told her interviewer that she had high self-esteem, and she encouraged her female peers to cease making the kind of complaints that Janis had articulated and—even as girls—to embrace the army:

> For the people who don't like the army and say that they're depressed because of it, I think it's because they don't get involved with it.... Why stand outside in the rain while the party is going on inside, when you

can go in and enjoy the party? Like, if you're depressed because the army is moving you around, why don't you get involved with the army and see why it's doing this, and do some research, and get more involved with the army, so you can understand it more? You'll probably enjoy it if you understand it.... It's so easy to go to Family Day and be a part of the army. You can support your family, you can support your parents, you can phone whoever is in Afghanistan and support them. It's not hard.

In speaking as they did, Janis and Jocasta raised an interesting question. Although their female peers attributed their low self-esteem to uncertainties about appearance, boys' treatment of them, and other girls' cattiness, is it possible that these common adolescent-girl uncertainties were weighing especially heavily upon girls within the overarching context of an army community in which female roles are undervalued relative to the dramatic contribution made to Canadian society by combat-trained male military members? In other words, might the male-dominated army culture of Armyville constitute more of an explanation for the gender differences in self-esteem than most of the girls, themselves, recognize?

Our participants' comments about their parents provide some support for this idea. Almost without exception, neither the boys nor the girls expressed admiration for their mothers as occupational role models (even if they belonged to the CAF). However, participants of both genders made it clear that they deeply valued the work their fathers did. We will begin with Fred, a recently graduated boy, who told us in answer to a different interview question,

We were in City X at a hockey tournament, and me and my dad were watching the game. And my dad just got back from his training in Alberta for his first tour. A parent came up to him, and she's like, "Why do you even do it? Why do you actually want to go?" He was like, "Well, it's my job. I've got to do it." We got in the car and I was like, "Why did you say that? Did you actually mean it?" He was like, "Yeah, I meant every word I said." I was like, "Wow."

He added,

Him being military, I see my future as me being military. That's just how I see it. That's what I want to be. I want to serve my country. It's the patriotic thing to do, I think.

Along similar lines, Joel, a senior boy, said,

I don't complain as much as I used to. I'm not a suck. Before, I used to see my dad as bossy, and I used to cry and stuff. But now I see him as

*more of a man and, like, a figure. And I try to be more like him. I suck
everything up. I don't complain.*

Amanda, the senior student daughter of an infantryman, added,

*I always used to love going to the parades and watching my dad march
around. You'd see people, and they'd be all dressed up. I wanted that
to be me. I used to wear his boots and stuff, and walk around the house
and get scuff marks all over the floor and get in trouble.*

It was the Afghanistan mission that had brought Marcia, a junior girl, to
the point of becoming devoted to her father's contribution to his country:

*I appreciate my dad a lot more.... I have more respect for my dad, and
I have a very healthy respect for our Canadian military. I am ashamed
when nobody's wearing their Support the Troops shirts every Friday,
when I know they have them. Because a while ago when all those soldiers were killed all at once, everyone was wearing them. But they don't
wear them any more. I'm like, "You guys, they're still over there!"*

When asked to account for gender differences in self-esteem at AHS,
most male and female participants who discussed this topic observed
that (1) girls are more likely to be affected by others' negative opinions of
them (especially the negative opinions of boys), (2) girls are more likely to
be "brought down" by the glamorous images of girls and women produced
by the media, and (3) some girls respond to the doubts that are thereby created by treating other girls badly in order to "pump themselves up." Only
two girls incorporated the wider community context of the male-dominated
army into their answers to the gender and self-esteem questions. However,
the interview excerpts displayed above reveal the possibility of a relationship existing among the facts that (a) Armyville is an army community, (b)
military men appear to be especially valued by their children, and (c) girls in
Armyville have lower self-esteem than their local and national male peers.

Geographical Transfers and Self-esteem

As we discussed in chapter 2, geographical relocations comprise one of
the unique stressors of military family life. Here we will make a brief
excursion into the topic of the geographical transfers of Armyville adolescents, in hopes of shedding additional light on the issue of adolescents
and self-esteem.

According to our survey results, as noted above, the AFS CAF adolescents had moved, and also changed schools, significantly more frequently
than their civilian peers. Similarly, table 3.6 indicates that almost two
thirds (39) of the 61 interview participants had experienced at least one

Table 3.6   Geographical Transfers across Provincial Borders after Age Six

	Yes	% of total	No	% of total	Total interviewed
One or more major moves during school career (after age 6)	39	64%	22	36%	61

geographical transfer from another province after the age of six. These findings are consistent with the literature on military geographical mobility that was reviewed in chapter 2.

How does the geographical mobility of military families relate to adolescent children's self-esteem? In brief, as we noted in chapter 2, changing schools wreaks havoc with some adolescents' academic progress, thereby robbing some youth of the mental well-being that comes with scholastic achievement at an early age. Mobile adolescents also experience significant losses in friendships and social networks each time they move, a reality that affects girls more negatively than boys (South & Haynie, 2004). As Joel, one of our participants, put it,

> *[We moved] in August, and I didn't get my first friends until, like, November. I hated going to school 'cause I just walked—walked around all by myself, and kept to myself.*

By way of explanation, Lorraine, another participant, added,

> *Since they've been there the whole time, they have their cliques.... So they're less accepting of you because they've been together all their lives and they know they're going to be together all their lives.... They look at you like, "You're going to be leaving, so why would I make friends with you?"*

Participation in extracurricular activities is a third important source of adolescent self-esteem (Eccles, Barber, Stone, & Hunt, 2003). Much of the school- and community-based social life of Armyville revolves around sports activities (Kwan-Lafond et al., 2011). Hence it is not surprising that some of our interview participants made remarks that underscored the extent to which they valued their participation on sports teams. They conversely mourned the absence of sports team membership from their lives, when this had occurred because they had moved to a new place. Ten of our 61 participants made a point of commenting either that moving had made it difficult for them to participate in sports (to be chosen for teams, etc.) or, on the other hand, that not moving had enabled them to easily make and keep good friends, because of their constant participation in sports. For example, when trying to explain why she had high self-esteem, Zoe, a senior girl, noted,

I guess I come from a really confident group of girls. Like, we all play sports, we're all kind of well-rounded, I guess.

Perhaps because she had been able to derive such high self-esteem from participating in sports, Zoe—unlike Jocasta—made it clear that she would never either join the military or marry a military member.

Along similar lines as the experience Zoe had had with sports, a few participants who had not moved, or had not had the experience of losing close friends to moves, spoke with joy and gratitude about the luck they had had in having been able to retain the same friends for several years. When asked to account for their relatively high self-esteem, two girls mentioned this fact as it had applied to them.

Notwithstanding the above comments, the impact of geographical mobility on adolescent self-esteem is not always negative. Adolescents who cope successfully with military relocations are frequently aware that their achievements have been significant, that they have demonstrated their ability to be resilient, and that they have met the tests of crucial challenges at an earlier stage in their lives than have their non-moving peers. For example, Mavis, a girl who had just graduated from AHS, told us,

I got used to the whole moving thing, and stuff like that that's different. Like I like it now—I like change. I like changing schools and I don't mind making new friends. I think it made me more used to that, where some people I know . . . that weren't military families were like, "I've lived here for 18 years, and now I'm moving for school, and I'm all scared!"

Similarly, Marcia, a junior girl, said,

I think we're different because we've learned some lessons that other people might need to learn later in life. We have had to move without any say in it, and that's gotta teach us something. I mean, I'm not exactly sure what, but "You gotta do what you gotta do!" Things like that.

Lorraine, a girl who had just graduated, believed that moves had made her a kinder person towards her peers who had subsequently found themselves new to AHS:

I'd like to think of myself as a better person. 'Cause I try to accept everybody and make friends with everybody, whether they're going to move again or not. And just like going to school, I've realized like this is going to be hard for everybody kind of deal. So, you have to learn to accept everybody and just go with everything.

As we noted earlier, our survey of AHS students found that students from CAF families had a more positive attitude towards school than their civilian peers. Janis offered a possible explanation for this when she made a link between her enforced move to Armyville several years earlier and her consequent enthusiastic engagement in a variety of school-based activities. She said,

> [If I hadn't moved] I would be a different person, most definitely, than I am today. I don't know if I would be as involved in the school. Because moving, you know, the school helps you out. And then you realize, well, hey, they have all these school activities. And then you get involved in that to meet more people. And then you just stay in those kinds of programs over the years. I wouldn't be in French Immersion, so I wouldn't have done my exchange. I wouldn't be graduating with my diploma with a certificate that says I'm bilingual. I wouldn't have done anything like that.

Janis's description of her involvement in the school lends support to what will emerge as one of the keynote themes of this book: the continuity that schools potentially provide to the lives of adolescents who have been challenged by military relocations and deployments.

The above contributions of Mavis, Marcia, Lorraine, and Janis are significant, as they suggest that the relationship between geographical transfers and self-esteem is a complex one for military adolescent girls. In support of this idea, we should note that the analysis of our survey results turned up no relationship between frequency of moves and level of boys' or girls' self-esteem. Moves certainly create problems in the areas of academic achievement, friendship, and sports team membership opportunities. However, they also provide adolescents with opportunities to measure up to unique challenges; some adolescents appear able to take advantage of these opportunities.

Conclusion

In this chapter we have introduced you to the town of Armyville and also to the various steps we undertook in order to carry out our Armyville research project.

We have also shared some links between our survey and interview findings regarding the Armyville adolescents' mental well-being. We had expected the Armyville CAF adolescents to score more poorly on the survey's mental health measures than their civilian peers, owing to what we knew about the stressors of military family life. We had formulated no expectations regarding how either the CAF or civilian Armyville adolescents would compare on these measures with their national NLSCY peers. To our surprise, the Armyville CAF adolescents scored the same as their

Armyville civilian peers on the survey's mental health measures. We were also surprised to learn that all the adolescents in Armyville scored more poorly on these same measures (self-esteem, depression, and suicide ideation) than their peers in the national sample. By way of explanation, we speculated that there might be a spillover of the impact of military life stressors from the population of CAF adolescents to the population of civilian adolescents who attended the same school. We attributed this possibility to the relative geographical isolation of the town, the single-industry nature of the town's workforce, and the military-civilian integrated nature of the town's culture. If a spillover effect existed, whereby military life stressors also impacted the Armyville *civilian* adolescents, this effect could account for both the similarity between the two subpopulations on mental well-being measures and the unexpected differences we found on these measures between all Armyville adolescents and their national peers.

We devoted some space in this chapter to discussing our survey and interview findings on self-esteem, especially with regard to gender differences. According to our survey results, adolescent girls in Armyville—both CAF and civilian—were found to have lower self-esteem than their male peers. Armyville adolescent girls also scored lower on self-esteem than their male peers in the national NLSCY sample. Several of the girls we interviewed confessed to being easily dragged down by other people's negative opinions of them; in contrast, most of the boys we interviewed claimed to care little about what others thought. When asked for explanations of this difference, both boys and girls mentioned girls' anxiety about their physical appearance and popularity, and their victimization by other girls' bullying and cattiness.

The relevance of the boys' and girls' above explanations to the tendency of girls in every community to suffer from low self-esteem is obvious. Thinking back to the survey results, however, one might still ask: Is there a reason, peculiar to Armyville, for the low self-esteem of adolescent girls? We used interview data to speculate that a contributing factor might be the organization of Armyville around the male-dominated single industry of the Canadian army.

Finally, this chapter explored the complex topic of the impact of geographical mobility on self-esteem. Our survey data turned up no relationship between geographical mobility and self-esteem in any member of the AHS population. We know from the research literature, and from what some of our participants told us, that geographical mobility creates problems for youth in the areas of school progress, friendships, and memberships on sports teams. In contrast, a few of our Armyville participants had found that geographical mobility had created opportunities that had enabled their self-esteem to be enhanced.

Certainly both our survey and interview data provided us with food for thought about adolescent self-esteem in Armyville, even if they provided us with little that was conclusive. The most notable finding of our survey was the fact that both CAF and civilian AHS students scored lower on mental well-being measures than their peers elsewhere in Canada.

We will discover in chapters 5 and 6 that deployments put considerable stress on the adolescents who are affected. An obvious question to ask would be, does this stress have mental health implications? Our survey results do not suggest any easy answers to this question because all Armyville adolescents—civilian and CAF alike—apparently share roughly the same level of mental well-being. Contrary to much research literature, our survey results point to nothing uniquely negative about the mental well-being of CAF adolescents. We will see in chapter 5 that previous research has found links between adolescents' (especially girls') exposure to deployments and heightened depression and anxiety. However, no links have been found (or explored) between deployments and self-esteem. Hence, no research has established that adolescent self-esteem is positively or negatively affected by deployments. Previous research has therefore found links between deployments and some—but not all—aspects of military adolescent mental well-being. And the results of our survey were inconclusive on *all* aspects of the mental well-being of CAF adolescents. We will revisit the issue of mental health later in the book, after we have had a chance to explore more of what our interview participants shared with us.

4

Life Just before a Deployment

We all went to a bunker. There was drinks and food there. We talked
to him, made sure he was okay. And we said goodbye. Like we hugged
him, made sure he knew that he was gonna be missed. And after that,
we went home and just tried to, you know, go on.
　　　　　　　—Roger, whose father was deployed to Afghanistan

In chapter 2 we made a distinction between the normative and non-normative life transitions in adolescents' lives. McCubbin and Figley's (1983) military-related distinction between normative and catastrophic life stressors may therefore be a good way to begin our first chapter on AHS adolescents and deployments.

A deployment can be regarded as a *normative* life stressor if it is one that the family considers to be routine and predictable. A deployment that qualifies as a *catastrophic* life stressor, in contrast, is one that has been brought on by a crisis, such as war: it is not predictable on the dimensions of length, location (sometimes), or level of danger, and it causes the family stress and anxiety (Wiens & Boss, 2006). During a deployment that can be categorized as a catastrophic stressor, children of all ages are at enhanced risk of experiencing behavioural problems and/or mental health issues (Lincoln, Swift, & Shorteno-Frazer, 2008).

As noted in chapter 2, a large proportion of CAF families live under a blanket of risk that during the last 20 years has increased the likelihood that a given deployment will qualify as a catastrophic stressor. A stressful deployment is especially disruptive to the lives of adolescents who, without the deployment, would have been free to concentrate on their growing-up tasks, their schoolwork, their extracurricular activities, their friends, and their first romantic relationships. This chapter focuses on our interview participants during the pre-deployment period, and it highlights the anxiety, or lack of anxiety, that they experienced at two stages of this period: receiving the news of the deployment, and getting ready to say goodbye.

The Military Deployment Cycle

Every deployment is unique, and it is experienced as an intensely singular event for every family that participates in it. At the same time, military family literature has developed concepts that have captured common aspects of the emotional side of a deployment in ways that have resonated with many military families' experience. The term *emotional cycle of military separation*, as used by Wiens and Boss (2006), incorporates the ideas that (1) distinct emotional stages unfold during each deployment, and (2) each emotional stage is associated with a set of recognizable experiences that are common to many military families.

Commentators disagree on the number of stages that characterize the emotional cycle of military separation and on how each stage should be conceptualized. The American Psychological Association's (2007) Task Force on the psychological needs of US service members and their families divided the cycle of deployment into four phases: *pre-deployment* (the period from notification to departure), *deployment* (the period during which the member is away), *reunion* (pre-return preparations), and *post-deployment* (the period following the member's return) (cited by Esposito-Smythers et al., 2011). Pincus, House, Christenson, and Adler (2005) divided the cycle of deployment into five phases: *pre-deployment* (the period from notification to departure), *deployment* (the first month of the deployment), *sustainment* (the second through eighteenth months of the deployment), *re-deployment* (the final month of the deployment), and *post-deployment* (the first three to six months following the deployment). Peebles-Kleiger and Kleiger (1994) built on Logan's (1987) earlier work by dividing the cycle of deployment into seven emotional stages of adjustment: *Anger/Protest* (immediate period after the news of the deployment has been received); *Detachment and Withdrawal* (final days before the departure, during which family members distance themselves from each other in fear of the separation); *Sadness/Despair* (the moment of departure and two to six weeks afterwards); *Recovery and Stabilization*; *Anticipation of Homecoming* (beginning six weeks before the reunion); *Reunion* (reunion day and six weeks afterwards); and *Reintegration/Stabilization*.

In this book we will simplify, and will emulate Norwood, Fullerton, and Hagen (1996) by focusing on a deployment's three main phases: anticipation (which we will term *pre-deployment*), separation (which we will term *deployment*), and reunion (which we will term *post-deployment*) (see also Johnson & Ling, 2013).

Receiving the News of the Deployment

The day that the military member receives notification of the deployment marks the start of the pre-deployment phase, and the pre-deployment phase spans a time frame that varies from several weeks to over a year (Laser & Stephens, 2011). If the deployment is a catastrophic stressor, all members of the family can be expected to begin this phase with feelings of shock and disbelief (Esposito-Smythers et al., 2011). As the pre-deployment phase unfolds further, high levels of anxiety will likely characterize the experience of children and adolescents, as well as of the parent who is staying behind (Laser & Stephens, 2011; White, de Burgh, Fear, & Iversen, 2011). The deploying parent may be preoccupied with training, bonding with his/her unit mates, and emotionally separating from his/her family (Laser & Stephens, 2011; Pincus et al., 2005). Both parents may be involved in negotiating household and administrative matters (finances, wills, etc.) (Pincus et al., 2005; Sheppard, Malatras, & Israel, 2010; Siegel et al., 2013), and may be less available than usual to their children (Amen, Jellen, Merves, & Lee, 1988).[1]

The pre-deployment period may therefore be an emotionally difficult time for children and adolescents as they cope with their fears and also learn to demand less than usual from both of their parents, each of whom has valid reasons to be preoccupied with other matters. In 1994, Michelle Kelley reported on research that compared children's behaviour during the period preceding a normative deployment with the behaviour of children the same age during the period preceding a catastrophic deployment. In the instance of the normative deployment, Kelley found that children aged 5 to 13 exhibited more externalizing and internalizing behaviours during pre-deployment than they did during the actual deployment. In the instance of the Persian Gulf War, in contrast, she found that the children continued with their externalizing and internalizing behaviours during the whole deployment. These findings suggest that children may settle down more easily during the deployment phase of a routine deployment than they do during the deployment phase of a wartime deployment. Based on their clinical experience, Amen and colleagues (1988) had earlier reported that, during the pre-deployment phase, children of adolescent age are likely to respond emotionally in one of three ways: (1) acting out (externalizing), (2) feeling sad and/or abandoned (internalizing), or (3) denying feeling any emotions at all.

Unlike the questionnaire-based research cited above, our interviews provided us with little information on how the CAF adolescents actually behaved after they had received the news of a deployment that they were about to experience. They also provided us with no systematic information on CAF adolescents' pre-deployment emotional states. They did, however, provide us with useful insights.

We will begin by sharing a small amount of background information on the parental deployment experiences of our interview participants. First, about two-thirds of them (42 of 61) had experienced one or more recent major parental deployments. "Major deployment" was defined as overseas, unaccompanied (i.e., imposed restriction) posting, basic training, or instructing courses in other provinces for at least 50 percent of each year. "Recent deployment" was defined as any deployment experienced by a given participant during senior elementary school (when aged 9 to 11) or subsequently. In practice, most deployments discussed by our participants had happened more recently than age 12. Of the 42 who had experienced a recent major deployment, 24 (or 57%) were girls; 18 (43%) were boys. Twenty-five of the 42 (60%) had experienced one or more parental deployments to Afghanistan. Fifteen (36%) had experienced recent parental deployments to Bosnia; 15 (36%) had experienced other recent overseas parental deployments; 10 (16%) had experienced a recent imposed restriction (IR) posting (parent was elsewhere in Canada, unaccompanied by family, usually for a year); five (12%) had experienced parents away for several months on basic training; four (9.5%) had had parents deployed to the West Indies; two (4.7%) had had parents deployed to the former Yugoslavia; and the parents of two participants (4.7%) had been deployed on ships. From the numbers, it is evident that some participants had experienced multiple parental deployments during the previous several years.

Our participants typically felt fear and anxiety when they received the news of an upcoming parental deployment. The degree of anxiety surrounding the news seemed to vary according to the danger of the deployment, the closeness of the adolescent's relationship with the deployed (as opposed to the undeployed) parent, relationships among siblings and other family members, and difficulties that were already affecting the family (e.g., illnesses, marital problems, the undeployed parent's stress, siblings' chronic conditions and/or behaviour problems).

Participants who were anticipating only a routine deployment tended to react to the news in a relaxed manner. Speaking of his father's nine-month posting to Alert, Hal, a senior boy, commented,

> There's lots of preparation and stuff. And I was all, "I'm going to miss you," and stuff like that. But I knew he wouldn't be gone for a whole long time. We'd be all right.... He was just going up to the North Pole. He loves snow to just plow—and stuff like that.

Zoe, a senior girl, commented similarly on her father's long deployment to Africa:

Military families are prepared for it. They know. They're expecting it. They know it's going to happen. So I don't think I was surprised. I was just like, "Oh, my dad's going to be gone again" type thing.

Exceptions occurred to the aforementioned relaxed reaction to a routine deployment in instances where the father's absence would create a special problem for the family. For example, Marilee, a senior girl whose mother had sustained a serious injury as a military member, recalled her fear, as a younger child, that her father would be sent on a dangerous tour and the family would lose its only able-bodied parent:

If my dad had said that he was going somewhere dangerous when I was little I would have said, "Then tell the military No!" 'Cause when I was little, I was extremely scared like if something bad might happen. 'Cause although I kept it to myself, I used to always think, "What if he hurts himself, what would we do then?"

Speaking of her fear of the possibility of her (now retired/reservist) father being sent to Afghanistan, Marilee added,

He still knows how to hold the guns. So it wouldn't take much to retrain him, 'cause things stick in his mind. I'm hoping that they pull out [of Afghanistan], so it doesn't happen for us or for anyone else.

Darlene, a senior girl and child of divorced parents, felt vulnerable as a result of losing her father to a European deployment only a year and a half after she had chosen to leave her mother's house and begin living with him:

I was with my boyfriend, and we were in his little car. We were driving out, and my dad's like, "I need to tell you something." I'm like, "Okay." And he just, "I'm going to be posted to Country X." I don't remember how the conversation went. All I remember is his walking away, and we were driving. I was looking out the window, and I couldn't stop crying. Because I'd gotten my dad, and now he was leaving.

Routine deployments therefore create stress and anxiety for an adolescent whose family is already experiencing difficulties, or has experienced a major recent change.

Canada's mission in Afghanistan marked a sharp rise in the stress level of deployments. Indeed, this event changed the meaning of *all* deployments for many Armyville youth. To begin with, the Afghanistan mission evoked strong emotions in adolescents who had not yet been affected by it, who were never destined to be affected by it, or who had been affected and did not expect to be affected again. For example, Darlene, quoted above, described how, after many years of living through her father's long deployments, she for the first time became fearful upon moving to Armyville and realizing that he could be deployed to Afghanistan:

> I felt like I was used to it. Like, "Dad's going to go away. He's going to come back." But then when I moved here and there was a chance of him going to Afghanistan, that's when fear struck that I was like, "If he goes there, it'll be different than before."

Bridget, whose father had already been deployed to Afghanistan, was fearful that her mother might also be deployed there and might miss the wrap-up of Bridget's high-school career:

> I don't want her to be gone next year, because next year I'll be in Grade 11. And if she leaves next year, she'll probably be gone until Grade 12. And I don't want her to miss my graduation, or our prom, or anything like that.

Joe, a senior boy whose father was in an occupation whose members did not deploy overseas, expressed guilt and discomfort that the father of one of his classmates had been killed in Afghanistan, whereas his family had been exempted from every aspect of the Afghanistan mission:

> I feel kinda bad. Like, my dad's been here for 23 years and he's never had to go to Afghanistan.

Several participants were in a position to express intense relief that their fathers or stepfathers had not recently, or would not in future, be deploying to Afghanistan. Mavis, a recently graduated girl, whose mother had been deployed to the Middle East, was relieved that, since the deployment had not been to Afghanistan, she knew that her mother would be safe:

> She didn't go to, like, Afghanistan or anything where I was scared. Like she was just working over there. So it wasn't scary like that.

Catherine, a junior girl, expressed relief that her father could not be deployed to Afghanistan because he had been injured several years ago in Bosnia:

> Getting injured in Bosnia at the time—we thought it was a terrible, terrible thing. But then, looking back, it was…a blessing in disguise, because he didn't have to go to Afghanistan now. He got out because he was injured. Like if that hadn't happened, my dad would've served in Afghanistan, or he could be serving now.

Similarly, when asked what it was like to have his injured father consequently home from Afghanistan "for good," Pete, a junior boy, quickly expressed his delight that he could never be sent there again:

It was nice to know, and with his [injury] they can't send him back,
because of that, because of the danger thing.

Likewise, Marcia, a junior girl whose father had been injured in Afghanistan, said,

[I felt] relief. It was kinda confusing, 'cause I shouldn't be happy that
he got his tour cut or whatever. But I was. I knew that I shouldn't be in
a lot of ways, but at the same time I was okay with myself feeling happy
about it.

For each of these participants, different circumstances would have created ongoing anxiety for them. This would have been the case if Mavis's
mother had been deployed to Afghanistan instead of to the Middle East; if
Catherine's father had not been injured in Bosnia and was still able to meet
the CAF's *universality of service*[2] requirement; and/or if Pete's and Marcia's
fathers had not already been injured in Afghanistan.

Significant relief—and, occasionally, guilt—characterized the reactions
of the above participants whose families had been spared from experiencing an Afghanistan deployment, or an additional Afghanistan deployment. Similarly, Jeff, a senior boy whose father had been deployed several
times to Afghanistan, had arrived, as a consequence, at the new opinion
that all non-Afghanistan deployments should be considered trivial events.
Although his father's recent IR deployment to another Canadian city had
been longer than any of his Afghanistan tours, Jeff reported "barely notic-
ing it." Rather than anxiety, he felt relief:

It was longer than any other time he's been gone, 'cause that was two
years. But it wasn't like he was in Afghanistan or something. So it wasn't
like, "Oh my God, he might get shot today!" Or something like that.
And, like, him and my mom talked every day. So my mom was still
kind of, like, okay. Like she didn't stress out, or anything like that. And
he would still come home every now and then.

As noted in the introduction, both the Armyville School District and the
adult members of the Armyville community had come to realize by 2006
that the Afghanistan mission would be different, and extremely dangerous.
It is not far-fetched to imagine that this realization trickled down to all
Armyville CAF adolescents, and that the parental deployment experience
of every one of them became transformed by this historical event. Given
some of the results of our survey, reported in the preceding chapter, *civilian*
Armyville adolescents may also have been affected by this mission.

For those participants whose parents did deploy to Afghanistan, a crucial factor affecting the level of anxiety with which they anticipated the

deployment was the amount of danger to which their parent was likely to be exposed. Some participants were able to reassure themselves that they had nothing to fear because their parents would be located in a safe part of Kandahar. For example, Mark, a junior boy, told his interviewer, "I felt like since he's a [occupation], he was safe—he wouldn't exactly be on the front lines." Leonard, a senior boy whose mother would be sitting behind a desk, was similarly able to reassure himself:

> I was pretty upset. I went through a week where I was pretty sad. [Then] I was like, "Oh, she'll be all right." 'Cause she was going to be on the base thing there the whole time. "So there's no huge possibility of her getting bombed or anything. So, okay, she'll be fine."

Jasmine, the daughter of a military police member, likewise believed that her father's job would protect him:

> I think he just makes sure that the military guys do what they're supposed to and, like, don't go out and get drunk all the time, and stuff like that.... Like, what else is he really gonna do? I think he just stays on base and guards stuff, or makes sure that everyone's doing what they're supposed to.... If he's stuck on base, I don't really think anything's gonna happen to him.

Other participants, who believed themselves unable to make such reassurances to themselves, were more fearful. For example, when asked how he felt when his infantryman father gave him the news, Sam, a senior boy, said,

> I was used to it from the other tours. But it was still kind of hard, because it's worse there than anywhere else. Like, you never know what's going to happen.

Jeff, introduced above, reported dreading his father's second deployment to Afghanistan more than his first, because by the time of his second deployment the Canadians had passed beyond the stage of setting up camp. As he put it,

> [His second tour] was...more difficult, because by this point things were moving. And the building that he was in was actually hit by a rocket attack while he was there.

Recalling how he had anticipated the Afghanistan deployment of his infantryman father, Brad, a senior boy, said, simply, "That was the worst one, 'cause he knew that he was going into hell." For her part, Marcia recalls being beside herself with fury that her infantryman father had *volunteered* for an Afghanistan deployment:

I'm thinking, "Man, what are you thinking? I know you joined the military to serve your country. But it's Afghanistan!! Can't you go do that somewhere else?"

Apart from the level of danger to which they believed their parent would be exposed, some participants had family-related reasons for being fearful about an Afghanistan deployment. Mark, introduced earlier, knew with a sinking feeling that, owing to his mother's demanding paid-work schedule, his household responsibilities would quadruple during his father's deployment and he would be forced to forego his extracurricular activities:

I was bummed that he was leaving—no extracurricular activities! I knew my brother and I were gonna fight a lot. It was just that gut feeling—ahh!

Reflecting some of the literature cited above, Petra, the daughter of an infantryman, knew that the whole family would have to cope with the acting out of her younger sister, who had been unable to accept her father's Afghanistan deployment. At the time Petra was being interviewed, her sister was refusing to go to school:

It's been hard with my sister, just trying to get her used to it. 'Cause it's almost like she won't accept the fact that [our dad] is going, and she can't do anything to stop it.... I don't know if she's doing it on purpose, but part of her is trying to be like, "Please stay home" kind of thing.... She hasn't gone to school this entire week. If my mom's not working, she stays there. And all day she tries to convince her, "You should go to school, you should go to school." And then she's like, "No I'm not!" But if my mom has to work, then she just kinda lets her stay there.... My sister doesn't talk to anyone, really, about her problems. She just kinda keeps it all shut in.

Petra was also afraid that her father would return from Afghanistan with PTSD, because he already had anger issues:

When my dad gets angry, he gets angry. It's like, try to avoid the anger with him. Because just the way he was brought up and with the military and everything, it's like everything has to be perfect almost. So when he comes home, I'm not really sure what to expect. Like I'm not sure if he's going to have any of the stress disorder kind of things, or if he's just going to be the same as he was.

Bridget, the daughter of two CAF parents, was fearful that her mother might be sent to Afghanistan and be killed there, because she knew that, in that event, she would be unable to live with her unnurturing father:

It scares me a lot more for her to go over, especially since she's a [occupa-
tion]. And she's out more. So it scares me quite a bit.... I'm afraid for
her to go in with the trucks and have to be out there. And your mom's
your mom. She could get hit, and it scares me. Because I don't know
what I would do without my mom. Like I'd definitely not live with my
dad if he was the only one there.

From the above excerpts you can see that the amount of anxiety accompanying the anticipation of a deployment to Afghanistan varied among affected
participants. It depended on the level of danger to which they believed their
parent would be exposed and such aspects of family dynamics as anticipated
stress on the parent who was staying home. It also depended on the participant's relationship with the parent who was staying home, the anticipated
stress on the parent who was deploying, and potentially negative impacts
of the deployment on siblings.

Lemmon and Chartrand (2009) distinguished among *normative, tolerable,* and *toxic* stressors that may affect families during various stages of a
deployment cycle. Tolerable stressors may include such anxiety-produc-
ing deployment events as war, long duration, or parental injury or death;
however, if adequate support exists for the family, these stressors can be
endured and overcome. Tolerable stressors become toxic, and create serious emotional consequences for families when they become chronic, and
when there is inadequate—or no—support available. For our interview
participants whose parents would be exposed to frequent danger during
the deployment, and who at the same time were living through or anticipating a significant family difficulty, there existed a risk that the deployment would be experienced as a less-than-tolerable, or even toxic, stressor
(cf. Drummet, Coleman, & Cable, 2003).

The experiences of Marilee and Darlene remind us that even a routine deployment can create anxiety when a family difficulty is already
present. In contrast, adolescents who are already coping with the catastrophic stressor of an Afghanistan deployment find their problems
compounded and rendered more complex by what, in other circumstances, would have been the relatively manageable situations of mothers' full-time jobs and younger siblings acting out. Just thinking about
the possibility of a parental Afghanistan deployment appeared to cause
stress to some of the youth we interviewed. Finally, it was sadly ironic
that a few of our participants were able to feel protected from the possibility of a parent being deployed to Afghanistan—or being deployed
to Afghanistan again—only by the fact that the parent had sustained an
injury on a previous recent deployment.

Our interviews taught us little about aspects of the pre-deployment period other than our participants' anxieties (or lack thereof) surrounding the fact that their parents would be deployed. The psychopathological tenor of some of the literature cited above on the pre-deployment phase (e.g., externalizing and internalizing behaviours) was seldom reflected in what our participants told us about themselves, because they spoke from their own perspective, rather than that of adults. Our participants also did not describe either of their parents as having been emotionally unavailable during a pre-deployment period (cf. Amen et al., 1988; Laser & Stephens, 2011); but this fact may have been a reflection of questions that they were not directly asked.

Getting Ready to Say Goodbye

If there was a *Detachment/Withdrawal* phase in the emotional cycle of deployment (as identified by Peebles-Kleiger & Kleiger, 1994, above) among/within their families, the two participants who discussed the final days before their parents' deployments did not mention it. Nor did they mention the feelings of anxiety they would inevitably have experienced during this emotionally fraught time. Instead, they focused on the family's awareness of the imminent separation and on how the parent who was leaving attempted to make the most of the diminishing time that remained, especially with his/her children (cf. Deployment Health and Family Readiness Library, 2006; Pincus et al., 2005). Amanda, a senior girl, recalled the period leading up to her father's deployment to Afghanistan:

> We definitely spent more time together as a family.... Everybody was trying to be happy. If something got them down, you just kind of picked yourself right back up and forgot about it. Whereas you usually wouldn't do that. We were always trying to be a lot more positive and doing stuff as a family before he left, because there's always that chance that that might be the last time.

Zoe described the special "alone" times she shared with her father before his long deployment to Africa:

> You know, I do things just with Dad. Like he'll take you on dates and stuff. And we would go to the beach just with Dad. Like, we'd have single dates. Or my parents would go away for the weekend together by themselves. Like, more family things, like family movie nights. They'd try to get us all together at once instead of just being like, "Oh you can go to your friend's house." Stuff like that.

Both Amanda and Zoe reported only positive pre-deployment interactions among family members. It is possible that, since both of them were describing a deployment that had occurred several years earlier, their negative recollections (if any) may have been mellowed by time.

When the actual departure day of a long and/or dangerous deployment arrives, it stands out as a major event. The details of the day their parents left for Afghanistan were recalled vividly by almost all of our relevant participants. Zachary, a junior boy, poignantly recalled his infantryman father cuddling him in bed the night before he left:

> The night before [he had to leave], he came up into my room and he [lay] there with me while I was going to sleep. And then I just didn't want him to leave.

Pete, introduced earlier, recalled not knowing the exact day that his father would leave, and therefore being surprised on that morning when his mother pulled him out of class:

> I was in the middle of a social studies class, and I just got called to the office. I knew he was leaving soon, but I didn't know he was leaving right that day. So I got called to the office; it was my mom. She said, "Go to your class and get your stuff. Your dad is leaving today, and I want you guys to have a little time together." So I was like, "Okay." I went to the classroom and got my stuff. And then we all went back to the house, ate a lunch, all hung out there for a while, and then we drove to the airport and saw him take off.

The day her father left for Afghanistan, Simone recollected the whole family's tears:

> We went on base and we drove him to one of the hangars where they were all getting on the buses, and everyone was crying. Even him. And I've only seen him cry twice in my life.... So he cried then, and I was so surprised. I was like, "Dad, you're crying. I've never seen you cry before." And then he got all embarrassed. And then this time he started crying again, and my brother was hugging him, saying goodbye to him and stuff. It was a really sad day.

Louanne, a senior girl, provided a chilling description of how the CAF micromanaged members and their families during the minutes leading up to the members' dramatic departure for the nine-month mission:

> I was angry at him for leaving. 'Cause I was like, "Why would you want to?" But at the same time I understood that he had to. And I didn't want him to see me cry. I wanted him to think that I was okay. I ended up

crying anyways, of course. But it was a long wait. We went into, like, the drill hall, and there was all these chairs set up. And you were basically just like counting down the minutes. And then they would announce it, like "Ten minutes!" They would announce how much longer you had. And [the members] would line up, and they would do the roll call or whatever. And then they would come back to their families. And then the bus came, and it was just like in the movies when they're like waving on the train. Except on a bus, basically. And then it was a really bad feeling. 'Cause then you were thinking, "Like, this could be the last time I see my dad. This could be the last time I hear his voice."

What comes through in this riveting account is the anxiety Louanne felt as the minutes ticked away and the lack of control and helplessness she experienced in relation to the unknown future that she knew would befall her family. In fact, as we will learn in chapter 6, Louanne's father returned from Afghanistan with PTSD, and Louanne's family life changed markedly. Even though her father went on an IR posting instead of to Afghanistan, Catherine (introduced earlier) similarly recalled being grief-stricken as his plane took off from Armyville:

He had to leave bright and early to get there. I remember I got up and I said goodbye to him. And I told him I'd miss him and I was crying. I remember I stayed up. Like, I would not go back to bed. I stayed up until I saw that first plane leave. And I literally went out on the step and waved to him, even though I knew I couldn't see him.

Just as not all participants experienced the same emotions when they learned that their parent would be deployed, the adolescents we spoke to also varied in their emotional responses to the moment of departure. One factor that seemed to influence this experience was family dynamics: On a day of crisis, *which* family members were expected to be strong? *Which* family members were expected to have been undiminished by internalizing emotions (e.g., fear or sadness) and to be able to play the role of "rock" vis-à-vis their more emotional siblings or parents? More than one of the girls we interviewed seemed to occupy this position in her family. Martha, a senior girl, recalled the day her father left for Afghanistan:

My mom knows what war is like. And she was really, really upset.... And my brother and my sister didn't know what to make of it. So everybody kinda went into a melodramatic kind of "whoohoo." And I'm the stubborn one in a way. I'm everybody else's rock. Because I don't really cry over stuff like that. Like, I will hug him and say, "You be careful. Please just lay flat. Don't get shot at. I really need you to come home," and that kinda thing. [But] when he got on the plane and everybody started crying, it was like... he was dead or something. He's going away to do something for his country! Like, I was proud of him. I was good, got in the car. Nobody went to school that day.... But I was also really...focused on school, so I didn't wanna miss any attendance or stuff like that. So I just missed the morning and then went back to school. My mom was like, "Are you sure? Are you sure?" And...two or three days later, the siblings all ganged up on me, "You don't even care! You don't understand!" I am like, "I understand. [But]...he's not dead." I was fine, really, the whole way through.

Bridget, introduced above, told a similar story about her reaction to her father's departure:

My mom, you know... 'cause now that she's in the military, she knows what goes on over in Afghanistan. She knows all the troubles.... And with all the people that died over there, she was terrified. And she had to have counsellors come in.... I kind of didn't really care. Because I'm used to them being gone. So, you know, my mom's like, "Oh your dad's leaving." . . . I cried and I felt bad and I was scared. But I didn't really make it into a big deal like some people I know. They cried for weeks after their dad left. It just...didn't affect me that much.

One wonders how Martha and Bridget processed their fathers' leave-takings, and why what they experienced was so different from what Simone and Louanne experienced. According to literature cited above (Amen et al., 1988), some adolescents deny feeling any strong emotion prior to the deployment. It is alternatively possible that every adolescent occupies a unique position in his/her family, and some adolescents derive self-esteem from possessing the ability to bolster their parents and siblings. What we will learn about Bridget in the next chapter would reinforce this latter explanation, as it would apply to her. Speaking about deployments in general (as opposed to Afghanistan in particular), Catherine noted that she, too, was the "rock" in her immediate family:

I'd take a day off school, and we'd literally cry all day—me and my sister. I missed my dad all the time. But I didn't want anyone to see me cry, 'cause I always felt I had to be the strong one. I was like, "I have to be a role model for [Younger Sister]." I don't want her to see that I'm upset, because I know it bothers her having him gone. So no one ever saw me cry except for the day when he'd leave. There would be nights I'd cry myself to sleep, 'cause I missed him. But nobody knew.

Finally, Jeff, introduced above, was also the "strong one" in his family. He attributed this status to the fact that, despite being the youngest child, he became the family's sole male member whenever his father left home. When asked which of his father's departures to Afghanistan he remembered most clearly, he replied,

> *Probably the third time.... It wasn't too bad, just 'cause we knew he wasn't going to be gone for very long. But it was still kind of an emotional thing.... Like, my mom definitely would have taken it the hardest, and then probably my sisters, and then me. Probably because I'm a guy.*

From the small number of interviews that touched in detail on the process of saying goodbye to a deploying parent, what came through for us is the emotional time this represented for the family. For Amanda and Zoe (who may or may not have been typical), it was a time when their appreciation of their deploying parent was heightened, and they were able to put aside the other priorities in their lives for the sake of spending as much quality time with this parent as they could. Similarly, the few hours and few minutes preceding their parents' actual departures were deeply engraved in the memories of the participants who shared their recollections with us.

Conclusion

This chapter has focused on how some of our interview participants experienced the pre-deployment phase of deployments that had recently affected their families. In particular, we learned something about their emotional states at two moments during this phase: the moment of receiving the news of the deployment and the immediate moment of experiencing the parent's departure.

The participants' comments shed light on how stressed and anxious they became upon hearing that their parent would be deployed. The news was easier to deal with if the deployment was routine (a "normative stressor"), unless the participant's family circumstances were already strained or the family had undergone a recent change or crisis. A mission—such as Afghanistan—that qualified as a "catastrophic stressor" created a degree of emotional turbulence for all Armyville CAF adolescents, even those who had no reason to fear that they would be directly affected. Participants whose parents had recently sustained injuries—and were therefore ineligible for an Afghanistan deployment—felt enormous relief. In contrast, participants who heard their parent utter the words "I am going to Afghanistan" became anxious, including participants whose parents' occupations would be expected to shield them from danger or bodily harm. The latter group of participants seemed able to use their knowledge of their parents' occupations to reassure themselves. In contrast, participants who were unable to make these reassurances to themselves were in an emotional situation that was more difficult; the difficulty promised to be compounded if the deployment threatened to put excessive strain on the resources of family members whose coping abilities were already overtaxed. Under these latter circumstances, it was possible that, in Lemmon and Chartrand's (2009) terms, what might have been expected to be a tolerable stressor would eventually grow into a toxic one. Participants' anxiety about the deployment, as well as the emotional burdens they were willing to assume for the sake of other family members, came through in their descriptions of their family's leave-taking scene, just before their deploying parent departed from Armyville.

After the buses and planes pulled away from Armyville, family members left behind were destined to face significant new challenges: assuming extra workloads, managing their emotions, and handling the tensions that threatened to divide them from one another.

In the next chapter we will explore in more detail the anxiety created by the Afghanistan deployments and how it combined with the even more difficult deployment-related stresses that our participants experienced.

5

Life during a Deployment

Trying to get used to him not being there. I come home and I'm like, "Where's Dad?" And my mom is like, "He's gone to Afghanistan." Just trying to get used to him not being there. And realizing that he's gone for six months.

—Zachary

It's luck. I mean, it's a really harsh way of putting it, but that's why it was so worrying. Because it doesn't matter how good my dad is at shoot-'em-up games; it doesn't matter that he was real fit for his age. It's luck! I think that's what was worrying me the most. No matter how much you hoped that he would come home, you had no say in it.

—Marcia

Once the departure has happened, the adolescent's anxiety about his/her parent's safety is augmented by the sense of loss that his/her absence has caused (Chandra et al., 2011; Huebner et al., 2007). This loved one, who under normal circumstances provides affection and mentoring, is suddenly gone (Houston et al., 2009). The adolescent is left behind to grapple with sadness, anger, and worry (Chandra et al., 2010; Chandra et al., 2011; Houston et al., 2009; Mmari et al., 2009).

In general, the deployment represented a quality-of-life loss that created enhanced anxiety and significant extra work. This chapter will focus on the losses, the anxieties, the extra work, and the process, successful or unsuccessful, of seeking support from individuals and institutions outside the home.

Experiencing the Loss

The deployed parent's role in the home had almost always been unique. The unique role noted by our participants ranged from the mundane level of the parent's share of the household labour (e.g., "Dad always drives and does the snow shovelling") to the deepest aspects of companionship: fun, togetherness, harmony amongst family members, the family's ability to function, and the family's ability to survive.

For Petra and Simone, when Dad was gone, disorder and crankiness prevailed:

> It's not as controlled as it was. Like, my dad can like control things very easily. He has this big yelling voice. And when he says one thing in his voice, everyone just kinda looks like, "Whoa!"... Now that he's gone, there's still some order. But a lot of it has, like, left.
>
> —Petra, father deployed to Afghanistan

> When me and my mom fight, it's mostly my dad that breaks it up. 'Cause me and her are like sisters...I steal her clothes, she steals my clothes. It's a vicious cycle. He would break it up and stuff whenever we'd get into a little fight.... When he wasn't there, our fights would be longer and we wouldn't like each other or talk to each other for a couple days.... It was just a stressful time. Everyone was cranky.
>
> —Simone, father deployed to Afghanistan

Cindy, a senior girl who has a poor relationship with her mother, missed the fun parts of family life that had been there when her father was home:

> [When my dad is away I miss] having fun. Because when he's home we have father-daughter things. Like I go shopping with my dad, and not my mom. And we do movies, we go out to dinner. When he's gone we don't do that.... I like it when my dad's home, so I can have somebody there with me. And it's really hard when he's gone, because it's basically just me and my brother.

Marilee had similar memories of her father's long deployments when she was younger:

> [When Dad was home] we used to always go out at least once every week or two and go to, like, Swiss Chalet or some restaurant. With just all of us. And we used to sneak steak bones out and give them to the dog. So that would be kind of fun for us. And usually [then] we'd go to the theatre and...be at the drive-ins. We used to love those. When he was away, we didn't do it as much.

Mom's or Dad's absence from an important event is also a hardship (Mmari et al., 2009, 2010; Wong & Gerras, 2010). Often a deployed parent misses a school graduation or the beginning of his/her child's life at a new school. The comments of Mavis and Fred, below, reflect the worry they had experienced over absences that in the end, fortunately, had *not* happened— the start of high school for Mavis and high-school graduation for Fred.

> *They wanted to keep her for an extra month or two. She came back the day before high school started.... And that was kind of stressful. I remember wanting her to be there when I started school. And she did end up being there, but for a while we didn't think she would be. I didn't like that very much.*
>
> —Mavis, senior girl; mother deployed to the Middle East

> *He almost missed my graduation. He just got back. He got back the very start of June. That's when it was. I remember that. I can remember being pretty pissed off because he wasn't going to be back for it. Because he missed my brother's graduation the previous year, because he wasn't living here.... [And] his tour kept being postponed. Like, oh man, he was supposed to be back, the first time was March. He was, "No, not going to be back in March." Then he was going to be back in April. Not April. And it was midway through May we finally found out he was going to be home like right soon, and then it was good.*
>
> —Fred; father deployed to Afghanistan

These comments reflect emotional turmoil, and reveal the disappointment Mavis and Fred would have experienced had their parents missed these events.

The deployed parent is sometimes "the only person I can talk to," and his/her absence is suffered especially profoundly. Leonard said,

> *She went to Afghanistan, and at the time I had a really shitty girlfriend on the go. So, Mom wasn't there to talk to—it was just Dad. And nobody wants to talk to Dad about girls. So I missed my mom a lot.*

When her mother was away on an Imposed Restriction (IR) posting, Bridget also had no one to talk to, at a time when she was losing some of her friends:

> *There was a lot of drama going on at school because it was Grade 7.... There was a lot of fighting between me and my friends. And I had to go to guidance counselling because of the drama that was going on with my friends. And I hated talking to my dad about that, because I knew he wouldn't understand.... So I was just by myself.... So it was really hard, especially when you go in a couple weeks from having someone to*

talk to, having a lot of friends, having someone to sit with at lunch.... And then the next week sitting by yourself, 'cause you don't have any friends.

Stewart and Paula had felt anxious enough during the Afghanistan deployment to imagine the dire consequences that would have ensued if their fathers had not returned. Stewart's mother suffers from chronic depression:

That was basically my only thought during the whole time. "I want him to come home: 'You better come home!'" Like, he's the only reason why our family stays together.... [If he didn't come home] it would make things a lot more difficult.

Paula, a senior girl, had fought with her father before his departure about her boyfriend, who her father had believed was abusive. Realizing that she might never see her father again, Paula had been so anguished at the fact that they had quarrelled that she had decided to end her relationship with her boyfriend:

I had a nightmare that my dad didn't come back, and he missed everything that was going to be important in my life. And so I sent my dad an email right away: "I broke up with my boyfriend." And that brought us a lot closer.... Like you don't realize how much someone does for you and how much someone means to you until the chance of them not going to be there any more is there.

The situation was sometimes made more poignant by the fact that the parent was permitted to return home during the deployment for a short leave. Catherine and Bridget found that, while this visit was temporarily comforting, their fathers' second departures broke their hearts:

He'd come home for two or three weeks at a time, depending on how much leave he got. And we only got three weeks. Like, he'd come home at Christmas, and he'd come home for three weeks. And we'd go up to City X, and he'd take two weeks off. And we'd stay another week...and he'd still be working. So we'd see him six weeks a year, five weeks a year, something like that. And it's just when you get used to being a family again he has to go back.

—Catherine; father on one-year IR

He came home and then he had to leave again, 'cause he was only home for two weeks. So him coming back from Afghanistan and then having to leave again—that was the hardest part. Because we were just having him home, and then it's just like, "Oh, nice to see you. You're gone back again." So it was really, really hard for me and my mom and my brothers.

And next time, like my mom said that if she goes, she's not going to come home. Because she knows how hard that would be.

—Bridget; both parents members of the CAF

"Worried Sick": Stress and Fear during the Afghanistan Mission

During the Afghanistan mission, participants worried a lot about their parents' safety. As Stewart, a senior boy, put it,

You don't know if your own dad's dead or not. I mean, it's like a dog that you love and he's not home one night. It's the exact feeling. You don't know what's going on.

Louanne, whose father also played a combat role in Afghanistan, felt continually physically sick. She explained how the "click" which preceded daily PA announcements at school always made her panic, because announcements of new casualties in Afghanistan were preceded in the exact same way:

Honestly! Even though somebody can tell me, "Oh, I'm going to call you at five," the phone will ring and your heart will drop into your stomach. And it will make you sick, because you're always walking on eggshells. And every time the PA goes off, even though you know "O Canada"'s coming on, it makes you feel sick. Like, you feel like you're physically going to throw up. And that's what it's like every single day.

Brad added that being summoned to the principal's office had a similar effect:

If you were called to the office, you were kind of like, "Oh yeah! Oh crap!" Like yeah, that was a big worry.

Daily media descriptions of the escalations of conflicts in Afghanistan made the adolescents' fears worse. This was especially true following the first instance of multiple Canadian casualties occurring in a single day. For Bridget, the two days between the media announcement of new deaths and the notification of next of kin created unbearable torture:

You can't help but be worried. Especially when you hear so much and you see so much on the news. You know, "four soldiers killed," and you're like "Oh my gosh!" And, you know, no names are being released right now, so you're freaking out for those couple of days. It was terrifying.

Brady, a senior boy, expressed strong anger at this time lag:

[One holiday weekend] we were all watching the news. And all of a sudden this thing goes on, "We have to interrupt this announcement. Four soldiers were driving in a... tank, and it exploded because they had

driven over a land mine. And we cannot release the names." Like, that is the worst part. I really wish they wouldn't do that.... That shouldn't be what I have to go through on [a holiday weekend].

The time lag was especially distressing when a phone call from a deployed parent occurred at a later time than had been expected. Shanda, a senior girl, recalled,

If we knew he was going to call on Monday morning and he didn't call 'til an hour later, then it was like, "Okay, why isn't he calling yet? He should be calling now!" Especially when we heard that someone died or someone got hurt. Then it felt like forever.

Fears of news briefings were connected with parents' potentially life-threatening locations, as well as with the possibility of hearing about their deaths. Amanda reminded us that security considerations prohibited members stationed in Afghanistan from revealing their whereabouts to their families, which meant that *any* locations identified as current sites of conflict by the media could create anxiety for an adolescent with a parent in Afghanistan:

I got to the point where I couldn't watch the news in the morning, because Dad could never tell us where he was when he would call.... I didn't watch the news because I didn't want to know what was going on.

Marcia added that these security considerations ensured that her father's contact with his family was very infrequent:

He's not really allowed to talk to us about much of that stuff.... And they had certain times that they were allowed to call us because, you know, there's terrorists over there. They could be watching the lines. So they had certain times that they were allowed, and otherwise the Internet was shut off or something like that.... [We talked to him] maybe once a month.

She elaborated:

Usually I'm totally fine with him going on tour, because he calls every now and then. And it's not like I really talk to him that much anyway. But because it was Afghanistan, it was really stressful. I was always thinking, you know, like, "Gee, I wonder what he's doing now."

Cindy added,

We barely talked to him. He would be able to send out emails, but it wasn't to hear his voice kind of thing.... He was able to send out those messages where he was like, "I'm okay and I'm doing okay" and everything. So that's how we knew.

If a deployed parent unwittingly revealed too much during a phone conversation with his/her family, the CAF, listening in, would terminate the call. Amanda told us,

> He could tell us a little bit of stuff. But I think there was one time, the first couple of calls, he told us what they were doing kind of in a bit more detail, and they actually cut him off. Because they listen to the phone calls.... Because satellite phones, it's easy for, say, the Taliban to connect into it and listen to where you are. So that way it would give away your position, or it could give away what you're doing.... There has to be a line drawn at some point, because you get some Joe Blow trying to tell you their exact position and exactly what they're doing. You're putting the lives of your troops in danger.

Coping with Worry

What emotional consequences ensue from worrying about a parent who is deployed? Previous research suggests that some adolescents in this situation experience mental health issues. For example, Anita Chandra and colleagues carried out a study of the children of deployed parents who were attending the US Military Family Association Operation Purple camp in 2008 (sample size: 1,507). They found a higher level of emotional difficulties amongst these children than amongst their civilian peers who had participated in national surveys of emotional well-being around the same time. The girls in particular reported symptoms of anxiety (Chandra et al., 2009; Chandra et al., 2011). Aranda and colleagues, who compared military children of deployed parents at a military treatment facility with their peers whose parents were not deployed (all children in the study were aged 4 to 16 years), reported similar findings (Aranda, Middleton, Flake, & Davis, 2011). In focus groups organized by Huebner and Mancini in 2004, of the 107 adolescent children of deployed parents who participated, one-third reported internalizing symptoms (e.g., depression) (Huebner & Mancini, 2005; Huebner et al., 2007). The school staff who participated in the research conducted by Richardson et. al (2011) found depression to be especially salient amongst the female adolescents of parents who were deployed. In 2009, Morris and Age compared young adolescents recently affected by a deployment with their unaffected military age peers. They found no difference between the two groups but notably higher levels of anxiety and depression amongst the girls. In their analysis of data collected for the Washington State 2008 Healthy Youth Survey amongst adolescents in Grades 8, 10, and 12, Reed, Bell, and Edwards (2011) similarly found that eighth grade girls with parents deployed to combat were comparatively depressed and at risk of suicide. However, in contrast with the results just cited, it was the male adolescents in Reed's study whose emotional well-being was more impaired (Reed et al., 2011). Similarly, in 1996 Jensen, Martin, and Wantanabe had studied 383 military children aged 4 through 17 and had found higher levels of depression amongst those who had had a parent deployed at the time of being measured (especially the boys).

Female adolescents with deployed parents tend to cope with their worry via internalizing mental health symptoms and behaviours (e.g., anxiety and depression), whereas boys, who are more likely to repress their emotions, focus on "acting out" and other externalizing behaviours (Chandra et al., 2010; Mmari et al., 2009; Richardson et al., 2011).

According to both Reed and Jensen, boys' well-being may be more negatively affected than that of girls by the loss of their father during a deployment, and also by the fact that they are likelier than girls to respond to the diminished supervision at home with risky behaviours. In contrast, the school staff who participated in the focus groups organized by Chandra and colleagues reported that older and female adolescents are more emotionally challenged during deployments than male adolescents because they are required to assume increased household responsibilities, take care of younger siblings, and become co-parents with their undeployed parents (Chandra et al., 2010).[1]

How had our own participants coped with worry? Zoe, a senior girl whose parent's life-threatening deployments had not included Afghanistan, shared an example of internalization. She believed that both her male and female peers who had been affected by the Afghanistan mission had responded by becoming fearful and withdrawn:

> Like, kids that I would usually see smiles on their faces, the next year if there's, say, 200 people from Armyville going, and you see that kid maybe with their hood up, or their iPod always in their ears, or never smiling or never answering the teacher, you're kind of, like, wondering, "Hey, did John's dad go to Afghanistan last year?" "Yeah, he's over there right now." Or, like, "Is she not eating? What's up with her? Why isn't she talking to us any more?" ... I have a good group of friends that didn't act that dramatic. But there are kids who act superficial, or act like they're not the same person they were before, just to hide the fact that no one's talked to them about it. ... You want to be alone. You feel isolated. You can't talk to anybody, or no one's giving you the chance to talk to anybody.

Zoe's recollection supports some of the literature that was cited above about adolescents, deployments, and internalizing emotional reactions.

Two of our participants told us that they had coped with their worry during the Afghanistan mission by "acting out." Amanda, for example, had gone out one evening and come home drunk:

As much as you try and put it out of your mind, the constant worry and anxiety is always there. So, yeah, it had to do, I'd say, about 75 percent with how [I was] feeling. At least 15–25 percent had to do with freedom.... That's kind of Mom's downfall. She knows that she'll let us get away with a lot more stuff [than Dad does when he is here.] [But] I really do think that it had to do a lot more with the emotions and how [I was] feeling.

Apart from her worry, Amanda mentioned her mother's disciplinary leniency during deployments as a factor that had affected her decision to get drunk; mothers' leniency is a theme that we will encounter again. Fred, a recently graduated boy whose father's Afghanistan tour kept getting extended, spun out of control, both at home and during his final term at school, because, in his words, the situation "got to me." He and his brother ran roughshod over their mother, whom they regarded as a very weak disciplinarian, relative to their father, who—being a male—commanded their respect:

My mom, she got pretty down. I remember her crying a couple of times because my dad...wasn't home to correct us. And we actually became pretty rebellious towards her, using a lot of profanity at her and stuff like that. Because... me and my brother, we think we're above our mom when my dad's not home.

He added,

I definitely felt like I had more freedom when my dad was gone.... The same with my brother. Like, we thought we ran the show for the longest time.

He also experimented with alcohol:

I did try drinking while he was gone. I thought I had the right to. Like, "Oh, I can do this. He's not home. I won't get into any trouble."

He skipped school and was suspended:

Hockey just finished at this point, so I had nothing else to do. I started skipping some school, and this is when I started to go downhill. I had a rough time just graduating. I barely graduated. I got suspended from school.

He clarified:

I found it hard to concentrate at school.

To make matters worse, after promising his mother that he would participate in counselling, Fred reneged on this promise after attending one session:

[The counsellor's] like, "We're gonna get another session," and I was like, "Sure." And I didn't even bother going again, because I knew it was stupid.

Several of our other participants said that they had "coped fine" with Afghanistan, and discussed the positive strategies they had adopted. For example, Roger had chosen to focus on the positive:

I've always thought that if you think negative, negative's gonna happen. So if that thought came, I was like, "No, he's gonna come back. He's gonna be fine."... I've always found if I'm thinking a positive thing, good things will happen. But if you focus on the negative things like, "Oh, what if he doesn't come back?"... Then you start to worry. And I found it actually comes true.

Shanda similarly believed that she had done the right thing by "keeping going" and avoiding focusing on her anxieties:

I see people now who have parents overseas. I dealt [with it] a lot better than they're dealing [with it] now, for sure. [I kept] my life going. I think that the people now focus almost too much on it. They don't focus enough on their day-to-day life that they should. I just kept focused on sports and school and going out with my friends and, you know, hanging out with my mom. I just kept going. I couldn't dwell on it, or I knew it would get worse.

Pete, whose father had been on several tours to Afghanistan, spoke of how he had kept himself busy, and his mind occupied:

I kind of took it all as it came at me. I just occupied myself with the kids and stuff, doing whatever and all that kind of thing. I spent a lot more time out in the woods, just kind of did whatever to keep my mind occupied and all that.

It is evident that the responses to worry over their fathers' deployments to Afghanistan had varied among our participants. Some AHS students observed by Zoe had become isolated and withdrawn. Amanda and Fred (especially Fred) had acted out. Roger, Shanda, and Pete had made a point of developing strategies that they were proud of, and that seemed to have worked for them. We will see below that, in keeping with much of the existing research, more of the girls we interviewed verbalized the emotional stress they experienced during deployments than the boys.

Unavailability of the Parent Remaining at Home

The deployed parent's absence creates a quality-of-life loss for every other family member. Especially in the case of a dangerous deployment (e.g., Afghanistan), the parent who remains behind usually suffers from stress. We found out that many of the undeployed Armyville parents were indeed stressed, and the stress levels of their adolescents rose accordingly.

During the Persian Gulf War, mothers whose husbands were deployed to the Gulf were more likely to suffer from depression than mothers whose husbands were away on routine deployments (Kelley, 1994). Since 1994, research has proliferated on the emotional stress suffered by the civilian family members of deployed military members: research on, for example, adolescents (Cederbaum et al., 2014; Chandra et al., 2010; Huebner & Mancini, 2005; Huebner et al., 2007; Lucier-Greer et al., 2015; Mansfield, Kaufman, Engel, & Gaynes, 2011; Mmari et al., 2009; Richardson et al., 2011); military couples (Allen, Rhoades, Stanley, & Markman, 2011); and female spouses (Dimiceli, Steinhardt, & Smith, 2010; Eaton et al., 2008; Everson, Darling, & Herzog, 2013; Jensen et al., 1996; Mansfield, Kaufman, Marshall, Gaynes, & Morrissey, 2010; Steelfisher, Zaslavsky, & Blendon, 2008). As participants in a recent series of focus group studies, school personnel discussed the difficulties they had observed in the lives of female spouses of US military members who were deployed to Iraq or Afghanistan. The school personnel described these mothers as frequently missing meetings with teachers, assigning a low priority to their children's academic performance, and keeping their children home from school as sources of companionship (Chandra et al., 2010; Richardson et al., 2011).

How and why do mothers'[2] emotional difficulties during deployments affect their adolescent children? Esposito-Smythers and colleagues (2011) recently used attachment theory to suggest that emotional stress experienced by the undeployed parent may weaken the attachment bond between the adolescent and his/her primary caregiver and may erode the adolescent's feelings of well-being and security (see also Lester & Flake, 2013; Paley & Mogil, 2013; Riggs & Riggs, 2011). Over the years, many studies have provided plausibility to the ideas of Esposito-Smythers and colleagues by uncovering associations between mothers' poor emotional functioning during deployments and emotional difficulties that have occurred amongst their children (Chandra et al., 2010; Chandra et al., 2011; Jensen et al.,

1996; Kelley, 1994; Medway, Davis, Cafferty, Chappell, & O'Hearn, 1995; Mmari et al., 2010; Morris & Age, 2009; Pedersen, 1966; Rosen & Teitelbaum, 1993; Wong & Gerras, 2010). In recent qualitative studies, adolescents have reported being significantly stressed by their anxiety about their undeployed parents' well-being (Chandra et al., 2011; Mmari et al., 2009; Richardson et al., 2011). We will see below that some undeployed parents become stressed to the point of being emotionally unavailable to their children, thus illustrating the concepts of parental unavailability and parentification that we discussed in chapter 2.

At the most mundane and least threatening level, our participants reported that their undeployed parents' available time had shrunk dramatically. Some of our participants (e.g., Mark) were unable to participate in extracurricular activities during the Afghanistan tour because their mothers worked full-time, and either they were now required to babysit their younger siblings (see also Huebner et al., 2007) or their mothers were unable to transport them (see also Knobloch, Pusateri, Ebata, & McGlaughlin, 2015).

A few mothers persisted, against odds, in chauffeuring their offspring to their sports practices, a chauffeuring that was essential, given the semi-rural context of Armyville and the surrounding residential areas. Paula recalled,

> She had two kids she had to take care of by herself. And my mom had never done any of the billing or anything with the money. My dad had always taken care of that. But while he was overseas my mom had to do that. And my mom had to cook every meal. My mom had to drive me everywhere. Like I play basketball, so she was driving me to basketball practices, basketball tournaments, basketball everything. And I played soccer that year too. She was there for all my soccer experiences.

Amanda added,

> At the time, she was working full-time. I still didn't have my driver's licence and [my sister] had a bunch of stuff. I felt really bad for Mom because she had a lot more responsibility on her. She was kind of the taxi driver for all our events and stuff. We're a big skiing family, so there was a lot of different activities and tournaments we'd go to, or school events. She had a lot more responsibility on herself and taking care of the house, when me and my sister should have stepped up more than we did. So, yeah, it was hard on her. It still shows the effects, and it's almost been three years.

Other parents compensated for their deployed partners with a less valiant spirit. Simone's mother and Leonard's father were described as "cranky":

She was cranky a lot. Like, she put a lot of stress on herself. And she felt deserted in a way, even though he was coming back. Because then she'd have to take care of both the kids, go to work. She had to uphold our family by herself for eight months.

—Simone

There was some times where I didn't really want to be around my dad. 'Cause he could get pretty grumpy. Because he had to do everything. He had to, like, make lunches, or whatever.

—Leonard

Leonard and Zoe reported having been less free to spend time with their friends:

[When you have only] one parent, you don't get to do as much stuff as you want to. It's kind of greedy, but you don't get to go out and do things, like go to the movies and stuff, because Dad's always like, "No, I gotta do this" or "I gotta do that" or "I've got to take your sister somewhere." It's always more work for them, less stuff for me kind of thing.

—Leonard

Things that normally we'd be able to do when my dad was there we weren't allowed to do. Like, some sleepovers or friends coming over after school. It was like, "No, no, you just have to come home and do your homework, and then we'll see." Automatically my parents would be like, "Yeah, of course, have friends over at the house, as long as you do your homework." But [now] it was like, "No, I'm by myself. You're not going to the movies tonight. No, you're coming home."... She didn't have him there, so it was like all the decision making was on her part. And she kind of just didn't want to make all the decisions.

—Zoe; father deployed to an African country

Mothers' reactions to deployment stress were often more complex than the above excerpts would indicate. Consistent with the advice that has traditionally been provided to military wives (Harrison & Laliberté, 1994), mothers whose husbands have been deployed often take great pains to hide their stress from their children. In describing her mother during her father's Afghanistan deployment, Cindy alluded to this fact:

[Deployments are] really hard on her. Like when we were younger, I would hear her crying at night when my dad was gone. So I knew that she didn't like it when he left. And she was happier when he was home and there was less stress on her. Because when he was gone, she was

more irritable.... [The Afghanistan deployment was especially hard on her] because we didn't get to talk to him as much.

Brady added,

[Our parents] don't really want us worrying about it. It's more just a casual, "He's at work." But every once in a while—I'm not sure if my siblings noticed this—but my mom would be on the phone and I'd walk by her room, the door was closed, and I could overhear her, and I could hear her crying. Like she didn't want to show that in front of us, but I knew it was happening.

It is legitimate for us to wonder if refraining from speaking of one's fears in front of one's adolescents has the effect of bringing the family closer together or, alternatively, of weakening the lines of communication amongst them (cf. Wertsch, 1991). Like Cindy and Brady, Louanne noted her mother's adeptness at concealing her fears:

As a kid you tease your mom, right? I would always tease her about her wearing his sweaters or his shirt to bed. And every time the phone rang and it was Dad, she would grab the phone from me. I'm like, "Hey, I want to talk to him, too." There's actually a [co-worker of my mom's] whose husband just went, and I guess she was, like, puking days before. I don't know if my mom actually did that because, you know, she's a mom, she has to hide it, she has to stay strong for all of us, and all that stuff. So she hid it well, I guess.

In the same interview, Louanne described how all of her family members failed to communicate with each other during the Afghanistan tour:

We never spoke, really... 'Cause like if one person starts crying, then the next person will start crying, and the next person will start crying, and we're all going to be crying. So everyone, I think, just kind of kept to themselves about it. I never really spoke to anyone. At the time I didn't have anyone to speak to. 'Cause me and my brother weren't that close. And me and my mom didn't talk. Me and my mom didn't get along, really. And me and my sister didn't talk. And there were no support groups then.

Along similar lines, Amanda berated herself for having communicated with her mother "too much" during the same deployment. Amanda had shared her fears about her father's safety with her mother, and she believed that, as a result, her mother had reverted to hiding her own feelings and being protective again, as if Amanda had reverted back to being a child, and had stopped confiding in her. Knowing that she had been her mother's only conversational outlet, and having become proud of the new close communication that had developed between them, Amanda regretted this episode deeply for the new barrier it had erected between her mother and herself:

I was the one person she could talk to, really, and trust. Because I never talked about stuff that we talked about with anybody else.... I kind of wish that I didn't tell her that I was scared. Because then she wouldn't have felt stuck—that she didn't have anybody else to talk to.

Stoicism during deployments has long been recognized as a military family practice (see, e.g., Harrison & Laliberté, 1994; Wertsch, 1991).

So far we have recounted what our participants told us about the stress experienced by their undeployed parents. These men and women (mostly women) struggled to juggle full-time jobs with housework, caring for their children, and maintaining their children's participation in extracurricular activities and friendship networks. Some of them were unable to live up to the last two of these expectations; those who went the extra mile did so under duress.

The difficulties our participants' undeployed parents experienced with multiple obligations were not simply a matter of having insufficient time to perform all their tasks. These parents were also stressed psychologically by having to make decisions by themselves that they normally made jointly with their partners, or that their partners normally made by themselves. They also often found their emotional aloneness overwhelming. As of yet we have learned little about how their adolescents were affected. We do know that they suffered as a result of being deprived of extracurricular activities and time with their friends; some of them were also made anxious by their mothers' secrecy around their own fears and distress.

In some cases, the parent who remained at home was stressed to the point of being emotionally unavailable to his/her children. At this point, we start to discern some of the effects of the stress.

Alluding to what he had missed from his mother (who worked full-time), Zachary described a typical bad day during his father's Afghanistan deployment:

You're really missing [your dad]. And then you go to school and nothing's really working out for you.... And then you go home and your mom has to work late, and you have to get yourself a sandwich for supper.

Similarly, when her mother had spent almost a year on an IR, Bridget had found herself living with a father whose loneliness for his wife had made it hard for him to provide any nurturing to his children. Bridget described her daily life:

It was pretty much leave for work, come back for dinner, go to bed, leave for work, come back for dinner. That was it. We didn't really talk. It was just "Here's your dinner. I'm going to go watch TV now."... That was it. I didn't talk to anybody. I was really, really lonely.

Joe's mother was chronically angry every time Joe's father was deployed:

She's very stressed out.... She just usually gets noticeably angrier. .... Like if I had small problems, she'd flip. And every day after work, she's just so angry and stressed out that she won't talk.... I can't really find a word to describe [how horrible it is]. Just constantly tension everywhere.

Lorraine had made a point of staying away from home during her father's second long overseas tour, in order to avoid interacting with her stressed-out mother with whom she is not close:

That was hard, because me and my dad get along. And me and my mom, we have a lot harder time of getting along. We fight more. So the first time, it was really really hard. And the second time, I wasn't home. I'd go to friends' houses, so I didn't have to deal with my mom and my sister.

She added,

She doesn't take the stress out on my sister because [my sister] just sits there saying, "Whatever. Like, you can yell at me, you can do whatever, but I'm not going to care." So she takes it out on me because she gets a response from me. I used to fight back with her, and that's what she liked, because then she wouldn't feel as bad.... So now I just sit there, and she yells at me and then walks away.

During the Afghanistan mission, Stewart and Bridget felt themselves dragged down by mothers who had been suffering from acute or chronic depression:

She wanted to act strong, and she was for a little bit. But towards six, seven, eight months, you could tell it really dawned on her that she wanted him back, and she missed him. And it was visible that that was occurring. [She was] just more mopey, more blah, sometimes more moody.
—Stewart; mother chronically depressed, father in Afghanistan

[The deployment] was very sad most of the time. Like when [Mom] was at work, and our babysitter was watching us, we were fine. [But when] my mom got home she was just sad, down, and just go to bed.... It kind of brought the whole house down.
—Bridget; mother acutely depressed,
father deployed to the Middle East

The above participants had experienced emotional suffering as a result of their undeployed parent's stress.

Some CAF parents are deployed overseas frequently. A few of our participants who were affected by this believed that the bond between themselves and one or both of their parents had weakened either severely or irreparably. For example, Cindy's father had been frequently away on tours. When asked, "Who is the mom for you?" Cindy replied, "Nobody really," elaborating,

> She tries to be there, but it's different. And now she's in school, so she's not here very much. She goes to school and then she has to pick up extra shifts, now that my dad is in Province X.... She's always working. And now she's always at school and she's more stressed than she was before.

Bridget's mother and father had been sent on back-to-back long deployments. When they had returned, Bridget had reacted by allowing them to focus on re-establishing their own relationship, repressing her need to communicate with each of them:

> We started getting really distant, and not telling him as much—and same with my mom. I didn't hide stuff from them. I just didn't tell them as much, so they could get back to being them again and not have to worry about me.... It's really hard, 'cause my mom and dad are gone so much. Like, my mom's gone on course. My dad's gone on course. My dad's gone to Afghanistan. My dad's gone to Country X.... It's never really stable.

This problem may have started much earlier when Bridget's mom had been away on an IR:

> I went to Province X that summer to go visit my grandparents and she was in City Y.... And so she came down and visited me, and it was the first time I had seen her. And, you know, we tried to talk about everything, and it's just, I don't know, it just wasn't the same. And I had just—I don't know. Things just started to get farther apart, like I said. 'Cause she was gone—my dad was gone.

A recent study of youth in US National Guard families found, similarly, that these youth withdrew emotionally from their undeployed parents during a deployment, after arriving at the conclusion that these parents could no longer provide them with nurturing (Thompson, Baptist, Miller, & Henry, 2015).

The previous few pages have provided examples of the quality-of-life loss that a parental deployment, especially a dangerous deployment, represented for our participants, from their perspective. Their words give us some insight into their experiences of loss, worry, coping with worry, and coping with the emotional stress that was suffered by the parent who stayed behind. An important question for future research would be the long-term impact of multiple deployments on the attachment bond between military adolescents and their parents (cf. Esposito-Smythers et al., 2011; Lester & Flake, 2013; Paley & Mogil, 2013).

Extra Household Chores
Additional to the losses and stresses they experience, adolescents find themselves working harder at home to pick up the slack created by the deployment (Chandra et al., 2010; Houston et al., 2009; Huebner et al., 2007; Mmari et al., 2009). They also miss out on extracurricular activities and time with their friends. Since we found gender differences in the extent and manner in which extra household chores were carried out, we will start with extra household chores, and what the boys in particular said about them.

On this theme, Roger (father deployed to Afghanistan) commented,

> I had to do a little bit more chores, which I didn't really mind. 'Cause I was getting $10 a week for cleaning my room and putting clothes away. So helping out felt a little more fair.... But other than that, no, it was pretty fine.

Zachary (father also deployed to Afghanistan) added,

> Usually me and my dad do [the dishes]. And then my mom will just like fill in his role. And my mom will do the laundry and I might clean—like dust like I do sometimes. It's pretty much the same.

Pete (father on same tour) added,

> Basically, anything he would normally do. Like sometimes he'd haul in the firewood. Anything that needs to get fixed or something that has to be dealt with, I kind of have to deal with it whenever he's not there. Or figure out how to deal with it, or call him and ask him how to do it.

In general, the girls took on a more intricate set of household responsibilities. For example, Simone, who lived in a babysitter's home when both her parents were deployed, carried out much of the care of her younger siblings during this time:

> I took on different roles by myself. I wasn't asked to. Sometimes maybe she'd need help with the kids, so I'd help her out. And I'd get the kids dressed for school or something, or get all the kids breakfast. And sometimes I had to be an authority figure to my sister because she wouldn't

listen. Because I knew what she was allowed to do and what she wasn't allowed to do, because we both live at home. So if she tried to act out or something and she wasn't supposed to, I'd be like, "Hey, you gotta calm down! You gotta listen!"

Bridget described a period when she was 12 and her mother was away on an IR:

I was like the mother role now, 'cause my dad was working. So I got up early in the morning, had to get my brothers ready to catch the bus...had to make lunches and...had to get myself ready for school. And then I would come home after school and my dad wouldn't be home yet. So I had to make dinner and had to make sure the boys did their homework. And they had time to play by themselves and stuff. And when my dad got home, I'd have dinner on the table.

Cindy, similarly, was 14 when her father went to Afghanistan:

I took on more responsibility, 'cause my mom worked a lot, and she wanted to start going back to school. So I was basically the mom.... [Mom] worked double shifts from, like, 7 to 3 and then 4 until 12. So she was never home. And she had to keep the money going while my dad was away. So it was just me and my brother all the time.

Describing a typical day during this deployment, Cindy said,

School, then come home and make supper for my brother. And then I'd have to get a ride to drama class, and come home and put him to bed. And then do laundry and dishes.

Janis carried out an impressive range of domestic tasks when she was just six, during the time that her father was in Bosnia and her mother had been disabled by a broken ankle:

He was gone when she broke her ankle, and he was gone for a month or two after that. And it was hard, because I had to try and deal with taking care.... I had to learn how to make my own food sometimes. Like my grandmother, she came and she visited, I think one Christmas, and she helped out a lot with that. But we had to rely on the neighbours that month or so. I had to make sure everything was cleaned up. I had to get us ready for school.

Both boys and girls described quality-of-life losses that had resulted from the extra chores they had had to perform. For example, Sam reported no longer having been able to spend time with his friends:

I pretty much prefer just to go and hang out with my friends. But then I've got stuck doing other stuff. And I can't do what I actually wanted to do, because it has to be done.

Roger, faced with the same problem because his mother was unable to drive him anywhere, had devised an intricate solution:

I would get off school an hour early. So I was able to go home, pack up my stuff if I was going to a friend's place.... And I'd head on the bus with them, 'cause the bus driver didn't mind.... Sometimes I'd have to stay the night there, so it wasn't really a problem. Like the bus was practically empty.... So I found a way to get to my friends' houses.

Mark, whose mother worked full-time, had to give up all his extracurricular activities to babysit his younger brother every day:

[I feel] extremely bummed 'cause I'm not able to do any extracurricular activities, 'cause I have to babysit my brother. After I get off the bus [every day], I have to wait at the bus stop until he gets off, which is anywhere between a minute to 10 minutes. And then, yeah, I babysit him.

Despite these complaints, Mark expressed pride in a new positive quality he had discovered about himself: the ability to resolve conflicts with his younger brother without their father having to intervene. Speaking while his father was still in Afghanistan, he said,

That's the good thing about me and him babysitting—we solve our own problems.... Me and my brother are learning to solve our own problems. But they're still arising, which we're still trying to work on.... Both of us sometimes overreact to something one of us say or do. Like, I would sometimes not even listen to him, 'cause he's talking about a story that I don't really care about. So I don't even listen, and he gets angry about that.... Of course, easy way to calm him down is play a video game with him. Then he's usually mellow.

In contrast with the boys, who complained mostly about lost freedom, the girls—e.g., Cindy and Amanda—bemoaned the fact that carrying extra responsibilities had forced them to grow up too soon:

It was just more responsibility than what I was used to.... My mom was working and I couldn't go out. I stayed home with my brother probably three weekends out of a month.... I liked helping my mom. But the down part was not being a teenager.

—Cindy; father deployed to Afghanistan

I didn't ask for the responsibilities that I got. They are just kind of given to you, and expected of you to step up to the plate. And that's what I did. So you see a lot of people going out on weekends, and that wasn't me. I was at home helping around the house, and doing what I could to try to step up into the responsibilities and into the shoes where feet were missing in. I was kind of taking Dad's role, because I was always the person who helped fixed the car, mow the lawn, all the stuff that usually they say guys do, or the father does. That's me. That was my job. So I kind of took that dominant role. At 15–16, those are big shoes to fill.

—Amanda; father deployed to Afghanistan

For Lorraine, the extra chore of looking after her sister had been compounded by her chronically poor relationship with her mother and the fact that her mother was stressed and emotionally unavailable whenever her father was deployed:

My dad went away for two weeks a little while ago. . . . And my mom was always at work. So I'd take care of my sister and I'd help her do her homework, and I'd cook for her. . . . And as soon as my mom would come home, and if [my sister] didn't have her homework done or something, she'd get mad at me for it. Saying, "Well, why didn't you help her with it?" . . . She'd go to work at 9 o'clock in the morning, from 9 to 5 go to her full-time job, and then she'd go down to City X right after work 'til 9 o'clock. Wouldn't get home 'til, like, 9:30. So I'd be taking care of [my sister] from the time we got home from school 'til whenever she got home.

However, Lorraine expressed pride in the greater adeptness she managed respecting her little sister's moods, relative to the habitually lesser adeptness of her mother:

Now that we're older we get along a lot better. And we sit there and we talk. So we find out more about each other. And she listens to me more than she listens to Mom. Like, if I tell her to do something there's a very good chance she'll do it. If Mom tells her, she'll just sit there and look at her like, "I'm not going to listen to you. I don't have to listen to you." . . . Whereas I'll make her do it. . . . And I make it easier on my mom too with [Sister]. Because me and her can talk. And she understands how hard it is for Mom, 'cause I explain it to her. . . . So I think Mom's benefited out of it, too.

For her part, Bridget learned that she had been able to run her family's household by herself during the year that her mother had been away on an IR:

I liked being in charge.... Because I was in charge a lot more than I was before. I could tell my brothers to do stuff around the house. You know, "Can you please come and do the dishes. Can you please sweep the floors. Can you go tidy your rooms." Stuff like that.

As a result of Zoe's contributions to the household during her father's long overseas deployment, her parents had developed a deeper level of trust in her ability to assume responsibilities, and had begun to allow her more freedom:

It obviously helped me, because now my parents trust me. Like, I can do things I want to do, because I respect them. Because they kind of set boundaries, and I followed them.... Some of my friends can't do the things I can do, but my parents trust me. It's just, like, little things. Like, I can go to City X by myself. My best friend has moved to Province Y. I can take the car to Province Y by myself. Things like that. I'm only 18, but my parents trust me with their car. My parents trust me that I will be okay. They know that I'm responsible enough to do those things, because I...proved to them that I can do it type thing.... So [Dad's deployment] sucked a lot of the time. But in the end we're fine—we're a happy family still.

Gender differences appear to exist in the kinds of extra household work that adolescents carry out when their parents are deployed. It would seem that boys take on a few extra jobs (mainly stereotypical, outdoor male jobs) and view their lives as being largely unchanged, except for reductions in quantities of extracurricular activities and time spent with friends. In contrast, girls appear to assume a significantly greater share of household responsibility and to resent both the accompanying lack of freedom and the fact that the extra work has deprived them of the pleasure of living the life of a teenager. Representatives of both genders express pride in their new accomplishments, however, and are able to identify lasting benefits that have come out of them.

Extra Emotional Work

As noted in chapter 2, parental emotional unavailability is often accompanied by the parentification of the older children and adolescents in the home (Hooper, 2007). Parentification is a set of interactions in which children are assigned roles and responsibilities that are typically considered the responsibility of their parents but which the parents have relinquished (Barnett & Parker, 1998; Broszormenyi-Nagy & Spark, 1973; Hooper, Moore, & Smith, 2014). Parentified children tend to be expected to fulfill caretaking and emotional roles, including the care of siblings and the provision of comfort, advice, or protection to a parent (Earley & Cushway, 2002).

Adolescents indeed carry out emotional (as well as instrumental) work during deployments (Chandra et al., 2010; Richardson et al., 2011). As already noted, some do so to the extent of being expected to co-parent both younger siblings and the undeployed parent (Huebner & Mancini, 2005; Richardson et al., 2011). Our participants' accounts were consistent with earlier research findings. With a few exceptions that we will note, the lion's share of the extra emotional work carried out was done by the girls.

Several girls mentioned making a special effort to spend less time fighting with siblings. Speaking about the time her father was in Afghanistan, Shanda said,

My sister and I probably got along more for the sake of my mom. 'Cause we're sisters and we're catty, but we definitely tried to pull together.

Amanda refereed between her mother and younger siblings while her father was in Afghanistan:

I'm actually kind of the referee in my house. If Mom gets upset with them, she comes and vents to me and vice versa. So I'm kind of the person trying to keep the peace in the house.

Amanda also described the intricate way in which she filtered communication received from her father while he was in Afghanistan, in order to protect her younger siblings from aspects of the message that might have upset them:

It's sort of like the chain of command in my family. My dad will tell my mom, Mom will tell me, and I'll tell [Brother and Sister]. That was usually how it worked, because a lot of times my father…just kind of mentioned it off to the side. And then Mom would vent [to me] about her problems, or [about] whatever Dad [had] said. If it was something important then, sure, I would tell [Brother and Sister]. But…if it was not important and it might threaten hurting them in some way, then I wouldn't. "It's okay, they don't need to know about that." So I was kind of like the filter.

Girls (e.g., Louanne and Cindy) participated in family collusions that were designed to hide explosive information about what was happening in Afghanistan from younger siblings:

We never told my sister, because at the time she would have been in Grade 7.… [She] actually had nightmares that my dad blew up, and he had no face and stuff. So we figured it was best not to tell her [when Dad got injured]. But when she did find out eventually, she got very angry that we never told her.

—Louanne

He was really mad because my dad was lying to him [about the danger level of his location]. And then I had to comfort him. And I stayed with him and I told him that Dad was safe. That he shouldn't worry, because it'll be okay.

—Cindy

Laverne, a senior girl, described the peacemaking role she played in her family during the months her mother was away on basic training. Through her description she revealed her belief that playing this role had been expected of her because she had been the only female in the house:

I felt there was pressure.... When my brother and my dad got into an argument, I felt I had to resolve it to keep them not fighting. I don't know why I felt that way, just felt like I needed to do something to make everyone get along.

Additional to diplomacy roles, girls had carried out the emotional work of censoring the information they conveyed to the parent who was deployed, to prevent him/her from worrying about what was happening at home and to keep him/her able to focus on the dangerous work s/he was doing, e.g., in Afghanistan. For example, Amanda described how she, her mother, and her siblings had communicated with her father in Afghanistan:

When my dad called, we talked to him and we'd tell him everything good that was going on. We'd never tell him anything bad, because that's the last thing you want them thinking about.... Like, he was just a couple hours away is the way that we made it sound when we were talking.

She added,

You'd always want to tell him, "Mom and [my brother] are fighting."...I remember somebody got in a car accident, or something, so I was really upset about that. You've got to watch what you say to them because you don't want to upset them.

Classic military family research monographs contain many examples of the self-censorship typically practised by family members during deployments (e.g., Harrison & Laliberté, 1994; Wertsch, 1991).

Taking Care of Mom

A special part of the girls' emotional work had to do with helping the parent remaining behind (usually a mother)—both instrumentally and emotionally—for the explicit purpose of helping her/him to manage the stress s/he was experiencing. For example, Simone, Shanda, and Amanda alluded to their mothers' stress in the context of describing the extra housework they had taken on:

Some nights I would make supper and stuff, just help out around the house. Like help clean the house and stuff. 'Cause I didn't really want my mom doing that all by herself.

—Simone; father deployed to Afghanistan

I'd get home from school, and I'd make sure that things were cleaned up and things were taken care of. And by the time she got home she'd make supper, and then we'd just hang out.

—Shanda; father deployed to Afghanistan

She finds it hard being alone. And because even now when Dad's gone to Province X she finds it hard, because she feels that there's so much more responsibility put back on her again. My brother and I are old enough now to do a lot of the stuff, so she doesn't have to worry as much. I find I do at least 50 percent of the chores, so it's not so hard on her.

—Amanda, father on an IR posting

As an exception to the female tenor of the above excerpts, one of the boys reported having provided heroic support to his mother during the weekend that persons deployed alongside his father had been killed in Afghanistan:

And of course it being Easter weekend, the Easter Bunny still had to come. And so that was kind of the first time that I helped Mom with that, but she really needed help. I mean, before that I believed in the Easter Bunny.... I didn't really care that he wasn't real any more. It was more my mom needed me.

—Brady

On the emotional side, Heather, Holly, and Petra described how they had become their mothers' best friends and/or confidantes during a major deployment. Heather, for example, had reorganized her social life in order to prioritize her mother's social needs while her father was away on an unaccompanied posting:

I don't like going out with my friends, so I usually bring my friends over. 'Cause I don't like leaving my mom home.... She says it's fine when I go out, but I think she'd be bored.... She has friends, but she doesn't go out much.

Holly's mother constantly asked Holly to spend time with her whenever her father was away on a course:

> *It's just like she wants to do a lot of stuff. I don't know if she wants the days to go by faster until my dad gets home. Or if she's just kind of lonely. So she wants to hang out with me, so she has somebody with her.*

Petra had acted as confidante for her mother while her father had been in Afghanistan:

> *She's going through a lot right now with my dad being gone and her mom [has a serious illness].... And things are going wrong at work, and she has all this stress, and she doesn't really have anyone to talk to about it. So I sit there and talk to her about her problems.*

Part of "taking care of Mom" involves a form of self-censorship similar to the self-censorship that surrounds the information that is conveyed by civilian family members to loved military members who are on a deployment. Participants of both genders (but mainly girls) reported having kept their own problems to themselves, in order to minimize the stress to which their mothers were being exposed. As Cindy put it, speaking about the Afghanistan deployment,

> *I didn't talk to my mom, because I know she had enough stress. So I didn't add mine onto her.*

Marilee, whose father deployed frequently and whose mother was chronically ill, did not tell her parents for four years about the severe bullying she had been subjected to in elementary school. She explained:

> *I think it's because [of] how independent I had to be once my dad had to constantly go. When he was in the military, he wasn't home till late at night some nights. So, to be honest, it was kind of just like Mom was dealing with all this stuff, so I'll just deal with my stuff alone.*

Because Marcia's parents had separated just prior to her father's Afghanistan deployment, Marcia had attempted to avoid sharing her thoughts about her father with her mother during the deployment, in an effort to avoid reopening the wound that had been caused by the separation:

> *Once Dad went to Afghanistan, it was kind of awkward. It wasn't like we couldn't complain about it to Mom, 'cause she's our Mom and she'd do anything for us, and I know it. But it was still weird. You hated to talk about him 'cause she was still hurting.*

Bridget and Stewart, whose mothers were, respectively, acutely and chronically depressed, had taken special care not to burden them with their own problems when their fathers had been away:

I kind of just did my own thing, 'cause I didn't want to stress her out more. So I kind of kept to myself. And I think that's why we started to get farther apart. 'Cause I wasn't really telling her as much. It wasn't like I was getting into trouble or anything. It's just I didn't want to stress her out. So I just did my own thing and let her be by herself. And if she needed anything from me, I'd be there for her.

—Bridget; father deployed to the Middle East

I guess I just didn't let it show. I didn't want to talk to Mom about it, because it would've just made her more depressed. I just soldiered through it.

—Stewart; father deployed to Afghanistan

Stewart had also tried to help his mother by forgoing sports practices, in order to avoid having to ask her for transportation:

Like, if I needed a drive to a certain sport I didn't want to ask my mom, because I didn't want to make her do that. Because it's not her daily schedule. It's not what she's used to, and my dad's used to doing it. And it almost makes her grouchy because she's not used to doing it. So it's a different ritual. It's almost like getting in a certain schedule. It's hard. I tried to make it easier.

For Stewart and Cindy, this latter form of self-censorship became an all-pervasive way of life during the Afghanistan deployment, and they commented on the energy that it had exacted from them:

Having my dad go away constantly, Mom being depressed.... It's almost like you're living with yourself. Because you don't want to talk to your mom about it because she's depressed, and you don't want to make her more depressed, and you don't want to make her think about it. And then you're sitting there like, "What am I going to do?" And you have to come up with your own reasons, your own answers.

—Stewart

Life throws you obstacles—you've just got to overcome them. You've just got to have adversity. Like, life's going to pile a whole bunch of things on your plate, and you've got to be able to handle it.... Like, Dad's going away for nine months. You've got to live with it. You can't really do anything about it.

—Stewart

I have days where I break down and just want to cry all day.... It's like a buildup, and then I just need to cry it out, and then I'm all good. Until something big happens, and then I need to talk to somebody. I don't usually talk about my feelings with people because... I'm the one who listens to people's problems. So when I cry, it's my way of letting my stress out, instead of talking about it or getting mad.

—Cindy

When asked if any of his friends had helped him through the Afghanistan deployment, Stewart answered:

Not about that stuff—no. It's really none of their business. It's nothing I couldn't handle on my own.

Brady did not specifically mention censoring himself vis-à-vis his mother during the Afghanistan deployment. However, his father had warned him that he might not return from Afghanistan, and Brady's present, and potentially future, existence as "the man of the house" caused him emotional stress:

He told me it was going to be dangerous. He told me it was going to be the most dangerous thing he's had to do in his life. And he wanted to prepare me in case something did happen.... Before he left, he pulled me aside and told me that I was supposed to be the man of the house now that he's gone.... A few weeks before he left, that's when he told me. And those few weeks I thought, "Yeah, this is so cool. I'm going to be the man of the house now, and I'm only 15," and all that. But when he actually left, it was one of the hardest things I had to do.... I felt [the responsibility] every day that he was gone.

In stark contrast, Zoe, whose mother had been strong and available during her father's long overseas deployment, expressed gratitude for the fact that the deployment had *not* created for her the kinds of extra emotional demands that had been grappled with by Heather, Holly, Petra, Cindy, Marilee, Marcia, Bridget, Stewart, and Brady:

[Mom and Dad] obviously knew how each other were feeling, but they never put it on me, which is nice. I have friends whose moms are like their best friend. And the moms tell them everything, how they're feeling. And they come to school more stressed than they were before, because the parent's not acting like the parent.... I can go to [my mom] for things. But she's still my mom and she would never put that on me. 'Cause [my parents] chose that life.

Alluding to the "taking care of Mom" work described by some of our participants, she added,

> Kids my age now, like 18, and my friends' dads are over [in Afghanistan], their moms don't know what to do with themselves. So like it's just hard, because at this age you don't really want to hang out with your mom every night.... So my friends now who have dads over there, they're like, "Want to go do something? Let's get out of the house! I don't want to be home! My mom's crazy! She's going through so much stuff right now!"

Zoe believed that her self-esteem would have plummeted if her mother had abdicated her role as parent:

> Obviously my self-esteem would go down if my mom cried to me at night, saying how much she missed my dad, or she would blame my dad and us for how she's feeling.... And if you were [continually] told it was your fault, your self-esteem would go down.

Zoe's comments provide insight into how parentified girls who "take care of Mom" during a deployment can find this temporary new responsibility enormously stressful. They also provide insight into a potential cause of the low self-esteem of adolescent girls in military families.

A few of our participants expressed pride in the emotional caregiving they had accomplished during their fathers' deployments to Afghanistan. For example, Brady commented on his newly close relationship with his mother:

> Over the last few years, she's seen me grow into the boy or man that she didn't expect me to grow into at the time before Dad left for Afghanistan. We grew a lot closer. I mean, we were close before Afghanistan as a mother is to her oldest son. But not that close. She needed me a lot when Dad was gone.

Amanda believed that the deployment had caused her to grow up faster:

> I probably wouldn't have grown up as much.... I definitely would not have gone into the program that I had now without [the] discipline I had when he was gone, and the responsibility, and the taking control, and all this kind of stuff. It changed me. I don't think I would have been as mature and responsible as before. I would have been your typical teenager.

Amanda also viewed her growing up years in the CAF as having comprised one of the great advantages of her life so far:

Being in the Canadian Forces is not a burden. Don't feel bad for us. I found that a lot of times people gave you pity because your parents were gone, or your loved one was gone. Don't pity us. We're normal human beings. Like, it's a career choice. It's a personal choice, and I didn't have the choice to go into a Canadian Forces family. Nobody has that choice. But, when you really think about it, it's a great opportunity. It may not seem like it at the time when you're a teenager or a preteen, or whatever they're called, but in the end you'll learn to value it.

These last excerpts suggest that adolescents' responses to the extra instrumental and emotional burdens that they assume during deployments are complex. On the one hand, the extra burdens exact costs on several levels and create stress. On the other, they represent sources of self-esteem and pride. The positive pole of this complexity (the self-esteem and pride) is borne out by a recent online survey of 559 US Army adolescents that was conducted by Wong and Gerras (2010). The survey found that adolescents aged 14 to 16 who had a parent currently deployed reported lower stress levels than their peers who did not have a parent deployed. The researchers speculated that these adolescents enjoyed their increased responsibilities, and decreased supervision, around their homes. In contrast, and on the emotional cost side of the equation, in recent qualitative studies school personnel reported to researchers that, in their experience, long deployments have negative effects on family dynamics. They also noted that, whereas many families acquire and display resilience in coping with deployments, extended and/or multiple deployments often have the effect of depleting this resilience and exacerbating the difficulties that have been described in this chapter (Chandra et al., 2010; Richardson et al., 2011).

In summary, most—but certainly not all—of the emotional work carried out during deployments had been carried out by the girls we interviewed. This emotional work had been additional to their extra household instrumental work. Both types of extra work had been thrust upon the girls (and some boys) during the vulnerable period when they were struggling to manage at home without the deployed parent, to live, in many cases, without the emotional availability of the parent who remained at home, and in the Afghanistan instance, to cope with their worry about the deployed parent's safety. In a few instances, the parent who remained at home had also mostly been physically absent from home, as a result of working two jobs, and had expected her adolescent daughter to take care of her younger siblings and run the household.

The extra emotional work carried out by the girls had repaired some of the damage to the family's equilibrium that had been created by the deployment. It had also represented an effort to cushion the stress that was being experienced by the parent remaining at home. As such, it had been found to be a source of pride, and at the same time a source of anxiety and stress.

An important theme that has recurred throughout this chapter has been the aloneness and isolation experienced by adolescent children during deployments. As Zoe eloquently told us, "You feel isolated. You can't talk to anybody, or no one's giving you the chance to talk to anybody." For the adolescent, the deployed parent often represents "the only parent I can talk to" or "count on." Anxiety about the deployed parent's safety is experienced differently by each family member, and the shared fate of being compelled to live through this anxiety typically fails to bring family members closer together, and sometimes drives them further apart. Anxiety about the deployed parent may engender mental health symptoms in the adolescent, such as depression, fear, and (for boys especially) "acting out" behaviours. The stress experienced by the undeployed parent sometimes leads to this parent becoming emotionally unavailable as a parent. Some of our participants made note of the self-censorship they had practised while they had been "taking care of mom": taking time to listen to her anxieties and problems; spending time with her instead of with their friends; and keeping silent about their own fears and difficulties. At the same time, these adolescents were prohibited from communicating openly with their deployed parents, when communication was possible. They also lacked their customary access to their friendship networks and extracurricular activities.

If much of the isolation adolescents experience inside the family is a product of family dynamics, outside the family they experience the feeling that too few people at school and within the community understand what they are going through (Chandra et al., 2010; Chandra et al., 2011; Krause-Parello, 2008). In the next section we will focus on sources of support for adolescents outside the home, especially the crucial support that is received (or not received) from their friends, their community, and their school.

Support from Outside the Home

Sometimes there are people that don't understand, because the people don't live in military families. I've grown up with people like that. And sometimes they don't understand why I'd be crying...because they haven't gone through it. But if only everybody got the chance to experience something like that just once, so that they knew, and everybody had the same outlook on it, then everybody would have at least a little bit of an understanding of how military families feel—how a military family feels when they go through something like that.... Because I've had people be rude to me about it.

        —Joanne, father deployed to the Middle East

[Middle school] was before the whole big [Afghanistan] thing, when they gave a lot of support to the kids whose parents were going away. So if I needed somebody to talk to, I just talked to my teacher, 'cause my mom told them that my dad was gone. But I didn't really need them, 'cause they didn't really understand what I was going through. It was easier to talk to my friends whose parents were actually already gone. And we were able to comfort each other. When I got to high school, there was more support. Because there's more teachers with, like, military spouses and everything. And then people were recognizing, like, all the troops going.

—Cindy

The quote from Cindy suggests that teachers' support is variable, depending on the broader community context and/or on how knowledgeable particular teachers are about military life. Friends, on the other hand, are people that can be counted on.

Receiving support from outside the home is an important antidote to the loss, stress, and extra burdens that change military adolescents' lives during a deployment. As the adolescent participants in Huebner and Mancini's (2005) focus group study pointed out, extrafamilial support is an important resource for adolescents to draw on as they struggle to create and maintain the resilience they need (see also Mmari et al., 2010).

Friends

Like their mothers, adolescents from military families become deeply involved in their friendships outside the home and give generously of themselves as they create and nurture these crucial connections (Harrison & Laliberté, 1994). During a deployment, one of the strongest desires of these young people is to have friends—whether from military or civilian families—whom they can talk to, friends who will be able to understand and empathize with some aspects of what they are experiencing.

Many of our participants believed that helpful support could be received only from friends who themselves had experienced a parent's deployment. As an exception to this trend, one or two participants believed that useful support was potentially available from "everyone" at AHS because, in a military community like Armyville, everyone knew about military deployments and would be able to empathize. For example, Lorenzo, a just-graduated boy whose father had been deployed to Bosnia when he was in middle school, said,

Everyone knows what they're going through. 'Cause everyone's seen it before.... It's not like [people] change their attitude towards them, but they just understand what's going on. People here know that they can talk to all their friends about it, because most people know exactly what's going on there. So they almost feel more comforted.... Because everybody knows or has been through it before.

The majority—for example, Bridget and Brad—believed that only adolescents from CAF families could be sufficiently understanding:

If you're in the military, then you kind of have the same feelings, like. You know how it feels when your dad goes away.

—Bridget

When you hear [that] a soldier dies in Afghanistan, it's kind of a different impact. You're more understanding when you're in a military family, I think, than when you're not.

—Brad

Brady identified what he perceived to be clear differences between his civilian and military friends:

I had friends that were military and not military. You could really tell the difference between the two, because the military guys would understand me more, what my situation was. Where the civilian guys, they still supported me, but they didn't quite understand why it was so hard. They thought I was more making it hard so that I would get extra time on stuff [from the school]. But my military friends really knew what it was like.

Brady and Cindy expressed the importance of a shared military experience:

Something that helped me through it a lot, not so much my family, 'cause they were going through it with me, but my friends that had family going overseas with my dad. And so we were in the exact same situation. A lot of them were the oldest [in their families], too. And so we kind of pooled together at school, hung out more. We grew closer. Whenever we heard that somebody died or was killed in Afghanistan, we stuck together a lot more than we would usually. Some of the people that I knew that I got closer to were people that were born roughly around the same time as me, in the same place as me. So I'd kind of known them my whole life, but not known them.

—Brady

My best friend, her dad went to Afghanistan and he wants to go back. And she's been moving around all the time, and she finally got to stay

here, and she's been here for three years. So we're really close, and she
helps me with anything I need help with.

—Cindy

Martha and Zoe also recognized that military experiences were unique, and they believed that a significant barrier separated military adolescents from their age peers:

Somebody else might look at it as being played up and overdramatic. But when your dad goes to his job behind a desk, he's not getting shot at. He's not trained to kill people. He's not trained to have to, you know, look at somebody else and not think about their family, and just shoot if you're in danger. Like, they don't have to worry as much about their family.

—Martha

The other night I was in [City] visiting my best friend, and her boy-friend's good friend was, like, the nth soldier to die in Afghanistan. And we all went to a bar, and we all just like toasted to him. And it gave me chills.... People in the civilian [world], like you read about it, and you have remorse for these families. But you don't really know until you're there, or you've gone through it, or you know somebody really close to you.

—Zoe

Shanda added,

There's definitely something that you can't talk about with civilian kids that aren't really close to you, that military kids would know about.... Stuff like how you feel when your parents are posted, or on a mission for six months, or they're gone living in [Training Base] for two years. They don't get it. They're like, "Oh, why can't they just come back?" Or, you know, "It's not that bad in Afghanistan." It's like, well, it kind of is. It kind of sucks when you can't talk to your dad for four weeks.

Several participants—for example, Bridget and Cindy—made analogous comments about the ability of the entire Armyville military (but not civilian) community—as an extension of individual military community friendships—to understand and support families during a deployment:

There are rough times. But everyone around you is military, so they all understand what it's like. So...you're not a loner because everyone around you is military. So they all know what it feels like to move.... And you're gonna fit in, no matter what. Because it's a military community. Everyone else in the community is military.

—Bridget

Because of the military, most of the families are like an extra family for one person. Like when my dad was gone, his military friends were, like, our extra family. They were there for us. So they supported my mom when she needed it.... And you get the other military children, and they're there for you, too. Because they're going through the same thing.

—Cindy

Reg, a junior boy, mentioned the crucial role played by the military community in supporting families that had been bereaved:

It's difficult sometimes, 'cause people move and people die. It's a real thing.... Someone died, and sometimes that guy's going to be your neighbour. Or you're going to know him, or someone's going to know him, and it's going to be difficult.... And it's kind of scary to get a phone call at midnight hearing, you know, "John has been killed," or "Bobby has been killed." There's always that little fear in the back of your head. He's not here, he's not home, he could be hurt right now. But I mean you've got to take care of each other when things go wrong. If something happens to you, they've got your back too, so you always have that little safe place to go. It's a good feeling.

Similar comments had been made by the adolescent participants in Mmari et al.'s (2009) focus groups. The main message of all these comments was that military adolescents receive positive deployment support from their community's adolescent and adult members.

Louanne and Amanda, however, were more cynical, to the point of expressing disappointment even in friends from CAF families whose parents had also been deployed to Afghanistan. In Louanne's case, the applicable friend had had poor listening skills:

I had friends, but no friends who would really understand. The one friend that I did have whose dad was over there—actually, I had two. One of them ... she didn't even know why they were over there. And my other friend, like if I would tell her about my dad's accident, she would be like, "Yeah, well, my dad, he was on this trip and he missed his bus, and the seat that he was sitting in was shot right where his head would have been." I'm like, "Thanks for listening."

Amanda's father's situation in Afghanistan had seemed so uniquely dangerous that Amanda had felt uniquely isolated:

There's a lot of people whose parents did go to Afghanistan, but ... they were on base. A lot of the guys that were with my dad's troop or my dad's platoon or whatever, they didn't have kids my age. My dad was

*one of the older guys there, so of course he had older kids in the fam-
ily. Whereas a lot of them were younger guys, early twenties.... So, no,
there wasn't a lot of people in my situation. So that's why it's so hard to
find people who understand to talk to.*

She added,

*[Afghanistan] has made me stronger, but at the same time I find that
I've also put up a lot of barriers and walls. It's really hard for me to let
somebody in.... Sure, I've had a lot of friends, you could say, but not
when I look at them now. I've never really had true best friends, because
I've been so much more grown up than they have. I don't get joy out
of making fun of people or stupid jokes. It's not me.... And, like, the
one time that you say something, your words get all out of context with
somebody else. And rumours start.*

Louanne's and Amanda's observations display some bitterness, and reflect
a degree of isolation during the Afghanistan mission.

Institutional Support from the CAF

From the section above, it would seem that the best peer support comes from
military community peers and the best adult community support comes
from the adult military community. We would therefore expect the CFB
Armyville Military Family Resource Centre (MFRC) to have contributed
to the deployment support our participants received. As we noted in chapter 2, military family resource centres (MFRCs) have existed on most CAF
bases and stations since the early 1990s. One of the key services each MFRC
provides is deployment support to the civilian members of CAF families.

The majority of our participants had not been to the Armyville MFRC
during their parent's most recent deployment. Of this set of participants,
Leonard's and Fred's comments were typical:

*They sent us pamphlets, but we didn't really need them. So, we were
all fine.*

—Leonard; mother deployed to Afghanistan

*Mom wanted to put me in the therapy through Canadian Forces,
because they offer that when you have a loved one, or whatnot. It's
completely free to go in.... They give you free resources and stuff like
that. I didn't take any of it because I didn't need it. I didn't think it was
necessary with me, although I did argue with my mom a lot. I thought
it was completely unnecessary for me to take it.*

—Fred; father deployed to Afghanistan

Bridget, on the other hand, had benefited from making use of the MFRC, both during her father's deployment to the Middle East and during his deployment to Afghanistan:

> *My dad got deployed to Country X. And they had a support system for that, 'cause I didn't know what to feel about the whole thing. I went there and they helped me out. I would go there Wednesdays, I think, after school. So I would just walk over, and there were a lot of other kids there too. And we'd just talk about how it was with our dads being in Country X and stuff.*
>
> —Bridget; when father deployed to the Middle East

> *My little brothers went [to the support groups], and I joined the volunteers. And so, you know, I got to help out my little brothers and stuff like that. So I learned more about what [Dad] was doing. Even though I wasn't participating in the program, I got to see what they were learning. And I helped out with cooking programs and... with dances and stuff like that.... Just getting my mind off everything.*
>
> —Bridget; when father deployed to Afghanistan

When his father was in Afghanistan, Brady had benefited as well, especially from the opportunities the MFRC had provided to enable him to talk to his father via video conferencing:

> *When he was gone, once or twice every two or three weeks we would go there. They would host a barbecue for us, and little activities for the kids, like hand painting or painting rocks—just little different activities. And one of the biggest things that they had there that really helped me was video conference with my dad. So I got to see him and talk with him. I thought that was really cool. Talking to him on the phone is cool enough, but to actually see him in person while he's in Afghanistan!*

Apart from during deployments, our participants generally did not participate in the Armyville MFRC, believing that MFRC programs catered mostly to younger children. On this theme, Joel's comment was representative:

> *They have stuff for, like, kids, but not for military families. They have absolutely nothing for teenagers. Well, nothing interesting. No teenagers show up to it. They have a teen centre and everything, but no teens go there because it's so lame.... I'd rather hang out at a skate park.*

Jasmine similarly noted,

> *Like, they have family stuff. It's usually for little kids, and it's so boring. And you just go there, and you're surrounded by a bunch of military*

people and their kids. It's annoying and it's boring, and they don't do anything. I went to this one thing—it was like this military thing. And we pretty much did this obstacle course. It was a military obstacle course. We had to jump over and under stuff, and like monkey bars. And go around. And then we had to run, and I was like, "Oh my God!" Like, "We're not military. Why are we doing this? This isn't fun!"

Fred recalled that he had felt connected to the MFRC as a boy, but in subsequent years had outgrown it:

I can remember when we had the tour in Bosnia. I remember [that] everybody's dad—a majority of people's dads were in Bosnia. So they had a family resource day when, like, there was other dads there, or whatever. And they were showing me all the tanks and stuff, because my mom obviously couldn't do it. My dad was gone. So that's when I felt connected when I was younger, living in the PMQs with my dad being away. Then for Christmas they had this thing. You'd have a bunch of activities, get like little gifts and stuff like that, to make you feel connected. But as you get older, you sort of drift away from all that stuff.

Bridget and Shanda disagreed with the "nothing for teens" narrative concerning the Armyville MFRC. They both had positive things to say about what the MFRC had to offer teens in 2009–2010, especially its course on babysitting and the opportunities it provided for teens to help out at younger children's parties:

I fit in to the community very fast. And, you know, I was in Armyville a couple times and, like, singing and stuff. And I got to dance. The Military Family Resource Centre—I started going to a lot of activities there and, like, cooking activities. And I used to go there like to, like, babysit. And my mom had a lot of friends there, and they had little kids. And so I liked that.

—Bridget

I like a lot of courses or stuff that I did—babysitter's courses, first aid. I did those all through the Military Family Resource Centre. We always went to Dad's family Christmas parties. You know, anything that was held by the base for kids and stuff like that, we always went to. Since I've gotten probably like 13, 14, I've been helping at those things. I've been, you know, an elf for Santa at the kids' parties and face painted and stuff like that... 'cause I know that it's fun for the little kids. So why not help out?

—Shanda

Our participants' views on MFRC programs and services were clearly mixed. We will return to the theme of the Armyville MFRC in chapter 7, when we discuss the community action undertaken by the Armyville School District and CFB Armyville in response to our project findings.

Support from the School

I just continued playing sports. I did better in school, and I worked. I was trying to keep busy so I wouldn't have to really think about it. And working hard in school, 'cause my dad's always the "do really good in school" type. Mr. 4.0 GPA.

—Paula

[Dad's deployment] was around exam time, so it was more stress of exams and tests and getting assignments done and worrying about him over there.

—Amanda

I was really bad in school. I was bad. I just was an arse.... I was like class clown, I guess. I guess it was just a way of handling the stress of not having my dad around. I got quite a few letters home from the teachers. I was also diagnosed with ADHD at the time.

—Brad; father deployed to Eritrea

The three school-related quotes above (two of them referring to an Afghanistan deployment) represent three distinct ways in which life at school could be affected by a parental deployment. Since Amanda's exams took place right after her father was deployed, she remembers being especially stressed. Brad acted out and tried to get attention at school, as a response to the stress of his father being gone. Paula worked harder in school than usual as a way of keeping busy and trying to forget about her father being in danger. In this sense, her life at school may have helped her. The variety among these participants suggests that there is no simple way to characterize how adolescents' lives at school change as a result of their experiences of parental deployments.

Some research has been carried out on how adolescents' school performance can be negatively affected by a parental deployment. For example, the heightened level of stress within the home can mean that adolescents have insufficient time to do their homework and/or insufficient homework supervision from their parents (Huebner & Mancini, 2005; Richardson et al., 2011). Both their grades (Ternus, 2008) and their school attendance (Richardson et al., 2011) may suffer. These outcomes have been most notably attributed to their increased household responsibilities during the deployment (Chandra et al., 2010; Huebner & Mancini, 2005; Richardson et al., 2011) and the emotional difficulties of the undeployed parent that they must cope with (Chandra et al., 2010; Richardson et al., 2011).

As we noted above, army communities tend to be closed, with their members believing that they have much in common (which civilians "do not understand"). Military families therefore typically look out for one another and assume parts of one another's burdens. We know that, as a military town, Armyville provided a generally supportive environment to adolescents during the time period of troops deploying to Afghanistan.

The generally supportive environment of Armyville would have benefited our participants and made Armyville a good place for them to live. However, the broader community would have been unequipped to reach, in one participant's words, "the real stuff that's making [the] kids [of deployed parents] sad." According to our participants, peers—and especially close friends—comprised a more vibrantly positive source of deployment support. While a few participants believed that "every kid in Armyville understands," the majority reserved their highest praise for their friends who were also growing up in military families and had, themselves, experienced parental deployments. A few participants were selective even among their friends who shared the experience of having had a father deploy to Afghanistan.

Despite the fact that no adult-initiated support system may be able to support adolescents as well as their peers and friends do, is it possible that the school—representing the environment in which adolescents spend their daytime hours five days a week—might be able to contribute anything useful? According to the school personnel consulted by both Chandra et al. (2010) and Richardson et al. (2011), adolescents at their schools who were affected by a deployment sought excuses to spend extra hours at the school and frequently solicited emotional support from the school staff. More recently, as noted in chapter 2, researchers in California found that military adolescents who perceived themselves to be living in a positive school climate—operationalized as relationships with caring adults, school connectedness, and feeling safe—were more likely than their peers to have a high level of mental well-being, to be free of depressive thoughts, and to be free of thoughts of suicide (De Pedro et al., 2015). The results of our own survey suggested that youth who had experienced a parental deployment were more likely than their peers to have a positive attitude towards school, to talk to their teachers, and to refrain from skipping school.

Our research team partnered with the Armyville School District in designing our research instruments and collecting our data. Part of what everyone involved in the project wanted to learn was how the CAF students attending AHS perceived the quality of deployment support that was being provided to them during the winter of 2009–2010—the period during which we were interviewing them. We also wanted to know how they thought the quality of AHS-based deployment support might be improved.

We received both positive and negative feedback about how well the school and teachers supported participants during deployments. We will start on the positive side.

"I'M NOT SURE WHEN, BUT THEY'VE GOT SUPPORT GROUPS"
For the most part, negative comments about the quality of deployment support provided by the school originated only from participants who had experienced recent deployments. In order to appreciate this qualitative difference, we will begin with some of the comments from participants who had *not* experienced recent deployments. In general, this latter group of participants either admitted that they knew little about the support offered by the school, or they assessed the level of support provided by the school as being higher than it was in reality. Isaac, a recently graduated boy whose family had experienced no recent deployments, commented,

> I never really had anything to do with them, 'cause my dad never went. I think they had some sort of support group for students whose parents went over, and they needed to talk about things. But I don't really know anything else.

Isaac's idea that AHS ran a support group for students whose parents were deployed was inaccurate. At the time of our interviews, AHS only ran a support group for offspring of CAF members with PTSD. Harper, a senior boy, made the same error:

> I think there's a group just for kids who have parents who have been on deployments, or are going on deployments. I'm not really involved in that because my dad hasn't.... But I've got a few friends who are involved. They say it's good to have someone who's on the same playing field they are. Like, me and my friends can't talk about it. I don't understand exactly what they're going through, because my dad's never been deployed or anything. But they say it's good to have people who are in the same boat they are.

Foster, a senior boy, said similarly,

> They've got support groups.... I'm not sure when, but they've got support groups for Canadian Forces family members who are at the school, who have family members deployed, where you go to that support group. And they talk and help you through it.

The positive comments about guidance counsellors' level of deployment support also tended to be from participants whose parents had *not* been recently deployed. Again, these students admitted knowing little about the subject, and/or overestimated the quantity and quality of support that guidance counsellors provided. Contrary to what several of these participants asserted, for example, the Guidance Office possessed insufficient resources to allow students to speak to a counsellor without making an appointment in advance. During the time of our research, the province in which Armyville is situated provided only one guidance counsellor for every 502 students enrolled at each secondary school.[3] Reg (a junior boy), Lorenzo (recently graduated), and Troy (a junior boy)—none of whom had experienced a recent parental deployment—made the following comments about deployment support and AHS guidance counsellors:

> There's a big guidance centre. People can go there sometimes if they're having troubles. But other than that, I don't know.
>
> —Reg

> Like, I remember them saying, "If you ever need to talk about it…" 'Cause they knew what was going on. Like, "Just come down and talk about it." And it's been like that throughout middle school and high school. But I never really looked into it that much, so I wouldn't be able to tell you.
>
> —Lorenzo

> The guidance program is supposed to be really good, apparently. I never went there, so I wouldn't know. But I heard it's pretty good. There's always someone to talk to.
>
> —Troy

As we will see below, the negative comments on AHS guidance counsellors were more specific, and appeared to be based to a greater extent on direct experiences. But before turning to that, here is some of the positive feedback about AHS teachers. For example, Frances, whose stepfather had severe PTSD, told us,

> The teachers are really good. They're really personal when it's appropriate. And you're just comfortable. I think it's a very comfortable school.

Darlene, whose father had recently returned from a deployment to Europe, told us,

> I find the teachers there care more in a way about every student, whether you're new or not…. They just go out of their way, I guess, to help people.

If it looks like you're troubled, whether you're troubled or not they're going to try and untrouble you.... It's like a family almost.

Joe, whose father had been on multiple deployments, said,

We had someone in the class and they lost their dad in Afghanistan, and [our homeroom teacher] just kinda took it really easy on him while he was trying to cope. 'Cause [Person] had a really hard time.

Roger, whose father had deployed to Afghanistan, talked about having received good support from teachers while his father was gone:

I find they're very supportive. Like, I know when my dad went overseas the teachers were like, "Yeah, I heard your dad went overseas recently." And stuff like that. They want to make sure you're okay.... They see you upset—they'll try and find out why. Like if it's related to family or military or anything like that.

Marcia, whose father had also deployed to Afghanistan, added, similarly,

They never let me know that they knew, but you know how sometimes you can just kinda tell.... They didn't really act any differently, except, like, say one day that I didn't have my homework done, they wouldn't scold me as much. They might've overheard me telling my friends, or something.

Reflecting, too, on when her father was in Afghanistan, Shanda added,

They know a lot of stuff is going on in the military, and they know whose parents are going where, and what they're doing for the most part, unless kids just don't talk about it. And they're willing to talk, and they know what not to talk about. And they just...they know a lot about what our families are doing.

Despite having recently experienced a major deployment, Shanda was in error regarding one aspect of the comment she made: "they know whose parents are going where, and what they're doing for the most part." In fact, at the time of our research, AHS teachers admitted freely to not knowing which of their students' parents were deployed overseas at any given time. This was also a finding of Richardson et al.'s (2011) interview study of North Carolina and Washington school personnel.

The positive feedback on AHS teachers quoted above reflects well on AHS. Some of it was detailed and specific; some of it was not. In contrast, all the negative feedback about teachers from participants who had experienced recent deployments was detailed and specific.

Some of the comments about the school from participants who *had* experienced a recent deployment were neutral or negative, along the lines of "the school isn't doing anything much." The remarks made by Jasmine, Heather, Stewart, Joel, and Pete—all of whose fathers had deployed to Afghanistan—all fell into this category:

> *I think everyone gets treated the same. So I don't think anything's different for military families.*
>
> —Jasmine

> *[The school does] nothing. Nothing that I know of, anyways.*
>
> —Heather

> *I haven't heard of or encountered any type of event that's actually going to help you.*
>
> —Stewart

> *Like the staff wears red on Fridays. But other than that, there's nothing they do.*
>
> —Joel

> *I don't think they're really doing anything. Like Remembrance Day ceremonies and all—that is good. And they recognize those who have fallen in Afghanistan and all that. So that's pretty good. But there is nothing like random assemblies about Afghanistan, and all that kind of thing.*
>
> —Pete

Bridget, whose father had also deployed to Afghanistan, mentioned only the 2008 survey that had been carried out by our research team:

> *Like, they did that survey last year. On the Forces. But they haven't really done anything else.*

Brad, whose father had deployed to Afghanistan, displayed stronger anger than the above participants at what he perceived to be the small amount of support the school had provided:

> *They never really drew attention to it. It's kind of something they didn't make public. The only time they really did anything was when they decided to have a thing where all kids could go who had their parents deployed. When they released it, it was by the time you were used to not having a support from school.... Like, it's kind of "Thanks for nothing."*

He added,

> I just know that if you're going to offer support like they did, timing is
> something.... Like, they didn't kick in until well after they were sent
> overseas.

Brad added that the school had also publicized the Afghanistan deployment
in such an upbeat fashion that civilian students had not been mobilized, as
they might have been, to offer support to their affected peers:

> The school is kind of sugar-coating it ... saying it's nothing too bad. Like,
> [the civilian students] don't quite understand what's going on there.

Zoe, whose father had been on a long overseas deployment several years
earlier, was not as angry at the amount of support that the school had
provided as she was at the lack of depth that had been evidenced by the
school's efforts. Like Brad, Zoe believed that the school's deployment support had not been targeted at the students' deep experiences and feelings
around their parents' deployments. In her view, the school had thereby let
the students down:

> We have, like, "Support the Troops." Or we'll have an assembly. We'll
> be like, "Raise your hand if your father's over there." So 400 kids will
> stand up: "Yeah, my dad's over there." Or "My mom's over there." Or
> "Raise your hand if your mom or dad have ever been deployed." Almost
> everyone stands up. We have a situation in our school like so many other
> schools in military towns, but we all have the same problems.... We'll
> have kind of a rally for "support the troops." And we all had Support
> the Troops stickers. We all wear red on Friday, and all that. But the real
> stuff that's making these kids sad, it just gets pushed under the table....
> Talking about it now makes me realize that there's so many kids that
> still probably aren't getting the support they need.

She added,

> They should have a list of what kids in your high school, or what kids
> in your middle school, have parents over there.... And [then] get all
> those kids into a room, and I'll bet you they'll all be sobbing within 15
> minutes of asking them questions, because they have it all bottled up
> inside of them.

Zoe's comments pinpointed the isolation that adolescents suffer from
during parental deployments, and the probability that too little emotional
community support exists for them. Like the other negative comments
shown above regarding support provided by the school, Zoe's were based

on observations that could be characterized as experience-based, relative to the vague positive observations that had been made by participants who had not recently lived through a deployment.

A few participants had some negative things to say about the quality of deployment support provided by individual AHS teachers. In the opinion of these adolescents, some AHS teachers were "uncaring" and were unable to empathize with what adolescents experienced during a deployment. For example, Joanne reported an incident with an insensitive teacher that had happened the day her father left on a long deployment, when she was in Grade 5 [in Armyville Middle school]:

> My mom brought me back to school after he left. And I was crying 'cause I was upset. And my teacher told me to stop crying because there was no reason to cry. And that it was stupid for me to cry over something like that. I got mad at her because my dad had just left to go to war for six months, and I'm pretty sure that's a valid reason to be upset. She was like, "Well, there's no need to cry at school. Stop crying in the middle of class!" So she was really rude to me about it. That made it harder to deal with. And my music teacher actually came up after school. And she pulled me aside and told me if I ever needed anything, she was there to talk to.... She saw [that] I was really upset.

Joanne added,

> It would be better if [the teachers] all did understand. Because they could comfort you and be like, "Why, I know exactly how you feel and I've been there before!" It's so different when there's somebody and they have no idea what you are talking about, because they have never gone through it. It would be easier if everybody did understand.

Stewart, whose father had been in Afghanistan, also expressed frustration at his teachers' ignorance. Some of them had promised at the beginning of the deployment to be lenient with the children of deployed parents regarding assignment deadlines but then did not follow through with the promise. The affected students were forced to plead for leniency for each assignment separately and ran the risk each time of having their requests denied.

> There's some that said they would [be lenient with children of deployed parents], but they really don't back it up. I mean, "Oh yeah, you can have time to do that assignment." "Okay, thank you." You get it done and that's the end of it. It's usually that one assignment.

As mentioned above, teachers often did not know whether a particular student was currently being affected by a deployment, or even if the student was a member of a military family. For example, Fred, whose acting out during his father's Afghanistan deployment was discussed earlier in the chapter, reported that he had been suspended from school partly because the school had not known that his father was on the deployment:

> I didn't really express myself too much that my dad was gone. They knew that something was wrong when I started cutting school. Because first term was okay, second term I cut school. In June I got suspended once, for two days' suspension. And then again for five days. I missed my entire grad week.

Amanda was fortunate to have a family friend who was a school secretary. Had it not been for the family friend, Amanda's teachers might not have discovered that Amanda was being affected by her father's deployment to Afghanistan:

> Our friend was actually one of the school secretaries. So she understood and she noticed, and she brought it up to somebody else. So the teachers kind of understood where I was coming from then. If she wasn't there, I would have ended up having to tell them. Because I actually got called in asking, "Why are you missing so many days of school?" Well, here's the thing—they didn't believe me.

While it generally seemed that participants wanted their teachers to know if their parents were deployed, one or two did not. Brad, for example, believed that some AHS teachers were "idiotic" for cornering individual students on the topic and putting them on the spot, instead of waiting for students to initiate the conversations:

> [Some teachers] were just really idiotic about it. Like, they asked me like what does my dad do, what's he doing down there. And sometimes I don't really want to talk about that when I'm at school. . . . You shouldn't approach someone and ask them these questions. Like, you should let them approach you and tell you instead. 'Cause you feel like the teacher's kind of an authoritarian figure. And when they're asking, you can't be like, "No, I don't want to talk about that." You feel you have to give them an answer. And if it's a teacher you don't feel comfortable talking about it, it's kind of irritating.

The adolescent participants in Mmari et al.'s (2009) focus groups were similarly divided on the issue of whether or not they wanted their teachers to know when one of their parents was deployed.

Amanda believed that teachers would be less ignorant about the impact of deployments on children and adolescents if they received appropriate training:

> *Teachers are supposedly trained about how to deal with kids whose parents have gone to Afghanistan. You need more training than that. You can't just have like a three-hour lecture on what to expect and then consider yourself qualified to deal with that kind of thing.*

Speaking of her younger brother's acting out during the Afghanistan deployment, Amanda added,

> *Teachers being untrained, they don't know how to deal with the situations. A lot of the times, my mom ended up calling the school and explaining what was going on. They knew for a fact, because my brother was never like that before. They weren't understanding; they just saw him as a troublesome boy, a typical boy who was causing disturbances in class.*

She explained,

> *They weren't trained for it. They didn't know how to deal with the situation. They didn't understand.... Because that was one of the big things to expect was that there was going to be changes in learning, or your grades may slip. Or recognize the signs of something bothering you, the stress of your loved one gone over there. They didn't recognize it. They were told about it, but they never recognized it.*

Like Amanda, Zoe believed that if teachers were better trained about deployments they would be better equipped to understand what was behind the acting out of military children whose parents were away:

> *If a kid is really obnoxious in class, or rude in class, there's obviously something behind it. There's some motive of why they may be acting out. Some teachers find it over and above their job to address it. Over and above like, "Oh, they're just a troubled child." Like, get them through this class with a 60, and then they'll be off to the next teacher.*

She added,

> *I know a lot of them are just acting out to act out. But some of them are probably acting out because they have problems at home because one of their parents are being deployed, or one of their parents are going through things in the military.*

The school personnel who participated in focus groups conducted by Mmari et al. (2009) believed—along with Amanda and Zoe—that teachers could benefit from more training on the impact of deployments on adolescents.

Moving on to AHS guidance counsellors, Amanda believed that they also lacked the background to appreciate what students with deployed parents were experiencing:

Counsellors, they think that they can help you deal with it, but not the same that you're looking for. Like the help you're looking for, you want somebody with experience and who knows how to deal with it.... I didn't trust the counsellors at school.... Usually, it takes me...time to get to know somebody, to kind of let this kind of thing out. I never got to know any of them, and just by, like, first impressions and meeting them a couple of times, I wouldn't trust them as far as I could throw them.

Disagreeing with their peers, quoted at the beginning of this section, who had not experienced recent deployments, Lorraine and Sam criticized the scarcity of counselling resources provided by the Guidance Department:

The guidance counsellors were always there, but they never took the initiative to realize like, "Oh, you're in the military." They just kind of said, "Well, if you need us we're here to talk."...Most of the time you can't just show up and be like, "Well, I feel like I want to talk." Because they'd be like, "Oh, you can go make an appointment then." Like, I'm going to make an appointment to talk to you about what I'm feeling right now? I don't think so.

—Lorraine

It's hard getting an appointment [with Guidance]. It's always filled.

—Sam

Along with Amanda, both the parents and the school personnel who participated in Mmari et al.'s (2009) focus groups believed that guidance counsellors lacked the training that would have enabled them to effectively help adolescents whose parents were deployed.

Our participants were therefore divided regarding how to interpret the deployment support they had received from teachers. Some participants—for example, Frances, Darlene, Joe, Roger, Marcia, and Shanda—had had good experiences with teachers they described as "caring." According to others—such as Joanne, Stewart, Fred, Amanda, Brad, and Zoe—students from military families had been damaged, to a greater or lesser extent, by teachers' ignorance. Participants also held differing views about the availability of AHS guidance counsellors. However, it would appear that the students who had truly needed them had often not found them, because the school had been under-resourced.

SUMMARY OF PARTICIPANTS' FEEDBACK ON THE SCHOOL

In general, those of our participants who had experienced stressful parental deployments tended to be both more specific and more accurate in their feedback about the quality of deployment support provided at AHS—and by

AHS teachers—as compared with their peers who had had little recent experience with stressful deployments. Many were also more negative. These contrasts would make sense, as it would be expected that participants who were in greater need of support from their school would be more aware of their school's shortcomings. Our participants' critical comments added up to (1) the school having implemented measures too superficial in nature to support students whose parents were participating in life-threatening deployments; (2) teachers who had known too little about the impact of deployments on adolescents; (3) teachers who had known too little about the impact of particular deployments on particular students; and (4) guidance centres that had been under-resourced.

We will return to the topic of school support in the next two chapters.

Conclusion

As we noted in chapter 2, adolescents experience parental deployments in ways that are different from the ways in which their younger siblings experience them. Unlike their younger siblings, adolescents are old enough to experience the full impact of the loss of the deployed parent in the home, as well as the present and potential future implications of this loss. They are able to imagine in detail how their lives would change if their parent never returned, and they recognize with full certainty that s/he may indeed never return. Adolescence is a time of growth and development, absorption in peers, new interests, new skills, and the beginnings of imagining life as an adult. Fortunately or unfortunately, adolescents are also old enough to be very useful at home during a deployment: taking on extra household tasks, co-parenting younger siblings, taking care of the undeployed parent, being discreet and restrained in their communications with both parents, keeping their worries to themselves, and often forgoing extracurricular activities, the companionship of their friends, and other carefree teenage pursuits. The girls in particular tend to take on emotionally useful roles in their homes, to devise strategies to compensate for the emotional unavailability of the undeployed parent (when this occurs), and to become parentified.

This chapter has provided a brief glimpse of the deployment experiences and reminiscences of some of the adolescent members of CAF Armyville families during 2009–2010, including the pride they took in their accomplishments, the despair they sometimes encountered, the isolation they frequently suffered, and the often-inadequate support they received from their friends, the Armyville military community, the Armyville Military Family Resource Centre, and their school.

An equally eventful and stressful component of the deployment cycle is the post-deployment phase, which begins when the deployed parent returns home. It is to this set of experiences that we will now turn.

6

Life after the Deployed Parent Returns Home

My dad doesn't consider himself a hero. I do. I think they're all heroes. I feel like [PTSD] may not be a physical injury, but he's injured. And they look at that as a negative thing. Whereas if he'd had his arm blown off, people would consider him a hero. And he might consider himself a hero.
—Louanne; father developed PTSD from experiences in Afghanistan

Despite often beginning as euphoric, the post-deployment phase is usually difficult, as the household rearranges itself to reintegrate the partner and parent (Daigle, 2013; Harrison & Laliberté, 1994). The military member typically returns as a different person from the person who left, and, as we have seen, the lives of his/her partner and children changed significantly while s/he was away.

Members returning from overseas experience complicated emotions related to what they may have witnessed, especially if they were injured or were present at the injuries or deaths of comrades or civilians. They return to what they often perceive to be mundane matters, and they may be anxious about their ability to carry out their parenting and household roles in the ways they did before (Daigle, 2013).

Spouses' and children's resources were taxed enormously during the deployment, and each family member was compelled to take on new roles. Upon the military member's return, roles and responsibilities must be renegotiated. Trust and intimacy must be re-established. As noted in chapter 2, it takes families between one month and over a year to return to the life they had before the deployment. Relationships with children and spouses are sometimes never again as good as they were before the departure. Just when an equilibrium is being reached, if it is being reached, the member often gets news that s/he is being deployed again (Daigle, 2013).

This chapter begins with the euphoria of the homecoming, the process of renegotiating family roles, and common parent-adolescent communication problems following repatriation. We will then look at the family dynamics between members returning with post-traumatic stress disorder (PTSD) and their adolescent children, and at how some of the adolescent children of members with PTSD who live in Armyville feel about the quality of extrafamilial support that they are receiving. For some adolescents (especially girls), the post-deployment phase may comprise the most stressful part of the deployment cycle (see also Chandra et al., 2009).

The Arrival

As would be imagined, our participants were excited to learn that their parent was safe and on his/her way home.

When Darlene's father returned from a long deployment to Europe, Darlene found out only as he entered their house:

> *Every time Dad comes home it's a big ta-da, even if he was gone and came home three weeks later. Me and my sisters were all upstairs, and we could hear this voice yelling at us. And we're like, "Who is that?" And we ran downstairs and it was Dad. And he had this big black truck, and we were all excited and crying.*

The more usual practice is to reunite with one's homecoming parents at CFB Armyville or the Armyville airport. Before leaving for the airport, Bridget, whose father was returning from the Middle East, had made some special preparations with her family:

> *We made a big banner. And we put it on the front of the house, and it said, "Welcome home, Dad!" And we made, like, a ton of balloons. And we had a big barbecue in the backyard, and we had all of our friends over. And we went to go pick him up at the airport. And they came in this big line. And they came down marching, and my mom started crying 'cause she hadn't seen him for so long. And then he saw us, and how big we'd gotten. It was only nine months, but they change.*

Louanne, Shanda, and Leonard described post-Afghanistan reunions that had occurred at the base:

> *There was these tables set up, and they had little papers to draw on to say "Welcome home, Daddy," or something like that. And they did countdown for this, too [just as they had the day my father had left]. And you could hear them in the room next to you. And you were just*

waiting, like, "Oh, my god, they're coming in!" And then there was a rope so that you couldn't cross the line.... They marched in, and then they stood there for a minute, and then they walked away. And you're just sitting there like, "Oh, my god! They're back! They're safe!" And we went and we stood at the line so that we had a good spot. We had a camera. We were ready! And then the bagpipes started, and they all marched through the door. And we were trying to look, trying to find Dad, and then "There he is!" And then again trying to play tough, didn't want to cry. Cheered up a little bit, 'cause you know that he's back and he's safe.

—Louanne

The day he arrived back, we waited in the drill hall. It was, like, midnight. And we waited in the drill hall for four hours, 'cause their flight was delayed and their bags weren't ready. And so we talked a lot with the other kids, parents. We just sat around, anxious. I was really, really excited. And I had something to show him, but I can't remember what it was. But I was really excited to show him. And then he got in and he was bald! He had shaved his head while he was over there, and I was so mad at him. I hated his hair! But it was really good to have him back. And there were people taking pictures and stuff. And I was like, "Don't take pictures. I just want to go home and be with my dad."

—Shanda

We were standing in that building that everyone walks through in their Afghanistan combat fatigues. I just stood there. I was by myself for some reason, I don't know. I just, like, walked out in front. And then my mom came out, and I started crying. And she started laughing at me, and crying with me, and I gave her a hug. And I was like, "I missed you." It was an emotional time.

—Leonard

Each of their descriptions captures the excitement of homecoming.

The First Evening and First Few Days

The euphoria continued during the first evening and the first few days after the homecoming scene. Brad, whose father had been in Afghanistan, described his family's drive home from CFB Armyville:

It's kind of like we just engaged in small talk. You know, I find that you don't ask the big questions until months later.

Felix and Zachary each described his father's first evening back home:

As soon as he got home, he dropped his stuff, he gave us all hugs and stuff, and he's like, "I'm gonna take a shower now." He did that—he had a nice long shower—and then we had a nice supper, and we spent the night watching movies and just being as a family again.

—Felix; father deployed to Bosnia for a year

We came home. My mom took some pictures. And then one of them, she blew it up and laminated it. And now it's in his, like, trunk thing that he puts all his stuff in. So when he opens it, he sees a picture of us, and it says Family.

—Zachary; father deployed to Afghanistan

Darlene and Bridget described the joy they felt during the early days after the return of their fathers:

It was awesome having him back. I just liked coming home and seeing Dad in the house—was just something good. You could hear him snoring outside. My bedroom was across the hall, and when I had to work at 6 o'clock in the morning it was an alarm clock. It was Dad being like, "Get up, get up!" And it was just like little things I missed. And it was good, because I didn't have to worry about my stepmom when my dad was there. 'Cause I didn't have to go to her for anything.

—Darlene; father deployed to Europe

It wasn't sad at the house any more. Everyone was happy all the time.

—Bridget; father deployed to the Middle East

Louanne, whose father had returned from Afghanistan, described her family's drive home from the airport in a slightly less jubilant way:

I remember driving home. I was really upset, because I was trying to, like, talk. And I just kept getting shushed, 'cause Mom wanted to hear all about Dad. I was really hurt, 'cause I was trying to talk with him, too.

Louanne's fear of being left out of the conversation as her parents became reacquainted with each other resonates with recent qualitative research. According to school personnel interviewed in two recent studies, many of their military-connected students had received less attention than they had needed from either parent in the immediate aftermath of their deployed parents' homecomings (Chandra et al., 2010; Richardson et al., 2011). We will discover more homecoming-related difficulties below.

Renegotiating Family Roles

Not long after the parent's return, it was time for some family roles to be renegotiated. Some of the renegotiating was a positive experience; for example, the moms of Darlene and Jolene recognized that they could relax a bit and ease out of some of their deployment household tasks, now that their husbands had arrived home:

> When he was gone, she was just so stressed. And, like, always had to be doing something. Was always on the go. Always worrying about something. And now there's four hands in the picture, as opposed to two. So she had to get used to allowing him to, I don't know, just help out around the house. Like do gardening and stuff. Our house definitely improved. She went back to doing housework and stuff.
>
> —Darlene; speaking about her stepmother after her father had returned from a deployment to Europe

> It was different, 'cause we were just getting adjusted to him not being there. So my mom found it weird. 'Cause now she was like, "Oh well, you can do this now, then—I don't have to do that." So I think she was happier then, especially like she didn't have to do it all herself. So if she had to do something, she'd be like, "You can help—you can do that. I'll just go do something else."
>
> —Jolene; father returned from Afghanistan

For Leonard, it was his dad who had learned during the deployment how much work was involved in running a house. After his wife had returned from Afghanistan, Leonard's dad continued to perform household chores, in order to make things easier for her:

> I guess it showed him what my mom was doing, because when she got back he helped a lot more than he used to. So he had to do a lot more stuff around the house.... Laundry and dishes and stuff like that, and all the regular stuff that moms normally do. And then when she got back, he just kept doing the same thing. And she was always like, "Oh, you're doing the dishes!" "Oh, you did the laundry!"

He added,

> Everyone started doing stuff around the house, not just my dad. We started helping her out more.

Cindy and Lorenzo had also taken on new household tasks during the deployment. After their dads returned, they happily kept on performing them:

I'd make [supper] for [Dad] too [as well as for my brother], because my mom would still work. So I'd just make supper for our family. And because he was home I was able to go out. But I didn't really want to, because I still wanted to be there.

—Cindy; father returned from Afghanistan

Oh well, of course, "Oh, you mow the grass now, okay?" Stuff like that. Like, he still did some stuff. But it was more like me and my brothers did more now, 'cause we were more mature.

—Lorenzo; father returned from Bosnia

Sam ungrudgingly retained his new chores because his father had been injured in Afghanistan:

I have to do most of the physical stuff [now], 'cause he just can't do it.... He'll try and do everything. But a lot of things—like when we're cutting wood, I'll have to move the log for him to cut it. 'Cause he can't actually pick it up and move it.

Not all aspects of renegotiating household roles were enjoyable. As explored in the last chapter, many adolescents had been quasi promoted to adulthood during the deployment, in the sense that they had taken on instrumental and emotional work that had required more skill than they had previously had to exercise. This new work had made them feel more grown up. The repatriation of the deployed parent often brought about a difficult transformation: either a reversion of the adolescent to a more childlike position in the household (possibly accompanied by feelings of disappointment), or no transformation at all: a situation in which the adolescent retained his/her deployment-related quasi-adult roles, and was also disappointed (or not). In other words, some of our participants wanted to remain quasi-adults once the deployment had ended; others did not.

Amanda, for example, had wanted to become a kid again after her father returned from Afghanistan:

When he got back, I wasn't doing all the same stuff that I was doing before, but I was still expected to have that responsibility. I was still expected to step up to the plate as much as I was before, when I was ready to step back down and be a kid again.

Bridget had wanted to remain a quasi adult, and in some ways resented her mother's return from a one-year IR:

It was hard for me to go back to being the daughter again because she was there. 'Cause I was used to being in charge of my brothers. So I was, you know, just the big sister again.

Mentioning conflict with her parents that we will elaborate on below, she added,

> I kind of missed it. 'Cause I liked having a lot of responsibility. I liked being in charge. And then I went back to not being in charge at all. So the transition was really difficult.... Because I would tell my brothers to do something, and Mom would be like, "Bridget, don't say that!" And I was like, "Oh right, I'm not in charge any more—I forgot." And me and my parents started fighting.

Cindy felt more ambivalent about how she had matured while her father had been in Afghanistan:

> Before my dad left, I was fun and I didn't want to be serious. And then he left and I had to be serious. Like, I had to kind of grow up. And then he came back and I still kind of stayed in that routine. Because if he left again, I didn't want to have to go through it all over.

The family dynamics also shifted, such that some of our participants found themselves being "put in their place" by parents who wanted to turn the clock back and pretend that the quasi-adult experiences of the deployment had never happened. Bridget had lost communication with both her parents during their back-to-back deployments. However, she believed that the "being in charge" experiences she had had at home vis-à-vis her younger siblings during her mother's long IR deployment had, in some ways, compensated her for losing her closeness with her parents, because she knew that she had acquitted herself well. To her horror, after her parents returned, they reacted to the long separation by treating her as a child to an exaggerated extent and becoming dramatically overprotective:

> I don't tell them as much, so they won't punish me as much. Like I said, I keep to myself most of the time. I just keep my life personal, and don't tell my parents. But if they do find out, then I can be in trouble.... They're just so protective, and they want to know where I'm going. They have a GPS on my cell phone, so they know where I am.... I'm not allowed to go on the computer when they are not home. I'm not allowed to be on my cell phone in my room by myself. And they took texting off my phone—I'm not allowed to text. Like, I have MSN, but that's it. And I'm not allowed to hang out with boys.

Bridget added,

> They yell at me a lot. And they're just always getting in my face. They "tag team" with each other. If I say something to my mom, then my dad will back her up.... They think that I'm always getting into trouble. They

assume. They think, because my marks are slipping and all that, that I'm getting into trouble.... They're concerned about boys. They're concerned about drinking. They're concerned about smoking. They're concerned about my marks and my social life. My social group. Because my mom wasn't in with the jocks when she was at school. She was a nerd. My dad was in with the nerds as well.... So they don't see, right?... Just even if I mess up a little bit. Like, don't clean the kitchen or something. They always yell at me, "I've told you before... blah, blah, blah."... Me and my mom used to be really close, but now she assumes so much. She assumes I'm getting into so much trouble. The assumptions add up, and she yells so much. And, yeah, it's really bad.

Similarly, following the end of Cindy's father's Afghanistan deployment, Cindy's mother failed to allow her relationship with Cindy to evolve and reflect the reality that Cindy had been the "mom" of the household and for her younger brother during the tour:

Her and I aren't so close. Like, she's a mom, but she tries to over-control me, where it's like she doesn't want me to grow up. Even though it's a little too late for that, because when my dad was gone I was the mom.... Now she just kind of tells me to do stuff, when I already know I have to do it. And she thinks that I don't listen to her. But I don't need to be told to do something, because I've already been doing it.

For Bridget and Cindy the insult was experienced as a double one: following the deployment, in their view, at least one of their parents treated them as younger than they were, and also failed to acknowledge and appreciate how much they had grown up and had learned how to contribute to their households.

Fred, too, was "put in his place" after his father had returned from Afghanistan. As noted in chapter 5, he had acted out during the deployment, as opposed to taking on extra household work, and his father's return had heralded the household's return to very strict discipline:

[My brother and I] thought we were the ringleaders. Then my dad came back and... he showed us who is boss.

He added,

I didn't get the car at all. If my dad ever caught you drinking, he would freak out. He would kill you if you were caught drunk or anything. When he was gone, I got drunk two or three times. [But now] I always have to worry about him finding out, so I don't bother doing it.

See Huebner et al. (2007) for examples of similar post-deployment family dynamics.

Some recent qualitative studies have found that, at this point in the deployment cycle, high-school students may feel uncertain about which parent is in charge of setting the household rules (Chandra et al., 2010; Richardson et al., 2011). Indeed, beyond household tasks, the whole structure of household interaction—and household relationships—usually needs to be renegotiated.

"Dad Came Home Different"

Some reintegration problems are more deeply personal than the ones we have just described. As Louanne implied above, some adolescents feel left out as their parents focus on reacquainting with one another (Chandra et al., 2010; Richardson et al., 2011). Other parents may find the process of becoming reacquainted rocky and conflict-ridden, and they may involve their adolescents in these conflicts (Mmari et al., 2009; Richardson et al., 2011). Some adolescents may find themselves unwilling to spend time becoming reacquainted with a parent who has changed during the deployment and now seems like a stranger. Some of these particular adolescents may have strengthened their attachment to their undeployed parent during the deployment and may feel unmotivated to develop a new attachment to the parent who has just returned (Chandra et al., 2010; Chandra et al., 2011; Huebner et al., 2007; Mmari et al., 2009; Mmari et al., 2010; Richardson et al., 2011). For example, Stewart, whose father had been in Afghanistan, resented the effort he needed to expend on becoming reacquainted with him:

> When I screw up, he always brings up the fact like I don't respect what he does for me, or things like that. But I don't want to bring up the fact, "Yeah, well you leave us for nine months at a time, and you expect me just to accept it. I know it's your job but you also have a family." I mean, it's hard to cope with it. It's almost like you're living with your family and then a stranger comes home. 'Cause nine months is a long period. It's almost as if you don't know him any more. You don't know his new habits.

Laverne's mother, similarly, had been away on basic training for eight months. After her mother got back, Laverne no longer felt able to open up and share with her in the way she had done before the deployment:

> My mom says I've changed a lot. She feels I'm really secretive now that she's gone and came back. I don't see how I am. Like, I try to tell her things. It's just so easy [not to] any more, so I don't. She thinks I don't tell her, like, how I feel, and things I used to tell her.

Some parents return home "different" from a deployment because they have been physically injured. When this occurs, it creates difficulties for every member of the family on multiple levels. Immediately following the injured parent's repatriation, his/her children may be exposed to uncensored information about the injury (e.g., a medical practitioner making a bald disclosure in front of them). Long-term negative impacts on the children may result (Cozza et al., 2013). Additionally, when a military parent comes home injured, both the "healthy parent" and the adolescents become compelled to assume new household responsibilities. The healthy parent's emotional availability to his/her children also lessens (Holmes, Rauch, & Cozza, 2013).

The fathers of two of our participants—Catherine and Marilee—had been permanently impaired by deployment-related injuries, in ways that had created significant and lasting problems for their family dynamics. Catherine's father had sustained spinal injuries in Bosnia and had become limited in the physical activities he could undertake around the house. For example, he could no longer mow the lawn or shovel the snow. No longer able to count on her husband's help, Catherine's mother felt perpetually stressed. Catherine said,

> She gets frustrated. And she feels there's a lot of pressure put on her, because he isn't helping out around the house. And the thing is, he thinks he is—but he's not.

The new dynamics between Catherine's parents had made the household atmosphere much more strained.

Marilee's father had worn himself out during many years as a CAF [manual labourer], and he had been medically released from the CAF. Marilee told us:

> [As a result of] injuries sustained in earlier years, he had to retire.... He wanted to retire at 50 or 60, but he had to retire at 40.... [His work had] kept him going.... He is [now] different, because he can no longer work. He's constantly on medication for his pains; he doesn't do a lot of the stuff he used to do, like when we were younger.

Marilee's father had become depressed as a result of no longer being able to work; the range of leisure activities he could pursue with his children had also narrowed significantly:

> He used to take us to his work baseball games when we were younger, and he'd toss the baseball around with us. And he can't do that any more.... We can't go to theatres any more, because even in the theatres medication puts him right out. So he can actually fall asleep in the front

row near the speakers because of his medication.... We used to go to restaurants. Now we just go to McDonald's, pick up some things, and go home.

The routine difficulties of renegotiating roles and reintegrating the returned parent are often temporary. In contrast, a serious and permanent deployment-related injury can catapult the family into a challenging long-term situation.

Have any effective ways been found to reduce the impact of this challenge? According to one recent study, children experience less stress following a parent's return from a deployment with an injury if the level of family stress during the deployment had been low, or at least manageable (Cozza et al., 2010). Similarly, a study of children of parents who had suffered a stroke found that children adjust more successfully to this event if the healthy parent has been able to do so (Visser-Meily et al., 2005).

Sometimes a deployment weakens the communication link between an adolescent and the parent who has been deployed. For example, as we have already noted, chronic communication problems had developed between Bridget and both her parents, because they had been on back-to-back deployments. What a military member witnessed during a deployment can also create obstacles to meaningful family communication. In this regard, Joel said of his father, who had returned from Afghanistan,

When he came back from overseas, he was a little different. Didn't talk much at all. He couldn't sleep.... The military will pay for some therapy if you need it, but he refused it. I think there's still something wrong with him in his head.... He said, "Oh, I don't need that. Just give me sleeping pills."

Fred, Amanda, Heather, and Sam all made similar comments:

He'd rarely talk about his tour—like what he did. A couple of times he'd talk about getting up and going under fire, and stuff like that. But he never got into detail. Never. Not once.
                    —Fred; father home from Afghanistan

Mom pretty much told us right off the bat, "Don't ask him about Afghanistan" afterwards. Because there was a good chance that he was going to end up having nightmares. So I never—I was always told that.
                    —Amanda; father home from Afghanistan

He doesn't show his feelings kind of thing. He just kind of sits there. He doesn't talk about Afghanistan much. I'm sure he's seen some things

that, you know, he doesn't want to talk about. . . . I kind of wish he would share the stories with me.

—Heather; father home from Afghanistan

That's the stuff he doesn't like to talk about. He thinks if he talks about it it's going to bring back memories, and it's going to cause . . . but I don't think it will. I think he actually should talk about it to help him get over it.

—Sam; father home from Afghanistan

Amanda's mother had told her that it would be best for her father not to be asked questions, and Amanda had accepted this. In contrast, Heather's and Sam's remarks revealed wishes on their part to find a way to do something to heal the communication rifts that their fathers' experience of the deployment had created. Sam added,

I think he's trying to use [drinking] to forget what happened, even though that's not going to work. He might forget for a little bit, but then it's just going to come back.

Fred was completely unable to communicate with his father following the Afghanistan deployment, because the latter, already a long-time sufferer of PTSD, had returned home even harder to live with. Fred elaborated:

I know my mom says, "Your dad has anger problems," and stuff like that. They don't ever go in-depth, because my dad doesn't talk about it. He doesn't discuss it. He says, "It's not something for you to know. It's my personal business. It's not for you to know." I am like, "All right—I don't really care."

Fred's anger and pain come through strongly here. As noted in chapter 1, Afghanistan was a uniquely stressful experience for CAF members who were deployed there. Despite the stigma within army culture that is associated with reporting a mental health issue (mentioned in chapter 2), a recent study published in the *Canadian Medical Association Journal* found that almost 30 percent of the 30,513 CAF personnel who deployed to Afghanistan before January 1, 2009, sought out mental health services upon their return (Boulos & Zamorski, 2013). In many instances, what the deployed member experienced in the operational theatre was so intense, and so unlike the life s/he had lived as a spouse and parent, that his/her communication with every other member of his/her family was damaged over the months and years following his/her return. When this happens, the adolescent may withdraw from the relationship, either temporarily or permanently. We will see below how this dynamic can be part and parcel of the operational stress injury of post-traumatic stress disorder (PTSD).

Parents Returning with Post-traumatic Stress Disorder

One of the questions we asked our interview participants was "Were there any readjustment problems after your parent came back?" Seventeen of the 42 participants who had experienced a recent deployment—10 girls and 7 boys—volunteered, without a further probe, that their father or stepfather was suffering from PTSD (post-traumatic stress disorder). They usually also stated that he had been diagnosed with PTSD and was being treated for it.

The above proportion—17 out of 42 eligible interview participants, or about 40 percent—should not be interpreted as implying that as many as 40 percent of CAF members who deployed to Afghanistan returned home with PTSD. Among other possibilities, the 40 percent may reflect the fact that CAF AHS students who had parents who were suffering from PTSD were more willing than others to volunteer for an interview.

As we noted in chapter 2, post-traumatic stress disorder (PTSD) is considered to be an appropriate diagnosis if two conditions have been met: (1) experiencing or witnessing an actual or threatened death or serious injury; and (2) responding to this trauma with intense fear, helplessness, or horror (cited in Gifford et al., 2011).

Military officials failed in their recent attempt to have the word "disorder" replaced by "injury" in the fifth (2013) edition of the American Psychiatric Association's *Diagnostic and Statistical Manual of Mental Disorders* (DSM). However, the Canadian Lieutenant-Colonel (retired) Stéphane Grenier coined the term *operational stress injury* (OSI) in 2001 to refer to "any persistent psychological difficulties (e.g., anxiety, depression, or post-traumatic stress disorder) resulting from operational duties performed by CAF personnel in Canada or abroad" (cited by Arrabito & Leung, 2014; Paré & Radford, 2013). Grenier had suffered an OSI during his tour in Rwanda in 1994 (Arrabito & Leung, 2014). Despite the technical inaccuracy of the term *PTSD* (for the reason just stated), we will—like our study participants—continue to use it as we move through this chapter.

The 2013 prevalence rates for Canadian veterans who reported and were diagnosed with an OSI were as follows:
- 23.6 percent for all Regular Force veterans released from the CAF between 1998 and 2007;
- 59.9 percent for veterans receiving disability benefits whose application for these benefits was approved after 2006.

These rates are significantly higher than for the active CAF population. Eleven percent of current CAF veterans are diagnosed with PTSD in the year following their release from the CAF. As of 2013, CAF veterans were also 45 percent more likely to commit suicide than either currently serving members or the general Canadian population (Paré & Radford, 2013). A June 2015 report prepared by the CAF Surgeon General noted that, between 1995 and 2014, Regular Force males in army combat occupations had been significantly more likely to kill themselves than their Regular Force male counterparts in other occupations (Rolland-Harris, Whitehead, Matheson, & Zamorski, 2015). Later in 2015, the *Globe and Mail* used Canada's Access to Information Act to obtain 162 pages of CAF email communication on CAF suicides; the emails revealed that at least 59 Canadian soldiers had killed themselves during the previous few years, after returning from a deployment to Afghanistan (D'Aliesio, 2015).

The possibility that a parent could return home from a deployment "different" is something that preyed on the minds of many Armyville adolescents during the Afghanistan mission. Zoe and Louanne both spoke about this fear:

> *Your friend's parent has PTSD, and your dad goes over—you're, like, worried… that your neighbour is different. So you're like, "Hmm, is my dad going to be different?" It doesn't matter what age you are. You're going to ask that question.*
>
> —Zoe

> *That was my biggest fear, actually, when he went over—that he was going to come back different. I didn't know what "different" was. Just, you know, changed. And then he did. I didn't know what it was—I just knew that he was different.*
>
> —Louanne

The fear of their parents returning home with PTSD adds to the stress that adolescents experience when their parents are away.

Making Sense of How It Began

Several participants told us how it was that their parents had become afflicted, according to their understanding of what had happened. Fred's father, an infantryman, had witnessed the sudden accidental death of his closest comrade during an overseas deployment many years earlier. Frances's stepfather had been involved in the cleanup of body parts that had occurred in the aftermath of a plane crash:

> *I know that he had changed drastically after that…. All the people died in the plane and stuff, so he had to help clean it up. I think it's something that he remembers. Like PTSD—I don't know what that is. I think that's what he had, but I don't understand it at all…. I know that there was dead people and stuff like that. And he had to carry them out and put them in body bags…. And I know that he has been affected by that.*

Brady's father had lost several of his unit mates on the same day in Afghanistan:

The whole post-traumatic stress disorder, that all started with [losing several buddies the same day]. That's what triggered it. When he came home, I think I was the only one, other than Mom, to notice a difference in him. Just the way he looked, the expressions on his face. You could see that he was worn out. It took a heavy toll on him. He didn't really show much at first, the first few months. It was more he was a little more agitated than normal. He got angrier more.

Roger's father had become afflicted with PTSD in Bosnia but had only sought help after he had returned from his deployment to Afghanistan. Roger described the tipping-point incident that had convinced his father to seek help:

[My friend] was having a little get-together. So I really wanted to go, because he was leaving on a vacation for a month.... I asked my mom if she could drive me, because she wasn't busy that day. She said she would, but [then] something came up so she couldn't.... So I asked my dad, and he said bluntly, "No, I can't do that right now." And I'm the type of person that wants to know why, so I get a better understanding. So I asked, "Why?" And he just said, "Because." And that's something where I'll ask "Why?" again. I'm immature like that. So I asked "Why?" again. Then he did yell at me. But then he sort of caught himself, and he realized it. So he ended up driving me. And I think after that he knew he had to get help, if he was yelling for someone asking "Why?"

Simone, whose father had developed PTSD in Afghanistan, described a similar incident, which was also a tipping point—the event that caused her mother to insist that her husband report his symptoms to the CAF:

One day...me and my sister started fighting—I can't remember what it was about—and he started freaking out. He started yelling at me, saying that I needed to act my age and stop trying to dumb myself down to fight with my sister. Like I'm old enough that I shouldn't be fighting with my sister and acting her age. It was different, and I didn't take it too well. 'Cause it was the first time.

The incidents described by Roger and Simone reveal a little of the impact of PTSD symptoms on family dynamics.

"Our Lives Changed"

PTSD interferes with daily functioning long after the traumatic event. The most common everyday symptoms of PTSD are (1) intrusive recollections of the event; (2) avoidance (e.g., withdrawal, psychic numbing, depression, and loss of interest in previously enjoyed activities); and (3) hyperarousal (e.g., concentration and sleep difficulties, startle reactions, anger, and outbursts of rage) (Dekel, 2007; Gifford et al., 2011). Our participants shared instances of several of these symptoms with us.

Marcia and Catherine recalled symptoms that could be classified as intrusive recollections of the event:

> *He used to love them shoot-'em-up movies—you know, he's a guy. And we watched District 9 a while ago, and he was frowning. And I was like, "What's up, Dad?"... I was kinda grossed out, 'cause people were blowing up. And he says, "That's just a little too realistic for my liking." So I thought, "Man, what did he see that he's not telling us?"*
> —Marcia; father deployed to Afghanistan

> *He's like, "No, I don't have it compared to ['these guys in Afghanistan']."... [But] you can tell. There's certain things on TV—even like commercials sometimes—he can't watch them. Like those things for sponsoring a child or something like that. He can't watch things like that.*
> —Catherine; father deployed to Bosnia during the 1990s

Brady recalled a significant—and very public—instance of his father's hyperarousal:

> *[On] Remembrance Day... they shoot off the big cannons and they start off the moment of silence. When they shot off those cannons [last Remembrance Day], his reaction right away, he was looking around, you could tell he was in Afghanistan mode. And then we managed to calm him down.... The big thing was at the end of the moment of silence. They shot [the cannons] off again. He wasn't expecting it, and he dropped down to the ground.*

The hyperarousal recalled by Louanne, whose father had returned from Afghanistan, had occurred at home:

> *One day he was in [the basement] by himself renovating. My brother came home, dropped his bookbag on the floor, was texting, and when he looked up, my dad was there with a baseball bat. He put it down right away, and he was like, "I'm going to go for the mail."... My brother had scared him. He... put it down right away like as if it was nothing, and then he tried to cover it up by saying he was going to go for the mail.*

Recent studies have isolated hyperarousal as a significant PTSD symptom. According to the fourth edition of the DSM, hyperarousal comprises "a tendency to be irritable, quick to anger, and hypervigilant [including such symptoms as]... sleep disturbance, concentration difficulties, and an exaggerated startle response" (cited by Savarese, Suvak, King, & King, 2001, p. 720). Recent research has found hyperarousal to be a predictor of partner marital dissatisfaction (Hendrix, Erdmann, & Briggs, 1998), poor family functioning (Hendrix et al., 1998; Taft, Schumm, Panuzio, & Proctor, 2008), and abusive and violent behaviour (Savarese et al., 2001).

Anger, a more difficult PTSD symptom to deal with, was the symptom our participants reported most frequently. For example, Fred described his father's destructive behaviour since returning from Afghanistan, and how his father's symptoms had escalated during the course of his past several overseas tours:

> [When he came back] I couldn't stand it. A lot of fights in the house.... He gets to this point—takes him a while—and he starts to get pissed off. As soon as he snaps, he snaps really bad. It's so bad I have to leave. And I don't come home for the night. It gets pretty hectic.

> If you say something—if you tell him that he's wrong—he doesn't realize it, but he'll break things. Like he threw something down the stairs and put a hole in the wall. He's punched through the bathroom door. He's broke this little ornament thing on the table that was china. He just freaks out.

> Every tour he takes, his anger level gets higher up and... what he's capable of through his anger. For sure.

Fred added a comment about how his own behaviour and attitude had modified accordingly:

> It gets so bad that I'll call Mom and like, "Yeah, Mom, I'm out." She's like, "Again?" and I'm like, "Yeah, I'm out." My mom says she likes it when my dad leaves for a week... like to Province X.... So do I.

He added,

> I can't be in the same vehicle with him—just me and him driving— because we'll get in heated arguments about just about everything.

Frances described a specific altercation between her stepfather and herself, during which he had treated her violently:

> I was trying to open a window, and me and my mom couldn't get it to work. He came in, and I was like, "Can you help me?" He said he couldn't do it. I really wanted to get the window open, so I kept on trying. And then my mom yelled, "Can you try? Like, can you even try?" He got it to work; he's like "You're fucking stupid!" and storms off. And I was like, "I'm not stupid. Don't call me stupid. I'm not!"... He had

left to go to the basement, and I was walking to the door to let the cat out.... And I swore. And he stepped out in front of me in the hallway, and slapped me on my face. And I fell. And I started crying and scream-ing, and then I think my mom knew. And she came and yelled at him: "Never touch her!" And I felt bad for my mom, because I was worried that something was going to happen to her.

By the time of Frances's interview, this altercation with her stepfather had not been mended; her stepfather had not apologized or otherwise men-tioned it. Speaking of her relationship with him in general, Frances added, "I'm nervous a lot. I'm scared and I always think 'Am I going to talk to him [today]? Or am I just going to be in my room or cause a fight?' It's always on my mind." She summarized,

Me and my stepdad don't have a relationship at all.

Following his suicide attempt (see below), Paula's father had become ver-bally abusive. Paula described the incident that had compelled her family to call the police:

We admitted him into the psych ward on a Tuesday, and he came home 'cause of good behaviour for a visit.... He got irate, smashing stuff, and really upset, 'cause we wouldn't take him to the gym, where he wanted to be. He got so mad at us, and we had to call the police. And the police dealt with it as if it was a domestic disturbance.... They frisked him in the driveway and cuffed him, and put him in the back seat.

The anger and violence that often accompany PTSD have a more negative impact on family dynamics than hyperarousal, and are more worrying. For example, Martha's father had become "a totally different person" following his repatriation from Afghanistan:

He's not the same person. I've seen him change so much. He used to be this nonchalant, really dorky kind of goofy guy. But now he's really angry, and he's really stressed out all the time.

Research has found PTSD-related anger to be a predictor of alcohol abuse (Bremner, Southwick, Darnell, & Charney, 1996), poor family functioning (Evans, McHugh, Hopwood, & Watt, 2003), and relationship violence (Taft, Street, et al., 2007; Taft, Vogt, et al., 2007).[1]

Depression is a PTSD symptom that has appeared frequently in research findings (e.g., Carroll, Rueger, Foy, & Donahoe, 1985; Price, Monson, Cal-lahan, & Rodriguez, 2006) and has been established as a predictor of poor family functioning (Evans et al., 2003). This symptom was mentioned only a few times by our participants. Louanne and Martha talked about how their fathers' depression and negativity affected how they interacted with family members:

There's different stages. First he was angry; now he's in depression. And he's actually saying that if he had to fight for his life, he wouldn't.

—Louanne

He's a really negative person. Like, he never, never hit any of us. He's not abusive. Not verbally abusive. But he's sarcastic, and he's just, "Oh well, that's lovely." He's not a happy person.

—Martha

Paula's father had attempted suicide several months after having returned from Afghanistan and subsequently had been diagnosed with PTSD. Paula recalled,

He got very stressed out at work, and we had to admit him into the psych ward. And then he was off work for six months, and now he's just slowly, gradually getting back to work. He's doing really good now. He just relapsed really bad in January.

Related to depression is the symptom of avoidance or emotional numbing—defined as "loss of interest, detachment from others, restricted affect" (Riggs, Byrne, Weathers, & Litz, 1998, p. 88). As an example, the wife of a New Zealand Vietnam veteran interviewed by Lesley Frederikson and colleagues (1996, p. 60) said this about how her husband had been interacting with their children:

The children [thought] their father didn't love them, that there was no love for them because he wouldn't touch them or talk to them or cuddle them.... He couldn't express it. It's all numb in that area.

Similarly, Louanne described how her father's depression had affected her relationship with him:

[My dad and I are not close] any more. [We never really were], but now I don't even like talking to him. 'Cause he's not understanding at all.

Citing one instance of her father's newly acquired way of treating her, Louanne added,

When he came back, I was venting about our school bandleader who was, in my opinion, very sexist. He was very rude, and actually he made the other girls in the band cry because he basically said that because we're girls we're slack, and the rest of the band has to make up for that. And I was talking to them about it, and he was basically telling me to get over it. "Like, who cares?"

Research has found the PTSD emotional-numbing symptom to be a predictor of poor marital functioning (Riggs et al., 1998), poor family functioning (Davidson & Mellor, 2001; Evans et al., 2003; Taft et al., 2008), and poor marital *and* family functioning (Ford et al., 1993; Frederikson et al., 1996; Hendrix et al., 1998). A well-known study carried out by Ruscio and colleagues (2002)—and subsequently replicated by Samper and colleagues (2004)—was able to isolate emotional numbing and identify it as the only consistent predictor, among PTSD symptoms, of strong parenting dissatisfaction experienced by afflicted veterans.

Depression and emotional numbing share an inherent negativity and passivity. Both these states of mind weaken the parent–child relationship and make it a disappointing experience in comparison with what it used to be.

Spouses and partners of persons with military-related PTSD experience their own psychological difficulties. These difficulties have been categorized as (1) psychological stress, (2) secondary traumatic stress, and (3) caregiver burden (Lambert, Engh, Hasbun, & Holzer, 2012). As defined by Figley (1995, p. 7), secondary traumatic stress is "the natural consequent behaviors and emotions resulting from knowing about a traumatizing event experienced by a significant other—the stress resulting from helping or wanting to help a traumatized or suffering person." Caregiver burden refers to "the extent to which caregivers perceive their emotional or physical health, social life, or financial status to be affected by their caring for their impaired relative" (Dekel, Solomon, & Bleich, 2005, p. 72). Secondary traumatic stress therefore comprises all the feelings and behaviours that result from being emotionally linked to a PTSD sufferer, whereas caregiver burden refers to a narrower spectrum of emotions—the feeling of being weighted down by a loved one's PTSD. The label *secondary traumatization* has occasionally been applied to partners' psychiatric symptoms (e.g., O'Toole, Outram, Catts, & Pierse, 2010; Rosenheck, 1986; Rosenheck & Nathan, 1985; Solomon et al., 1992; Waysman, Mikulincer, Solomon, & Weisenberg, 1993). However, after administering the PTSD Checklist (PCL) (Weathers, Litz, Herman, Huska, & Keane, 1993) to the wives they studied, Renshaw and colleagues (2011) discovered that the PTSD symptoms reported by most of those wives referred to traumatic events that had happened in their own—as opposed to their husbands'—lives. Renshaw and colleagues therefore advised researchers not to use the term *secondary trauma stress*. It is perhaps safest to use the simple expression *psychological stress* to describe the emotional state of partners of PTSD sufferers (Glenn et al., 2002; Renshaw et al., 2011; Solomon et al., 1992; Verbosky & Ryan, 1988; Waysman et al., 1993; Westerink & Giarratano, 1999).[2]

Given the symptoms described above, pertaining to both the PTSD suf-ferer and his/her partner, military members afflicted with PTSD often report dissatisfaction with the quality of their parenting and with their relationships with their adolescents (Gewirtz, Polusny, DeGarno, Khaylis, & Erbes, 2010; Ray & Vanstone, 2009; Ruscio, Weathers, King, & King, 2002; Samper et al., 2004; Sayer et al., 2010; Sayers, Farrow, Ross, & Oslin, 2009; Taft et al., 2008). Their spouses/partners report corresponding dissatisfaction (Frederikson et al., 1996), and so do their adolescent and young adult children (Davidson & Mellor, 2001). A keynote reason for relationship dissatisfaction from the spouses'/partners' standpoint has been the injured partner's reduced ability to communicate emotionally (Daigle, 2012, p. 45; Gerlock, Grimesey, & Sayre, 2014; Ray & Vanstone, 2009; Riggs et al., 1998).[3]

Research has also correlated PTSD symptoms with relationship conflict (Gibbs et al., 2012)[4] and relationship violence (Teten et al., 2010).[5] Along these lines, Louanne reported frequent arguments between her parents:

They would fight and wake me up at night. Their bedroom was in the basement, and I could hear them. They would go to bed at 8:30, and by 10:00 they were arguing. I'm like, "You're supposed to be sleeping. What are you doing?"

What Fred had to say was similar:

Most husbands and wives, I think, do argue. But my dad… being in the military, I think plays a role in why he gets so angry, and why the major-ity of the fights will start. On average, there's an argument in my house probably five times a week, maybe, or once a day.

As a result of the afflicted member's PTSD symptoms, his/her part-ner's psychological stress, and the difficulties that evolve in the partners' relationship, the entire family atmosphere becomes affected, and becomes more stressed. Paula described the new atmosphere within her family:

We walk a little more on eggshells, 'cause you don't want to make him mad. And we're more aware of what ticks him off, and how to do things better around the house.

A study carried out by King and colleagues (2006) asked the question, Do low levels of social support inhibit or prevent the recovery of a veteran with PTSD, or, alternatively, do veterans with PTSD symptoms often "drive others [including family] away" from them, as a result of the symptoms, and thereby reduce the (likely already low) amount of social support that is available to them? King et al.'s research found that the latter is probably the case: in their study, it was the symptoms of the veterans that, over time, appeared to weaken the quality of the social environment around them.

The stressful family atmosphere surrounding PTSD is made worse by the impact on the family of the stigma that surrounds PTSD diagnoses in military communities (Baker & Norris, 2011; Blais, Renshaw, & Jakupcak, 2014; Chapin, 2011; Daigle, 2012; Harrison et al., 2014; Marin, 2001, 2002, 2003; McFadyen, 2008a). Although the rank-and-file culture of the CAF (especially the army) has recently become more understanding of and accommodating towards PTSD as an operational stress injury, afflicted members remain hesitant to report their symptoms to the chain of command. In the recent words of the CAF ombudsman,

> No matter how successful the CF is in increasing awareness and reducing stigma, it is unlikely to ever completely disappear. Within the military environment there will always be an element of the membership that...cannot reconcile being a warrior with succumbing to an injury of the mind. (Daigle, 2012, p. 59)

Apart from the stigma attached to mental health problems within the military (and Canadian society generally), the CAF's universality of service requirement (the need for the members of most CAF occupations to be deployment-ready) means that reporting PTSD symptoms often comprises the first step towards being medically released from the CAF. Most CAF members who no longer meet the military's universality of service requirement are eventually released from the organization; their military careers are terminated against their will (Daigle, 2012, p. 23). Unsurprisingly, the first major mental health survey of CAF members (in 2002; a supplement of the Canadian Community Health Survey) found that one third of members suffering from PTSD had never sought treatment (cited in Fikretoglu, Brunet, Guay, & Pedlar, 2007).

An additional practical problem is that the number of mental health care providers currently available to CAF members falls between 15 and 22 percent short of the level of mental health care that would be deemed necessary to carry out a mental health care program that would be adequate for CAF members *without the extra demands on the system that have been created by the Afghanistan mission*. The shortage is therefore significantly larger than the 15 to 22 percent figure would indicate (Daigle, 2012, pp. 28–30), and its impact on the CAF community has been profound.

Martha and Amanda commented on the culture of silence that surrounds the issue of PTSD and other mental health problems in the rank-and-file CAF:

I think before Afghanistan, nobody was really aware about how to provide adequate health for everybody. Especially psychologically. Because a lot of people really don't want to talk about it. Because they're taught to be strong and to take it. And they think, "Oh I'm weak—because I've trained for this."

—Martha

The military is a man-dominated career. It's a man's world. What kind of guy that you know would want to give up his pride and his dignity and say, "I need help"? When a lot more of them do need help, but they don't seek it. They think that they can deal with it themselves. That is one of the biggest problems.

—Amanda

Simone explained how the typical CAF workplace silence around PTSD creates mental stress for the sufferer (who has perhaps not reported his or her symptoms), which in turn adds to the stress experienced by his/her family members:

He holds it all in at work. Because if you say you have PTSD, that's embarrassing around your friends. Like, they make fun of people for having it. So he holds all that stress in. And then when he comes home, lets it all out, and that affects us.

CAF members' under-reporting of PTSD adds to the stress suffered by the members of their families. It also precludes those family members from receiving help or counselling from the CAF. The relatively new CAF *Member Focused Family Care* policy, developed in 2007, provides a limited amount of counselling to family members of CAF members who have PTSD, but only in instances where the CAF member has requested care from the CAF himself or herself (Daigle, 2012).

In one of her comments to us, Martha referred to her PTSD-afflicted father as "damaged goods." Two of our participants—Amanda and Louanne—summarized, each in her own way, their fears of the long-term nature of the damage that had been inflicted, either on themselves or on other members of their families, by their fathers' PTSD. Amanda believed that there was now "something missing" for every member of her family. About her younger brother she said,

I find his personality has changed. He used to look at pictures and stuff when he was younger. He'd have the big toothless grin and the mushroom cut. He looked cute, but now he doesn't smile as much. I find there's a spark that's gone, and it's been gone for a long time. But it's the

same with everybody. There's something missing. I've always wondered if it would have stayed, or wouldn't have left if Dad hadn't gone.

Louanne mourned the fact that she could already no longer remember her father the way he had been "before":

Before he went off to Afghanistan, I was still really young. And I don't remember much about him—how he was before—which really sucks. So I wish he'd went later, so I could remember who he was before.

She added,

I don't actually remember what it was like with my dad there in the morning getting ready for school. I remember him being gone and I remember him now, but I don't remember what he was like before.

We do not yet know what the future will hold for adolescents who currently live with parental PTSD. We do know that, after he had studied the short- and long-term impacts of fathers' PTSD on 12 adult children of American World War II veterans, Rosenheck (1986) concluded that the adolescent experiences of these adults had occupied a position of "enduring significance" in their lives, at least until they had reached middle age.

Making Up for Parental Unavailability

In chapter 2 when we first introduced the idea of adolescents performing extra instrumental and emotional work during deployments, we made a distinction between the concepts of *parentification* and *young carer*. A young carer is a child who takes on family caregiving roles as a result of crisis circumstances that affect the family, but whose parents remain at least somewhat emotionally available. A parentified child is a young carer who receives very deficient (or no) emotional mentoring from at least one of the parents who lives with him or her, and who takes on parenting responsibilities that have been relinquished by one or both of his/her parents. Rosenheck, whose research was mentioned above (1986), created what could be considered a link between living with parental PTSD and one or both of these concepts when he identified a subgroup of the adult children he had interviewed as "rescuers": children who assumed personal responsibility for their fathers' well-being during their childhoods and throughout their fathers' lives, and who sought out "rescuer" identities for themselves in their adult relationships.

When speaking of their relationships with their fathers, post-PTSD diagnosis, Louanne, Frances, and Paula described carrying out emotional work that could be classified as young caring. For example, Louanne told us that she was angry with her father for doing too little to help himself get better:

I don't know if it's my dad or the depression, but I feel like he needs to get off his butt and try to help fix himself. You can't just sit on your butt the rest of your life. All he does is sit on his butt and go on the computer. It's getting really old and frustrating.... He goes to a psychiatrist apparently, but I think he needs to do a little bit more than that.

However, she felt the need to shoulder responsibility for her father's state of mind, censoring her reactions to him in case he should be pushed too far. In deference to her father's depression, Louanne was therefore trying to take care of him by suppressing her anger in his presence:

I'm afraid to get angry at him, because if I get angry at him, then I'm afraid that I'm going to push him off the edge.

Their relationship had changed so much that Louanne believed it was she who had become the parent:

Sometimes I feel like I'm the adult 'cause he's very childish a lot of the time. And I have to treat him like a child.

For example:

If we'll be in the kitchen, and we're making supper...he's in there fooling around, joking, punching you, like, playing around. I'm like, "Did you want me to burn you?" Like, "You need to stop. You take things too far." And then he goes and [sulks] on the couch.

Louanne had also felt the need to assume a parental stance vis-à-vis her mother, who had gone through the process of thinking about leaving her husband:

It was getting to the point where I was actually like, "Can you please leave?" Like, "Stop! It's almost like you're taunting. Threaten all you want to, but packing your bags, sitting there, and then saying, 'Okay, I'll stay' is getting really old. Like, pack your bags, say you're going to leave, leave, and make himself fix himself. Like, you can't baby him!" It was getting to the point where I was like, "Can you go now?" Because she would say it so many times.

In relation to her father, Louanne may actually have been a parentified child, given her father's emotional unavailability to her that was described earlier in the chapter.

Frances, whose stepfather had behaved violently towards her, took responsibility for the negative impact of his resentment of her upon his relationship with her mother. Referring to the dynamic within their family, Frances explained that, whenever she and her mother had even "the littlest argument,"

He'll come and stand at the door, and I'll instantly be quiet. And he'll [be] like, "Don't talk to your mother like that!!"

Frances' mother had become traumatized by her husband's way of treating her daughter and had become obsessed with trying to prevent his predictable outbursts of anger towards her daughter from happening:

When me and my mom fight, she gets nervous that something's going to happen.... When she hears him walk by, she'll be like, "Quiet down!" 'Cause she knows what would happen. She doesn't want him to become involved.

Frances consequently blamed herself, and her own presence in the family house, for worsening the quality of the relationship between her mother and stepfather.

I think in a way that I'm interfering with their relationship. My stepdad's mad at me because of how I treat my mom, but my mom is mad at him by the way he treats me. And it's just like a big circle.

She was thereby assuming responsibility for aspects of her mother's life over which she had no control. Frances' relationship with her stepfather appeared to be so often toxic, and so devoid of nurturing on his part, that Frances might be described as parentified.

Like Louanne, Paula reported suppressing her "real" desires for the sake of her father's PTSD—in her case, her desire to leave home and move in with her boyfriend. Paula believed that she needed, instead, to remain at home to protect her mother from having to live alone with a husband who had become verbally abusive:

I see eventually me and [my boyfriend] moving out and starting our lives. And eventually I'll be going into social work after I'm done at University #1. And I just see me having my own life, like anything regular, you know. Come back to visit every Sunday, maybe, to have supper with the parents and everything. But it's a little scary moving out from home, thinking that my mom's going to have to deal with him all by herself. That's the thing I'm very worried about. 'Cause out of all of us, the one who gets the most heat is her. Like, the most painful things that get said are to her.... I don't want her to have to be alone.

Like Frances, Paula was taking responsibility for her mother's emotional well-being. Paula also took on a caring stance vis-à-vis her parents in a more general way. She decided to focus on her father's suffering, thereby setting aside her own grief at the quality of life she and her family had lost as a result of his injury:

At first you can do the whole "Why is this happening to me?" And you've got to think "It's not happening to me, it's happening to him." Whatever I'm going through, he's going through it a hundred times worse—like, in an unimaginable way.

Paula added,

When did this become my life? It's so surreal at times. You're, you know, this can't be real and this shouldn't be happening to us. We've never done anything wrong. Why is this happening to us? But you deal with it, and you've got to stop being selfish about how it's hurting you. And you've got to try and help your family member. Like, it's all about being supportive.

Roger commented in a similar way, after having being asked how he would advise other adolescent children of CAF members who were going through the same experience. Rather than directly recommend that they take care of their afflicted parent, Roger instructed his peers to "overcome it yourself," as well as recognizing the work that your parent would have to do in order to get better. He implied that parents with PTSD would be unable to recover successfully unless their adolescents contributed their own part and "toughed it out":

[Your parents coming home] may seem different. But they are still your parents, and deep inside they do love you. It's a challenge, not only for them to overcome, but you have to overcome it yourself.... Tough it out. Because they're gonna end up coming back to reality soon enough, and then your relationship's probably gonna become even better.... Don't feel down about what's going on. Stay high-spirited.

Brady reminded his peers that, as Louanne commented at the beginning of this chapter, their military fathers, even with PTSD, should be considered much greater heroes than the fathers of their classmates and friends:

It's hard mentally on the family left at home, not knowing if your dad or mom is going to come home. Or even if they do come home, not knowing if they're going to be healthy like they left, or sick or have something changed in them. It's scary; it's frightening. But at the same time I'm more proud of my dad than I am of a lot of other dads out there, just 'cause of what he does.

In the last chapter, Zoe expressed gratitude for the fact that her mother had remained emotionally available during her father's long deployment to Africa and that she had not expected her children to take care of her or become parentified. Adolescent children of parents who have returned from a deployment with PTSD are, by definition, members of a family that is in crisis, and they are unlikely to be in the enviable situation that was described by Zoe. Indeed, the material presented in this last section has suggested that, just as some adolescents take care of the family members who remain behind during a deployment, adolescents often feel compelled to take care of both parents after one parent has returned with PTSD. In the next section we will review what past research has taught us about the possible mental health outcomes of being the adolescent child of a military member who has returned home with PTSD.

Possible Mental Health Outcomes

During her interview, Frances expressed the fear that she was in the process of developing an anger problem which would require therapy:

> I think it's gotten worse as I've gotten older, because I kind of speak my mind more. And if he was to say something, I'm not going to let him. I know I should just let it go, because maybe it's just because of whatever he has. But now I can't handle not saying anything back, because I don't want someone to talk to me like that.... I'm worried that I'm going to have some sort of anger problem, which scares me.

Indeed, the CAF ombudsman's 2008 national investigation into support available to the families of CAF members and veterans with PTSD noted that a number of the parents they had interviewed had commented that their children were in need of courses in anger management (McFadyen, 2008a).

Consistent with Frances' fears, an American study of children of Vietnam veterans with military-related PTSD found that, compared with same-aged members of the general population (aged 14 to 35), the veterans' children scored significantly higher on measures of emotional distress, depression, interpersonal problems, problems with authority, and excessive energy (Beckham et al., 1997). Much earlier, when 107 male Vietnam veterans filled out Child Behavior Checklists (CBCL) (Achenbach & Edelbrock, 1983) regarding their children aged 6 to 16, it was discovered that, among the adolescent subgroup of these children (aged 12 to 16), the girls were significantly more depressed and withdrawn, according to their fathers, than their peers in the general population; the boys were significantly more hyperactive, impulsive, and immature (Parsons, Kehle, & Owen, 1990). More recently, in a study conducted by Westerink and Giarratano (1999), adolescent offspring of veterans with PTSD reported psychological distress, relative to their peers; in a study carried out by Ahmadzadeh and Malakian (2004), they reported anxiety and high levels of aggression, relative to the members of a control group; and in a study carried out by Glenn and colleagues (2002), they reported hostility, relative to those of a matched age and gender in the civilian population. Only one major study of Vietnam veterans' offspring, carried out in Australia, found that the self-esteem and PTSD symptomatology of these youth were no different from the self-esteem and PTSD symptomatology of a same-aged group of the children of civilian men (Davidson & Mellor, 2001). Several of the 12 adult children interviewed by Rosenheck (1986) about the impact upon their lives of their fathers' World War II–related PTSD stated that they had been permanently emotionally traumatized by the rage, depression, guilt, and affective dyscontrol suffered by their fathers when they (the adult children) were adolescents.

In March 2007, the Ontario ombudsman felt compelled to launch an investigation into the unacceptably long wait times for mental health services that were being endured in Pembroke, Ontario, by the children of CAF members stationed at CFB Petawawa (McFadyen, 2008b).

Huebner and colleagues (2007) recently applied Boss's (1999) *ambiguous loss* theory to adolescents living through parental deployments. According to this theory—also applicable to living with a parent with PTSD—the combination of (a) the *loss* of the parent as s/he was (e.g., because s/he is away on a deployment or has returned from the deployment "different") and (b) the *ambiguity* inherent in the fact that, despite this loss, the parent is still "there," still very much present in the adolescent's life—is a potent emotional brew. According to Boss, the confusion inherent in loss coupled with ambiguity erects a barrier to effective coping and grieving, and leads to mental health problems such as depression and conflicted relationships. It is not unexpected, then, that parental PTSD would create emotional difficulties for adolescents. The research literature, though sparse, suggests that it does.

Support for PTSD Received from Outside the Home

In chapter 5 we explored the quality of support our participants received from outside their homes during deployments: from friends, the military community of Armyville, the CFB Armyville Military Family Resource Centre, and their school. Accessing this support had been difficult or impossible for some of them. For adolescent children of CAF members with PTSD, an extra layer of isolation is created by the understandable reluctance of many CAF members to report PTSD symptoms. Living with PTSD at home is also a unique experience; almost all civilians, and even many military members, know little or nothing about the characteristics and dimensions of this experience. It is therefore not surprising that adolescent children of afflicted military members tend to keep silent among their friends and in the community. The consequent isolation adds to the stress experienced by these adolescents at home, and it widens the gulf between themselves and extrafamilial support that they might have taken advantage of under other circumstances.

Frances, for example, said nothing to almost anybody about the time her stepfather had treated her violently:

> I told my best friend—and that's it.

She had decided not to discuss the incident with counsellors for fear of getting her stepfather in trouble with the CAF:

> I don't consider him an abusive person. Maybe he actually is—or if it's just because of this disorder. Like, I don't know. I wouldn't necessarily want to talk to someone about it, because they might not know what it is. Or something might happen to him just because of a disorder that he had.

She worked hard to ensure that her friends learned as little as possible about her stepfather's anger when they visited her house:

> I'm cautious about when my friends come over. We normally just stay in my room.... We have a skating rink, so in the winter we're at my house a lot more. But when it's not winter, we're normally at someone else's house.

Similarly, Simone had chosen not to share the experience of her father's PTSD with her civilian friends:

> I don't [talk about it with my friends]. 'Cause I feel like they don't understand. Not because I don't like talking about it. I'm not embarrassed to say, "Oh, my dad has PTSD." But it's just that they don't understand what it is. They haven't experienced it.

She added,

> Personally I don't like saying that my dad has PTSD. Not because they'll make fun of it, but people like to think, "Oh, if your dad's got PTSD then he's abusive, or he's not a good father," and stuff like that. So I don't talk about it to friends who don't understand.

Similarly, Paula reported,

> Talking to my friends who don't have family members struggling with this.... It's like they try to understand. But they'll never understand unless they see it, or unless they're experiencing it.

Civilian kids...don't know what it's like to have a sick parent with something like this. Like I know post-traumatic stress disorder can happen anywhere. But the majority of the time it happens in the military. And [civilian kids] don't understand what it's like to lose a piece of someone you love.

Louanne felt a lack of confidence even in her military community friends:

One of my good friends, her dad was in the military and then he got out. I don't think he ever had to do any tours, but he's gone away a lot, like on training and stuff. But [my military friends] don't really understand, 'cause their dads don't have PTSD and stuff.

As noted above, the CAF do not provide counselling to family members of CAF members who have not reported their PTSD to the CAF. The only counselling available to family members in this situation is the Canadian Forces Member Assistance Program (MAP), which provides six to eight telephone counselling sessions, on request, to civilian members of the families of CAF members. The telephone counsellors, however, have no expertise in military family issues (Daigle, 2012, p. 62). Since Amanda's father had not reported his PTSD to the CAF when we interviewed her, Amanda had so far had no other resources available to her except the MAP telephone line; she had found the MAP line to be very unsatisfactory:

Even the military—they're putting those signs out: "If you need to talk to somebody, go talk to somebody." Well, the hard part is finding someone to talk to who has actually been through it—who can help you deal with it. Counsellors, they think that they can help you deal with it, but not the same that you're looking for. The help you're looking for, you want somebody with experience, and who knows how to deal with it.

She added,

A friend of mine's father was actually on suicidal watch for, I think, a couple of months, because he tried to commit suicide so many times. Because the resources are not there, and they should be.... Obviously you're going to need the weapons and all that kind of stuff. But at the same time get some [mental health] funding from somewhere, because it's much needed.

Paula, in contrast, had been able to access some support for children at the Armyville MFRC, because her father was being treated for his PTSD by the CAF. She therefore reported having been set up with a peer mentor through the MFRC program:

The Family Resource Centre set me up with another girl. She was 23 or so, and they set me up with her to talk to her. 'Cause her dad has post-traumatic stress disorder, too, from Afghanistan. And she was really helpful—just telling me that it seems really bad right now, but it'll get better. It always does get better. And so it made me see, well, you have hope—that it wasn't going to be as tragic as it was forever.

It goes without saying that the support from friends and community that is available to most adolescent children of CAF members with PTSD is seriously inadequate and that the isolation experienced by some of these adolescents is profound. Improved support originating from outside the family would seem to be essential (cf. Charles et al., 2012). In the next section, we will consider the support that is now available to Armyville adolescents at their school.

Support from the School

When considering the support AHS provides to them, our participants commented most favourably on the PTSD peer support group, which was briefly mentioned in chapter 5. The PTSD peer support group, which meets once a month during the school day and is facilitated by an AHS guidance counsellor, was started during the 2007/08 school year by this counsellor, who was moved by what he was hearing in the media about "invisible wounds" and advertised his new initiative during the school's morning announcements, through posters, and through conversations with other guidance counsellors. The CAF parents of potential members of this support group did not need to have reported their PTSD to the CAF; the perception of PTSD symptoms on the part of their AHS student sons or daughters was the only requirement for admission to the group. Six or seven students were members during the group's first year, 2007/08.[6]

As we have seen, the theme of isolation pervaded participants' narratives of their experiences with friends and CAF telephone Member Assistance Program counsellors. In contrast, it was with great enthusiasm that they described what belonging to the AHS peer support group had meant to them. Amanda and Simone commented on the group's origins:

[One of the guidance counsellors] started it, because I went and spoke to him. And there were some other parents who went and spoke to him. Because our troops are supposed to go sometime soon—they're supposed to go again. I told them that there was a lot of times that I personally could have used it. And I know that a lot of people could have benefited from it. So why not start something and get something ready now? Tell

them what they're going to expect. Give them a heads-up, so it's not as big of a shock as it was to me and a lot of other people.

—Amanda

I never even knew that there was a PTSD group at all, until this year they announced it in an assembly. Like, they did an assembly separate for each grade. So Grade 9, Grade 10, Grade 11, and the guidance counsellor came out and started saying, "Like, if you want to join this group that we have—come." And I was like, "Wow!" Like, this is a place that I can go to talk about my experiences and stuff.

—Simone

Amanda had been a catalyst for getting the group started, even though, as a student about to graduate, she had known that she would be unable to benefit directly from its existence. It is interesting that Amanda, and a few participants who were cited in chapter 5, described the group as a deployment support group instead of as a PTSD support group. At the time of her interview, Amanda's father had not reported his PTSD to the CAF. Even though the PTSD peer support group represented an end to isolation for the students who belonged to it, it is possible that the secrecy surrounding PTSD accounts for the way they described the group to their peers, such that their peers (some of whom were quoted in chapter 5) believed that the group had been structured around general deployment support instead of around support for the stigmatized problem of parental PTSD.

The group was fulfilling several important functions for those who were attending it. Most importantly, it was counteracting their isolation. As Brady put it,

My sisters went to this, I went to this, some of my best friends went to this that I didn't even know, or they didn't know that my dad had PTSD. I didn't know theirs did. And that's [something] that really brought us together.

Paula shared,

It's one of those things that when you find out your dad has post-traumatic stress disorder you keep it secret. 'Cause you don't know what people are going to think, and you just try to keep it confidential. But when we got into that group last year, it felt like you could finally breathe. And you could tell people, "It really sucks."... It [had been] really traumatic telling my friends about it.

She added,

When we had that group and 10 people came into that room, I was like, "Oh my God, I thought I was the only one who's dealing with this. I never knew!"... But no, you realize it's on a much larger scale, that there's many people coming home from Afghanistan with post-traumatic stress disorder.

Along the same lines, Louanne said,

People were going through like, "My dad is sick." And I'm like, "Mine too." It was really weird how it can be such a relief just to hear somebody else say, "My dad's nuts!" and actually mean it and understand.

An anecdote related by Zoe showed that there had been a compelling need for the group at least a couple of years before its meetings had begun. A classmate of hers had been able to present his experience of parental PTSD to his whole class, as a result of having had the prior experience of opening up about it in the group. Despite the fact that Zoe had been a close associate of this classmate for years, she had had no idea of what his family had been suffering since his father had returned from Afghanistan:

For sociology we had an exit project. And one young guy did his exit project on PTSD, explaining it to the class, saying his dad has it—that he's known about it for years. And he just recently, in the last year, has been going to these PTSD meetings. His dad's been home from Afghanistan for three and a half years. This is the first year that he's been able to talk about it. Obviously [the group is] helping, if [he's able] to be standing in front of a class of 30 and telling everybody what it's like. There's obviously growth in this kid, and he just opened up to everybody. But it took a while. And before then I hadn't even really heard of it. Even me. I [knew him quite well]. But I hadn't known anything about his dad. And I hadn't known anything about my friends' dads, other than in my small tight-knit group of girlfriends.

Second, the group was validating the participants' efforts to be patient with their parents and encouraging them to recognize what they could not control. As Paula put it,

Some nights you spend your night crying yourself to sleep because you miss your dad, and you miss who he used to be, and you miss that he used to be really happy all the time. And sometimes when they're having a bad day, it gets taken out on you. It's just, you have people [now]. It's a support group.

She added,

*Talking to someone who's had their dad lash out at them for no rea-
son…you get so low on yourself, sometimes thinking, "What did I do
wrong? I did something wrong." But then you talk to this other person,
and they're like, "We did nothing wrong. It's them. They're sick." And
you have to realize that.*

Finally, the fact that its members were peers who had lived through parental
PTSD made the group more trustworthy as a source of support than adult
professional counsellors who lacked this personal experience. Louanne
commented,

*The guidance counsellor can talk to you, but really they won't under-
stand. They can say, "I understand," but they really don't. And it's different talking with an adult than it is with somebody your own age who
knows exactly what you're going through.*

The PTSD peer support group was the most positive initiative for students
affected by deployments that AHS had undertaken by the time our interviews had taken place. The group was a vehicle whereby its members could
share and ventilate, to paraphrase Zoe, "the real stuff that was making
them sad."

Apart from the PTSD peer support group, a couple of participants mentioned AHS teachers and guidance counsellors who had been understanding and caring. Paula described how her teachers had been lenient with her
late homework and assignments:

*I was over my days by that many days of the week for exemption. And
I had a meeting with all my teachers and my principal, and they said,
"We understand. We'll just forget about it, and we'll let you exempt."
So they made my whole course load a whole lot easier. And they under-
stood about the homework. They said, "Just hand it in whenever you're
ready and whenever you have it finished. Don't be rushed to get it done.
Like, we understand." And it was good.*

Brady described how an AHS guidance counsellor had always made time
for him on the mornings following troubling episodes with his father:

*There were moments. Like of course we have bad nights and good nights
with him. There were some nights where I couldn't get my homework
done, because it was a bad night for him and I went to bed early. Or I
got in an argument with him over something really dumb, and I felt
bad about it 'cause of his position that he's already in. So I'd go to bed
early. And when that happened, the next day I would go to the guidance counsellor first thing in the morning. And I would miss a period or*

two—it depends on how bad it was the night before. A lot of the time it was 'cause I felt guilty for what I had done, and I had got him going when I shouldn't have. But my guidance counsellor, she was always there for me, and I really appreciated that.

Brady also described how a particular teacher had learned to give him the leniency he needed as a result of an unexpected conversation he had had with him in the guidance office:

Most of the teachers were very supportive of me. They understood my situation. One of them, my second-period teacher, he had a substitute in one day, and I was wondering why he was gone, 'cause he never told us. It was right after one of those nights that wasn't so good. And I went to my guidance counsellor, and it was my second-period teacher. He had filled in for my guidance counsellor, 'cause my guidance counsellor couldn't be there that day. This is a teacher that I really trusted. And so I sat down and I explained to him my situation—kind of what I'm doing with you. And he was extremely supportive. Whenever I didn't get homework done, he gave me extra time, because he knew my situation. If I was late he wouldn't dock me too hard. For tests he'd put me in the resource room, 'cause I would need extra time. 'Cause I might not have had that much time to study. So he would give me a few extra minutes to study before I did the test.

The material presented in this past section is encouraging, and it displays a positive side of life at AHS. It also helps to make the case for the appropriateness of the school as a source of deployment and post-deployment support. The crucial role played by the PTSD peer support group is underscored by feedback participants provided when they were asked how AHS could improve its support to the children of deployed parents. Janis, who had experienced no parental overseas deployment since early childhood, suggested that the school institute a deployment peer support group for all adolescents who could benefit from it:

They should have a group or something where you can just go and have someone who has family in the military.... Maybe, you know, once every couple of weeks, have some of the kids get together and just talk about stuff. Because you do feel lonely a bit when your parents are gone. And you don't really have anyone to talk to about all that stuff. And it's hard talking to a civilian about what's going on, and using, you know, all the terms and stuff, when they have no idea of what you're saying.

Zachary, whose father had deployed to Afghanistan, added,

Maybe make, like, a program for people that have parents deployed. And they can come in and talk about it if they feel that they need to talk about it. Like a coffee night kind of thing.

Not quite all the comments about the support provided by the school regarding parental PTSD were positive. Zoe and Louanne believed that the school had shown insensitivity to the issue of PTSD by instituting the peer support group for students "too late"—that is, after the problem had become very well entrenched within some of their lives:

I have two friends with parents who have PTSD from Afghanistan. And just recently, a year ago, they've been attending meetings at the [CAF] Family Resource Centre in [Armyville] that's not affiliated with the school. And just up until recently, the school has not recognized that this is an issue. And Afghanistan has been going on for how many years?... The school just realized why kids are rebelling in class—why kids are not showing up to class in the first place.

—Zoe

It was almost too late. 'Cause about three or four of the people in the group were graduating, and they [had] loved the group. They were like, "I am so glad that we did this, but it's kind of too late 'cause I'm graduating and I'm done." So they should have tried to do it sooner, I guess, through the year. 'Cause now those people are gone, and they don't have that support any more.... They don't have anybody to talk to.

—Louanne

Only one participant—Brady—shared a negative comment about a teacher who had shown no understanding of how his father's PTSD had been affecting him:

There was the odd teacher who said, "You know what? There's a lot of people in that situation. Get over it! You still have to do your stuff for this date. No excuses!" I mean, she couldn't possibly understand what I was going through or what my family was going through.

Amanda and Zoe would have characterized Brady's experience as an example of a teacher who lacked appropriate training. In doing so, they would have concurred with the recent recommendation of psychologists Lincoln and Sweeten (2011) that, given the current magnitude of children affected by military deployments, specialized training should now be provided to all professional practitioners who work with military children and adolescents. Along similar lines, the school personnel who participated in the focus groups conducted by Mmari and colleagues (2010) recommended the development of improved communication strategies between schools and the military bases in their communities.

Conclusion

As we saw in chapter 5, deployments are times of stress, anxiety, sadness, and frequent loneliness for military adolescents. It is easy to imagine the joy and relief felt by all family members when the parent returns home, apparently safe and sound. The loss represented by the parent's absence has been healed, and home life functions smoothly again, with new happiness having grown out of everyone's deeper appreciation of what each family member contributes. Unfortunately, the new happiness is often soon marred by the realization that life has shifted for every family member during the deployment, and still more emotional work will be exacted from each adult and child to accomplish the returning parent's successful reintegration into the home.

Two of the most dramatic changes that can occur as the result of a deployment are a physical injury and PTSD. Unlike the usual changes undergone by a household after a deployment, the impact of a serious physical injury, or of severe PTSD, can be permanent. For families who experience these latter dramatic changes, the end of the deployment represents only the beginning of the burdens they must find a way to shoulder effectively. As some of them did during the deployment, adolescents affected by parental physical injuries or PTSD take on long-term instrumental and emotional caregiving roles. Some of these adolescents take responsibility for their parents' emotions, and some of them can be described as parentified, with accompanying and understandable psychological stress. The fact that the experience of living with PTSD is socially isolating dramatically underscores the need for improved community-based military and civilian mental health support for PTSD sufferers and the members of their families.

The question we posed towards the end of chapter 5 was, Can the school do anything to fill the voids created by the quality-of-life losses suffered by adolescents whose parents have been deployed? The resounding success of the PTSD peer support group at AHS suggests that extending the model of small-group peer support to a broader range of students living through deployment-related issues—including issues that arise upon a deployed parent's return—might be a good way to begin to answer this question.

In the next and final chapter, we will expand on the theme of school support by discussing how the academic and school district members of the research team jointly followed up our research findings and instituted some changes at AHS.

7

New Beginnings at Armyville High School

As previously noted, the academic members of our team carried out this project in partnership with the Armyville School District (ASD). Once the survey and interview data had been collected and provisionally analyzed, we, the academic team members, were anxious to share our interim findings with our partner, in hopes that the latter might be able to begin to make some use of them. As discussed in chapter 3, Armyville is a single-industry military community. According to some of our survey findings, the Afghanistan mission appeared to have had an impact on the lives of every adolescent who lived there. Accordingly, all the members of our team were hoping that tangible benefits for all AHS adolescents might result from the research we did.

The academic team and the ASD jointly organized a two-day symposium in Armyville in March 2011. The objectives of this event were (1) to discuss the team's findings and (2) to make recommendations aimed at improving school-based services to adolescents who are affected by military deployments. The 30 attendees included most research team members, personnel from Armyville High School (AHS), other school and district staff from the ASD, and a representative from CFB Armyville.

During the morning of the first day, Karen Robson presented the 2008 survey findings. This was followed by a presentation of the interview findings by Deborah. Both presentations were followed by discussions. During the lunch break, the partners jointly announced the main research findings at a national media conference.

In the afternoon, each attendee participated in one of the three breakout groups, titled Deployment Support, PTSD Support, and Gender Issues. In each group, attendees were asked to begin by reading individual scenarios, each of which represented a compilation of real-life experiences of adolescents who had participated in the study's interview phase. It was hoped that the scenarios, along with the morning's presentations, would serve as a vehicle for getting each group's discussion kick-started.

One of the scenarios presented to the Deployment Support group was as follows:

> Janie has been missing school regularly since her mother left for Afghanistan. She seems listless and uninterested in her school work or playing on the basketball team. When she does come to class she is very tired and seems defeated. When confronted with her absenteeism, she says she has to stay at home to help get things done around the house.

Life at home during her parent's Afghanistan deployment had apparently created a temporary rupture between Janie and her life at her school. Part of the problem may have been Janie's fear that no one at the school would be able to understand the stress she was experiencing at home during the months her parent was away. Janie may also have been uncertain as to whether or not her teachers knew that her parent was on the deployment.

One of the scenarios presented to the PTSD Support group was as follows:

> Charlie was never the best of students, and his dad, who has been on several tours in the last few years, recently returned again from Afghanistan. Charlie has been skipping classes and skipping school, and he responds only with anger when confronted about (or disciplined for) this behaviour. He looks in bad shape, and does not seem to be sleeping.

As was the case for Janie, Charlie was likely having a hard time at home. In Charlie's case, his father may have developed PTSD when he was in Afghanistan. For whatever reason, Charlie felt unable to communicate with personnel at the school. If Charlie's father had refused to report his PTSD symptoms to the CAF, the aloneness and helplessness experienced by Charlie, his siblings, and his mother would have been hard to bear. Charlie may have been expressing his frustration by acting out.

It took little time for group members to move away from the scenarios in order to focus on the issues that seemed most urgent to them, based on each member's experiences with CAF adolescents. During its discussion, each group was also asked to seek tentative answers to such broad, open-ended questions as these:

1. Building on what we already do, how could we best support students whose parents have been deployed?
2. How could we better support the students' parents?
3. As teachers, counsellors, peer students, and school staff, how could we help each other in supporting these students?

4. In what ways could our community help support these students and their families?
5. What do we need (resources, information, etc.) to be able to provide better support?
6. Given the large and varied contributions girls make to the household during deployments, what special support could we provide them with?
7. Are there any steps we could take to increase girls' self-esteem?

During the morning of the second day, representatives from each of the three breakout groups made presentations to a plenary session on the recommendations arrived at within their respective groups; they then answered questions from the floor. These discussions were followed by a final plenary session, which condensed the recommendations made by the three groups into 18 recommendations that were agreed upon by all, considered important, and deemed to be suitable for follow up (see appendix 2). The ten most significant recommendations were as follows:

1. The Armyville School District (ASD) should create a joint committee of representatives from the school district, the Military Family Resource Centre (MFRC), CFB Armyville, teachers, parents, and students. Purpose: to oversee and enhance the well-being of students from CAF families.
2. The ASD should appoint an employee from each school that is willing to liaise/share information with the MFRC.
3. CFB Armyville should add a "notify school" check box to the MFRC pre-deployment checklist that is distributed to CAF parents.
4. The ASD should organize a booth at every CFB Armyville Departure Assistance Group (DAG) function, to solicit voluntary information sharing with schools and teachers about the deployment as part of each military member's pre-deployment checklist.
5. The ASD should request voluntary information about upcoming deployments from students and parents on annual intake registration forms.
6. The ASD should update its current deployment binder to include information on the post-deployment phase and PTSD; information on our team's research project; and deployment-related information from the MFRC.
7. The ASD should make deployments and other military adolescents' issues part of professional development (PD) days on a regular basis (e.g., with keynote speakers).
8. The ASD should provide resources to Grade 10 Personal Development teachers on the topics of (a) Military Deployments; (b) PTSD

Information; and (c) Stress, Juggling Responsibilities, and Mental Health (including women and domestic-labour issues), to help them incorporate these topics into their curricula, should they wish to do so.

9. The AHS Guidance Department should start a monthly pre-deployment and deployment peer support group for interested eligible students during the school day.

10. The ASD should continue its monthly PTSD peer support groups during the school day for high-school students. Middle schools should initiate a monthly PTSD peer support group during the school day for middle-school students.

As we saw in chapter 5, most of our interview participants believed that students who were experiencing a parental deployment would be better served by their school if their teachers knew about it than they would be if their teachers did not know. Recommendations 3, 4, and 5 in the above list represented three possible strategies for increasing the chance that school personnel would be informed about relevant CAF deployments. Recommendation 3 proposed that the Armyville MFRC take steps to encourage CAF parents to report to each of their children's schools the fact that a deployment was coming up. Recommendation 4 proposed a new communication link between ASD personnel and CAF members, which would enable the ASD personnel to solicit the members' voluntary sharing of deployment-related information during the period just prior to a deployment. A Departure Assistance Group function at an army base typically takes place during an evening close to the departure date, when the deploying CAF member and his/her spouse visit a succession of administrative and professional tables (staffed by, for example, social workers and chaplains) and are interviewed, in order that the CAF may reassure themselves that no issues exist in the life of the member, or in the life of anyone in his/her family, that should cause the member to be held back from the deployment. Recommendation 4 proposed to add a School District table to every Departure Assistance Group event.

Finally, Recommendation 5 proposed a mechanism whereby the ASD could solicit voluntary upcoming deployment-related information from all its CAF parents on an annual basis, via an expanded annual intake registration form.

The AHS Guidance Department's PTSD peer support group had been lauded highly by those of its members we interviewed, as you will recall from the preceding chapter. Accordingly, Recommendation 10 proposed that the PTSD peer support group be continued at AHS, and be extended to middle schools in the ASD.

Recommendation 9 was also important. The intent of this recommendation was to extend the benefit of guidance-counsellor-facilitated peer support to every AHS student who was in the process of experiencing a parental deployment and believed that s/he could benefit from belonging to this kind of group. If this recommendation were implemented, AHS adolescents from CAF families whose quality of home life had diminished during a deployment would gain access to a strong source of adult-facilitated support, as provided by a group of peers.

As noted in chapter 5, some of our participants believed that teachers and guidance counsellors would be able to provide better help to affected students if they could receive face-to-face training about the impact of deployments on members of military families. To this end, Recommendation 7 proposed that regular professional development days about deployments and other issues pertinent to the lives of military kids be instituted in the District. If this recommendation were implemented, teachers in the ASD would be provided with regular opportunities to discuss, and achieve new insights into, the family dynamics set into motion by deployments and other military lifestyle events.

Lastly, Recommendation 8 proposed the use of an existing school course to educate all AHS students about deployments and other military family issues. If Recommendation 8 were implemented, every AHS student would have the opportunity to learn about military family life issues. If the course included military family issues on a regular basis, one of the consequences might be a "ripple effect" whereby Armyville's culture would become suffused with enhanced understanding of the challenges experienced by the members of military families—and the adolescent members of these families would thereby find themselves less isolated.

Follow-up after the Symposium

A few days after the symposium, David, the ASD superintendent, contacted the CFB Armyville base commander in the hopes of initiating a dialogue about how the ASD and CFB Armyville could co-operate with one another to implement the symposium's recommendations. The base commander replied and delegated his senior staff officer, a senior operations and training officer, and the executive director of the CFB Armyville Military Family Resource Centre (MFRC) to meet with David briefly. A larger meeting organized by the executive director of the CFB Armyville MFRC would take place in the fall.

Before the planned fall meeting at the MFRC, David took the following steps towards implementing some of the symposium's recommendations:

1. He advised all ASD staff that military family issues (especially deployments) would be treated as a notably high ASD priority during the 2011/12 school year.
2. He facilitated the organization of a PD day for all ASD teachers at the end of August, at which MFRC staff members made a presentation about the mental health of military children whose parents are deployed (re: Recommendation 7 above).
3. To the intake form that the ASD sends annually to all parents, he added boxes that parents could voluntarily tick to indicate (a) CAF membership and (b) deployment during the current school year (re: Recommendation 5 above). From now on, this information would be routinely entered into the ASD database, and relevant school and district staff would have access to it.
4. He directed the ASD Student Services team to update the district's deployment binder, in keeping with Recommendation 6 above. This action was carried out during the 2011/12 school year; the new sections of the binder were distributed to each school. They included information on the emotional cycle of deployment and on the potential impact on children of living with a parent with PTSD.
5. He appointed an employee from each ASD school to liaise with the MFRC (re: Recommendation 2 above). As of 2015, this channel of communication still existed, but was seldom used.

In September 2011, David, a few of his staff, and Deborah attended a half-day meeting at the CFB Armyville MFRC, hosted by the MFRC's executive director. Following a tour of the facility, the visitors sat down to a discussion with the executive director and eight members of her staff.

David both chaired and structured the discussion, which focused on the symposium's most important recommendations. By the end of the meeting, the MFRC had agreed to the following:

1. Prepare a resource binder on deployments for each ASD school.
2. Add "notify school" to the pre-deployment checklist it gives to the applicable military families (Recommendation 3 above).

David had agreed to the following:

1. Initiate the process of implementing Recommendation 1 above—the joint committee.
2. Ask the AHS guidance staff to implement Recommendation 9 above—the during-class-time deployment peer support group.

As of September 2014, the MFRC had not implemented its proposed actions. Recommendation 4 above—that the ASD should organize a booth at every

CFB Armyville Departure Assistance Group (DAG) event, to encourage deploying members and their spouses to identify themselves (and their children's names and schools)—had been rejected by CFB Armyville as impractical, on the grounds that spouses no longer routinely attended DAG events along with deploying members.

Following the August 2011 professional development day that was mentioned above, Shanyn (the school psychologist mentioned in the introduction) organized an after-school event in March 2012, which was facilitated by the Armyville MFRC. Thirteen ASD staff members attended it. As of September 2014, no subsequent deployment-related professional development events had occurred.

In February 2012, David scheduled a meeting with all the principals in the ASD to discuss the recommendations from the symposium, especially those that had been intended for initiation by schools. The minutes of this meeting described Recommendation 7 (about professional development days) as "will continue to be on our radar." The minutes described Recommendation 8 (about Grade 10 Personal Development course curricula) as "still on radar." Around the same time, David met the new commander of CFB Armyville, discussed our research and the symposium, and gave him a copy of the recommendations. In March 2012, David requested a progress report from Gary, the AHS guidance counsellor who facilitated the PTSD peer support group. Gary told David that the 2011/12 PTSD peer support group had grown in size over the previous year; it now had 20 members who were divided into two groups. During 2012/13, 22 students belonged to the PTSD peer support group; the 22 were divided into two groups. During 2013/14, the support group had 10 members. Gary noted that the group was now being publicized by middle-school district staff; hence, more younger students were now joining it than in previous years. During 2014/15, the group had 16 members, divided into two groups of eight; the trend of students joining immediately after arriving at AHS from middle school was continuing.

Subsequent to David's February 2012 meeting with the ASD principals, Recommendation 8 was addressed. The provincial Department of Education and Early Childhood Development revised the curriculum of the Grade 10 Personal Development course, such that it now included at least four learning outcomes that would be compatible with the military family issues content proposed in the recommendation: (1) how change and personal growth affect one's ability to engage in learning and work; (2) strategies for achieving positive mental health/well-being; (3) how an individual's various roles and responsibilities may interrelate with work, family, and leisure activities; and (4) gender stereotyping in work and family settings. A teacher who wished to do so would have no difficulty using the topics suggested in Recommendation 8 to achieve these learning outcomes, with the help of the resources located in the deployment binder. In the fall of 2014, David sent an email to the district school staff to remind them of the possibility of incorporating military family issues content into this and other courses they were teaching.

Reflections on the Symposium and Its Follow-up

There was considerable momentum in the immediate aftermath of the symposium. Only a few years later, however, progress had slowed, and at least three important recommendations had not been implemented. The Armyville joint committee, whose purpose would have been to enhance the well-being of students from CAF families, had not been created, because not all Armyville community stakeholders had believed that it would be effective. Apart from the updated deployment binder, the enhanced deployment-related training that had been recommended for teachers (Recommendation 7) had materialized only to the point of one professional development day in 2011 and one after-school session in 2012. The recommended deployment peer support group (Recommendation 9) had also not been initiated.

How might these disappointments be explained? One reason is that, in some respects, our symposium happened too soon. By March 2011 we had indeed collected our data, done some of our data analysis, and compiled some of our findings. However, it is only now—more than four years later—as we come to the end of the process of reflecting on our findings through the writing of this book, that we (the authors) believe that we are fully able to appreciate the need for improved school-based support for adolescents affected by deployments, and for enhanced deployment-related education for school staff. Were we able to undertake the symposium now instead of four years ago, it is possible that the academic members of the team would present their findings in a different way, the questions assigned to the breakout groups would be different, and the recommendations would be created in a more compelling atmosphere.

In the years following 2012, Canada's role on the international military stage was also transformed. Not long after our symposium, Canada began withdrawing its troops from Afghanistan, and by the spring of 2014 the last of the Canadian troops had returned home. Despite recent evidence that the violence and instability in Afghanistan are continuing (Simpson, 2014; Smith, 2013), the opening of the NATO summit of September 2014 had leaders declaring that the Afghanistan mission had been a success. Canadian troops have shifted their attention away from Afghanistan, to conflicts in Iraq and Syria, to Russian and Ukrainian actions in eastern

Ukraine, and to more than a dozen task forces currently occurring around the world (Department of National Defence, 2014). Relevant for our purposes is the fact that the end of Canada's combat involvement in Afghanistan marked the end of the sense of urgency that had surrounded the issue of military deployments in the town of Armyville and in the offices of the Armyville School District.

A second monumental event occurred on July 1, 2012, when the province, which had been traditionally divided into 14 school districts, woke up to an amalgamated new world, consisting of only seven school jurisdictions. The province's teachers and administrators had had only six months' notice to prepare for this new reality. The main relevant consequence of the amalgamation was that the old Armyville School District, consisting of 18 schools, became part of a much larger school district, consisting of 74 schools. This meant that the province no longer contained a school district that was dominated and driven by a military family presence.

For the above reasons, the symposium's three remaining important recommendations were not implemented by the ASD personnel who now worked in a larger school district with a different name. While conversations would always continue between school district personnel and CFB Armyville, and close co-operation would be expected to reoccur in the event of another crisis of the magnitude of Afghanistan, the joint committee recommendation was not implemented. Within the new larger school district, other topics for professional development days were considered to be more timely and relevant, at least for the foreseeable future, than PD days devoted to military family issues. Unfortunately, all the impetus from the symposium towards improved deployment-related training for teachers and guidance counsellors had been concentrated within the one basket of this recommendation on professional development.

The deployment peer support group was also not implemented. However, in September 2014 Gary indicated to Deborah that he would consider inaugurating such a group at a future time if students indicated that they would be interested in it, and if another guidance counsellor were willing to co-facilitate it.

On the financial side, the ratio of guidance counsellors to students in the district continued to be one counsellor for every 502 students. As we learned in chapter 5, this number of guidance counsellors is insufficient to meet the needs of adolescents who are experiencing a deployment of the magnitude of Afghanistan. A difficulty that was discussed at the symposium is that, in Canada, National Defence is a federal responsibility, whereas the cost of all public education is borne by the provinces. In England, in contrast, the federal Department for Education allocates annual monies to each child from a military family, through the child's school. This money is used for such purposes as resources to support military children, training in military family issues for school staff, and the employment of special support workers to liaise between military families and the school.[1] Similarly, in 2008, a memorandum of understanding was created between the US Department of Defense and the US Department of Education, to empower the Department of Defense Education Activity to provide large school partnership grants to public school districts that serve students from military families. By early 2012, over $100 million in grants had been provided to US school districts under this program. The Interstate Compact on Educational Opportunity for Military Children (ICEOMC) was also established in 2008, to "reduce and/or eliminate barriers to educational success for children from military families as they transition between schools and across state lines" (Esqueda, Astor, & De Pedro, 2012). In Canada at the time of writing, no provincial school districts receive assistance for military children from any federal government source.

Despite the historical events we had been unable to foresee, and the fact that no federal support exists for school attendees from Canadian military families, our project can be considered a tentative success for several reasons. First, the efficiency and co-operation between the academic team and the ASD during the data-collection process, the wrap-up symposium, and the writing of this book were outstanding. Second, the symposium went well. It produced well-thought-out recommendations, which had resulted from a decision-making process that was participatory and democratic. Third, at least one lasting policy outcome can be attributed to the symposium: the fact that a mechanism now exists to enable CAF parents to inform their children's schools that (if applicable) a deployment will be occurring during the current school year. Fourth, the ASD's deployment binder was updated with new information about deployments and PTSD. Fifth, the curriculum of the Grade 10 Personal Development course was revised, to make it easier for military family issues to be incorporated if the teacher wished to do so. Sixth, despite the school district amalgamation, the PTSD peer support group was continuing in 2015, and its facilitator believed that it was filling a need that was even greater than had existed in 2007.

Seventh—and finally—our project was a solid example of collaborative action research (CAR), which was structured from its first beginnings to lead to action outcomes. While both discrepancies and convergences existed among the respective agendas of the academic team, the ASD, and CFB Armyville, the three entities were sufficiently able to focus on the convergences amongst their agendas to work co-operatively to carry out the research, the symposium, and some useful post-symposium follow-up. Our efforts showed that meaningful findings and action can result from the process of an academic research team collaborating with a school district that is located in or near a military community. As laid out in this book, our findings also make the case that, at this point in Canadian military history, the need for civilian-driven research on the impact of deployments on the civilian members of military families is very strong. We hope that this research will soon happen, and that sound policy recommendations will emerge from it.

Conclusion

This monograph has provided a glimpse into the lives of Canadian military adolescents during a historically unique time. It has attempted a partial answer to the question What was it like to grow up in a CAF family, attend a particular high school, and experience parental deployments during the first decade of the twenty-first century?

Deployments create significant challenges for the military adolescents of Armyville. These young people cope with deployments resourcefully, by assuming new instrumental and emotional household tasks and by becoming family caregivers, at exactly the same time as they are grieving the loss of the parent who is deployed; worrying about this parent's safety; coping with the stress and emotional unavailability of their undeployed parent; foregoing extracurricular activities; spending less time with their friends; and experiencing isolation and loneliness.

When the deployment is over and the deployed parent has returned home, the stress continues, as the adolescent is compelled to renegotiate family roles. S/he may lose, happily or unhappily, the quasi-adult position in the household that s/he occupied while her/his parent was away— or s/he may want to "become a kid again" and be prevented from doing so. The adolescent may witness conflict between his/her newly reunited parents or, alternatively, feel excluded as the two of them re-bond. S/he may need to work at developing a new rapport with a parent who has returned home different.

If the deployed parent returns home with a physical injury with chronic implications, or with serious PTSD, the long-term situation for the adolescent, and for the "healthy" parent, will be hard. In the case of a parent returning home with PTSD, both the research literature and our own findings identify isolation as a serious problem. The PTSD of a returning parent has the effect of weakening relationships both inside and outside the family. PTSD, after all, is a mental health issue, and a stigma continues to surround mental health issues in the CAF and civilian communities. The adolescent therefore continues to feel isolated, as s/he struggles to provide emotional caregiving to both of her/his parents and to take responsibility for some of their feelings.

The term *ambiguous loss*, as coined by Boss (1999) and applied to parental deployments by Huebner and colleagues (2007), helps to illuminate the stress and mental health difficulties that are experienced by the adolescent of a military member who has returned from a deployment with a physical injury or PTSD. The *ambiguous loss* concept expresses the contradictory reality that the parent has been, in some senses, lost but in other ways remains present. According to Boss, the confusion inherent in this contradictory reality creates a mental obstacle that stands in the way of what might otherwise have been the adolescent's progress through the normal stages of coping and/or grieving.

The literature has identified mental health consequences for adolescents who are affected by parental deployments, and also for adolescents who are affected by parental PTSD. The simplest and most common of these consequences are internalizing and externalizing psychological symptoms. Boys, for the most part, are the externalizers, who are more likely to engage in risky behaviours. Girls, in contrast, tend to perform more of the extra household emotional work, become parentified, and feel, as internalizers, depressed and anxious.

Some adolescents are more able than others to develop a healthy level of protective resilience during an overseas deployment. According to the adolescents interviewed by Huebner and Mancini (2005), resilience may be achieved if reliable and nurturing sources of extrafamilial support can be found. On the other hand, resilience that has already been achieved may subsequently be weakened by a deployment that is too long, or by multiple deployments occurring within a family during a short period of time (Chandra et al., 2010; Richardson et al., 2011). Our participants identified same-aged friends—especially those from other CAF families—as their most important sources of extrafamilial support.

Being the adolescent of a parent with PTSD makes it more difficult to find nurturing support outside the home. Given the ignorance about PTSD that is shared by most people who are not directly affected by it, our participants' experience suggests that same-age friends are unlikely to be equipped to provide the kind of support they may have been able to provide during the same adolescent's parental deployment.

For students at AHS, a notable exception has been found in the PTSD peer support group that was discussed in chapter 6, consisting of adolescents and a guidance counsellor facilitator. As some of our participants told us, this group is deeply cherished. The group provides support and validation for each member's experiences of living with a parent with

PTSD, and its existence counteracts the almost-total isolation that otherwise often surrounds them.

As yet, there is no school-based peer support group at AHS for students who have a parent who is deployed. Those of our participants who had experienced a recent parental deployment were more critical of the quality of deployment support provided by the school than were participants who had not. While many individual teachers were described as "caring," several participants remarked that the school's response to the Afghanistan mission had been "not much." A couple of them believed that the school's approach to supporting students with parents in Afghanistan had been too superficial, and that the school had missed out on the opportunity to reach out to the students and engage with "the real stuff that is making them sad." According to one student, the school had "sugar-coated" the Afghanistan mission to the extent of discouraging unaffected students from taking the situation seriously enough to offer needed support to their suffering peers. Several participants noted that they would have been better served if their teachers had known that their parents were deployed, and that teachers would need specialized training in order to be able to understand enough about the impact of deployments on military families to provide their students with mentoring that was meaningful.

In chapter 1 we learned that the Canadian public was kept in the dark about the level of violence Canadian soldiers experienced in Afghanistan and about the depth of anxiety and suffering that was experienced by the soldiers' families. AHS teachers and other school personnel would have been members of this Canadian public.

As was noted in chapter 3, we found in our survey that CAF adolescents who had experienced a parental deployment scored higher on school engagement measures than their CAF and civilian peers. Along with our interview data, this finding suggests a readiness on the part of youth affected by deployments to take advantage of improved school-based support, should it become available. This suggestion is supported by the recent California research of De Pedro et al. (2015), which found that a positive school climate—operationalized especially as relationships with caring adults, school connectedness, and feeling safe—exercises a beneficial influence on military-connected students' mental well-being, even if it is not able to counteract all the negative mental health effects of their experience of a deployment.

Our interview participants were relatively few in number, and they were also self-selected. We are therefore unable to make any claims to the effect that what they told us was representative of the experiences of military adolescents, CAF adolescents, or even the CAF adolescents who attended

Armyville High School in 2009/10. However, as the reader can see from the excerpts reproduced in this book, many of our participants spoke genuinely from their hearts. Since much of what they told us was consistent with the research literature we cited, it is likely that other military adolescents will find echoes of their experiences in what they said.

Some aspects of our interview data contained nuances that supplemented the qualitative data of earlier studies. For example, our participants provided us with windows—from several different angles—onto the anxiety they had experienced during the Afghanistan mission. They also suggested a few ways in which the reduced quality of communication between the undeployed parent and his/her adolescent during a deployment might exacerbate the interaction occurring between their respective stresses. As related by Joe and Lorraine, an undeployed mother can push her adolescents away, and possibly alienate them, by taking her stress out on them. Alternatively, as in Amanda's case, a mother can repress her stress to the extent of inhibiting the sharing that otherwise might have occurred between herself and her child. For reasons that are unclear, although the mothers of Zoe and Brady also made an effort to avoid burdening their children with their own anxieties, communication in their families continued to thrive.

As noted in chapter 6, in March 2007 the Ontario ombudsman felt compelled to investigate the excessively long wait times for mental health services that were being endured by the children of CAF members stationed at CFB Petawawa. Relatedly, in chapter 3 we learned that military-connected California students sampled in 2011 were more likely than their civilian peers to be depressed and/or to think of committing suicide (Cederbaum et al., 2014; see also De Pedro et al., 2015). In contrast with the California study, our own 2008 survey found that *all* Armyville youth—CAF and civilians alike—were more likely than their national NLSCY peers to be depressed, to have low self-esteem, and to have thought of suicide. The uniqueness of our survey finding may be explained by the fact that, unlike California, Armyville is a geographically isolated single-industry army community, in which all families are at least somewhat affected by the stresses of a life-threatening combat mission. In Armyville, in other words, there may be a spillover effect. Our survey finding raises the possibility that mental health services should be enhanced for all adolescents who live in military communities—not merely adolescents who belong to military families.

Before deciding to seek collaboration with the Armyville School District on this project, the academic members of our team explored the possibility of collaborating with a school district in another province. After many weeks of negotiation, the most generous offer of co-operation we could receive from this district was an offer to mail our surveys home to the adolescents' parents, accompanied by a letter that stated that the district had had no input into the design of the study, and that the district's co-operation (by mailing the surveys home) should not be interpreted as an endorsement of our work. In contrast, our genuine and constructive collaboration with the ASD turned out to be second to none during our project phases of collecting data, planning and executing the symposium, and writing this book. As noted in chapter 7, at least two changes in district practice have resulted from the follow-up to our symposium. First, CAF parents have been provided with an annual opportunity to submit information to the district that will make it easier for district staff to know if one or both of them will soon be deployed. Second, a greater possibility exists than previously that the Grade 10 Personal Development course will incorporate material on military family life.

As discussed in chapter 7, we conclude the project with a few feelings of regret and disappointment. The need for deployment-related training for teachers and guidance counsellors was an important issue to emerge from previous research, our interview participants' experience, and the discussions at our symposium. The fact that the recommendation from the symposium that attempted to address this need might have been better crafted, coupled with the amalgamation of the school districts and the end of Canada's mission in Afghanistan, led to the outcome that our work did not succeed in addressing this need in a long-term manner. Another important need left unsatisfied by our project was the need for improved support to adolescents who are living through deployments. We are heartened to know that improved support during deployments remains on the table as a possible new direction to be taken by the high school.

As noted in chapter 1, Canada's military role has changed since the end of the Cold War. The decade of the 1990s brought both a higher operational tempo and more dangerous missions to members of the Canadian Forces. From 2001 to 2014, Canadian foreign policy supported the "War on Terror" waged by the United States and its allies. Even before 2001, Canada had begun to transition from its traditional job of peacekeeping into a peace-building role that has involved higher levels of force, missions of indefinite length, casualties, physical injuries, and post-traumatic stress disorder.

Although the medium-term future of Canadian military involvement is uncertain, chances are low that the peacekeeping era of the Cold War will soon return. The findings of previous research, our 2008 survey, and our 2009–2010 interviews—plus the continual need for children's mental health services in locations such as CFB Petawawa, as documented by the CAF ombudsman and the media—suggest the existence of a need for school-based mental health support for adolescent offspring of CAF members and veterans. The ideal solution would be a deployment support program, including both staff training and support services, that would permanently exist in every military community and would require all school staff to possess at least a minimal level of deployment-related expertise. The advantages of this policy would include the availability of mental health support for CAF adolescents who had been affected by past deployments, and the maintenance of a culture of deployment-related expertise within the school district that did not rapidly have to be reinvented whenever the district was faced with a crisis of the magnitude of Afghanistan. The most effective way to create and maintain a school-based culture of expertise would be through the provision of a form of federal financial support to school attendees from military families, of the kind that now exists in England and in the United States.

The adolescent members of Armyville military families grew and developed as a result of the extra responsibilities they took on at home during the Afghanistan mission, and they were justifiably proud of that. Nevertheless, our findings suggest that these young people also struggled with overwork, stress, anxiety, and aloneness; and, like their civilian counterparts, some of the girls struggled with low self-esteem. The struggles continued—and still continue—for the adolescents whose parents returned with physical injuries or PTSD to a community that has in many ways moved on from the Afghanistan mission and believes that the crisis has passed. The fallout from future volatile deployments will add to, rather than subtract from, the difficulties that these Armyville families are experiencing.

The current generation of CAF adolescents will soon become some of the adults whose lives will determine the vitality of Canadian society during the second half of the twenty-first century. They deserve more visibility—and more support—than they have achieved to this point. And they deserve the most competent resources that our Canadian society can provide.

Afterword: Some Reflections from David McTimoney

There are significant events in our world that are considered to be "unforgettable moments"— occasions when, upon reflection and with simplicity, you can remember exactly "where you were" at the time. For my parents' generation, the event was likely the tragic assassination of President Kennedy in 1963. For the longest time for my generation, it was the explosion of the space shuttle *Challenger* in January 1986. We can remember where we were, who we were with, what we were doing... all the details of that moment when we learned about the world-changing event. For many of us now, that vivid memory is in place for the morning of Tuesday, September 11, 2001.

Nine Eleven changed our lives forever. The sights of New York City, the Pentagon, and a field near Shanksville, Pennsylvania, were evidence of a new type of war that was playing out in the safety of North America. The response of Canadians to the tragic event was as expected—one of kindness, caring, and giving of oneself.

I had two connections to the Canadian response. I remain proud of my uncle who, at the time, was the principal of a school in Halifax, Nova Scotia, and played host to the passengers of a grounded flight for a week. He rarely left the school (if at all) and maintains friendly connections from that week to this day. Likewise, a childhood friend who is an air traffic controller in Gander, Newfoundland, gave of his time and energy to serve stranded travellers.

The response of Canada, as a nation, to a new war on terrorism, was also one that could be expected. It was a response that was firm, confident, and unwavering. Together with coalition forces, Canada would send a message that could be heard loud and clear: terrorism will not be tolerated. Sadly, but also expected, this message came with a cost. This cost was evident in my hometown.

I can't think of a better place to grow up than in the small, military town of Oromocto, New Brunswick. While the military is what brought my family to Oromocto and CFB Gagetown, my father left the armed forces in 1975 to further his education and embark on a new career. I was three years old at the time, so I don't really have a memory of being in a military family. In the midst of his successful career as a psychologist and consultant, my father spent a period of time working at CFB Gagetown as a civilian, in service to soldiers who needed mental health support, including those who battled with post-traumatic stress disorder (PTSD).

Both of my grandfathers served in World War II. One was a sailor on HMCS *Prince David*. My father was subsequently named after the ship, and I was named after my father. My other grandfather was in the army. I cherish the framed picture I have of him on a Harley-Davidson motorcycle during a quiet moment overseas. Both grandfathers returned from the war and went on to lead quality lives in different careers. I was fortunate to be able to know both my grandfathers during my boyhood.

As a civilian kid with three sisters growing up in Oromocto, we had a mix of friends from military and civilian families alike. During that time, there were no real noticeable differences from a "kid perspective." I had a few close friends who had to move due to a posting. We would keep in touch for a while (in that pre-social-media era), and then time would pass and we would lose track of one another. Sometimes they would move back. In other cases, there were no further postings for military dads, such as that of my childhood best friend, who stayed in Oromocto for the duration after his arrival in the fifth grade. To this day we remain close friends as he pursues a career in service as a sergeant with the Fredericton police force.

There were also times when a father went away to train, be it "out in the field" or even leaving New Brunswick or Canada for a short period of time. While I don't recall missions from my early years, I do remember soldiers from my town going to peacekeeping missions in places such as Bosnia, Cyprus, Eritrea, and Rwanda. Until 2001, I didn't recognize the dangers associated with the service of our soldiers.

The mix of civilian and military kids happened naturally, and we had a great time growing up in Oromocto. Living in a military town had its perks, and I was lucky to call it my home.

Some of my friends went on to join the Canadian Armed Forces in a variety of trades and professions. Many continue to serve today, including my youngest sister.

After a summer trip in Europe (which provided me with a different perspective on history and war), I returned home and began my career as a teacher in the fall of 1995. For the first four years, I taught high-school math and science at a small, rural K–12 school in the village of Cambridge-

Narrows. Located approximately 35 minutes outside of Oromocto, the village contained very few students who belonged to military families. In 1999, I moved to Oromocto High School (OHS) as a teacher and stayed for the next two years. Naturally, I taught many kids who were part of military families. Some had been in Oromocto for a while. Others moved in and out. We did our best to align the curriculum for newcomers and ensure they got the courses they needed to graduate. As a young teacher, I realized that every student was an individual and that I needed to be mindful of the differences they might be experiencing in their lives outside of school, regardless of whether they were in a military family or not.

In August 2001, I moved across the street to Ridgeview Middle School, where I had earned my first assignment as a permanent vice-principal. Again, I was working with a variety of different kids, mostly from military families. One morning, shortly after 10:30 a.m. (Atlantic time), I went outside to do a walkabout. There, I bumped into a couple of fellows who worked with the town recreation department; they were repairing a basketball net.

"Did you hear?" Steve called out.

"No," I said, "what is going on?"

It was September 11.

From 2002 to 2008, I worked at Oromocto High School as a vice-principal and principal (four years and two years, respectively). During those six years, I continued to grow as an educator and school leader. I knew we had to be mindful of kids who had parents—no longer just dads, but moms and/or dads—who had critical roles in active duty in a real war that was rolling out a world away. We heard the news daily, and we all knew friends, neighbours, parents, and former students who were serving their country in a very dangerous setting. Our kids were impacted. Our staff was impacted. Our town was impacted. How could we, as teachers and educational leaders, make a difference?

Oromocto High School (student enrollment: 1,200) was the largest school in the medium-sized Anglophone School District 17. The district office was located in a wing of OHS, and there was always a close connection. Marilyn Ball, the superintendent of schools at that time, and her team recognized a need to put something in place that would help respond to the stresses placed on military families and their children enrolled in our schools. Marilyn was fortunate to have an outstanding Coordinator of Student Services, Ed Griffin, who also knew that it was critical to have in place both a crisis-response plan and a comprehensive response to the deployment. With that, Ed and his team conducted research and put together a framework that helped guide our schools during this time of active war. The "deployment binder" helped serve all teachers, school-based Student Services team members, and educational leaders as we continued to try to serve the children of our schools and district. There was training. There was personal follow-up. There were highs, and there were lows. Ed's work was groundbreaking, and now, in his retirement, he should be proud of these contributions. A very competent group of Student Services staff continue to have oversight of this framework, under the direction of Catherine Blaney.

During this time, Marilyn made the connection with Dr. Deborah Harrison and facilitated her work as Deborah and her team pursued their research on the impact of military deployments on adolescents. I was fortunate enough to get involved in the work as well, through my roles as principal, as a district coordinator, and as superintendent of School District 17, a position that I assumed in August 2010 upon Marilyn's retirement.

As the team's research continued, the response to deployment by our school and district officials continued. There were four elementary schools, two middle schools, and one large high school in the town of Oromocto. There were five other schools on the outskirts of town that would also host a number of students of military families. There was also a K–8 school in Oromocto that fell under the umbrella of the Francophone School District 1.

As principal at OHS, I vividly remember the Easter weekend of 2007, when four Canadian soldiers were killed as their reconnaissance vehicle struck a roadside bomb 38 kilometres west of Kandahar City. I remember wondering, early on, how intense will our response need to be? Will this loss include the parent of one or more of our students?

As it turned out, a former OHS student lost his life in this blast. Trooper Patrick James Pentland, 23, was a member of the Royal Canadian Dragoons, and he died on April 11, 2007. I had taught Pat. I remember him well, and I liked him. He was a quiet, reserved student. He was not demanding. I, along with the community, mourned his loss. All were proud of his service.

Another local loss that stands out was that of Cpl. Chad O'Quinn, 25, who died in service on March 3, 2009, in Afghanistan. A roadside bomb detonated near an armoured vehicle during a patrol in the Arghandab District, northwest of Kandahar City. Chad was with the 2 Canadian Mechanized Brigade Group Headquarters and Signals Squadron, based at CFB Petawawa in Ontario. I had also taught Chad at OHS. I can recall his contributions to our class. I know he is missed by many. His parents and brother continue to remember him with pride, and Mr. and Mrs. O'Quinn are recognizable community members who show a continued dedication to acknowledging soldiers—both those currently serving and those who have died in the line of duty.

As mentioned above, I had the opportunity to work with Dr. Harrison and the research team in a variety of different capacities, and I see the value of this important research. Deborah is a dedicated, experienced, and intelligent academic who cares deeply about the work she does. She saw value in this study from the outset and took responsibility for providing leadership to her team and to the educators in our school system. Her team was also very committed to the project.

As the current superintendent of Anglophone West School District, I recognize the responsibility of caring for students who are impacted by military life and deployment. My response is shaped by my life experiences, both as a youngster growing up in a military community and as an educator and school leader in a system that serves students who are part of military families. Being a part of this research experience and reading the finished product has added a new dimension. Soaking in the comments and thoughts of real students who have lived through real experiences is a humble reminder of how important it is to support our kids who are impacted by their parents' commitment to our nation as soldiers in the Canadian Armed Forces. Many of the students' comments had an impact on me. Some of their statements I had expected. Some of their statements made me proud, as I knew we had some good things in place. Other statements caused me to reflect on how we could do things differently to better meet their needs. Reading this book reminds me of the critical responsibility that I currently hold.

The recommendations and new connections with experts in the field have helped, and they will be a source of guidance as we continue to move forward. There are some great supports in place. I think in particular of the PTSD peer support group at OHS that has helped affected students who are in search of others who might be experiencing the same relations and circumstances at home. The deployment binder is a professional document that serves as a tremendous source of guidance in times of need. As mentioned above, our Student Services team has shown a tremendous ability to respond in times of crisis.

Canada is no longer involved in an active war on terrorism in Afghanistan. That is not to say Canada will not need to respond actively again— and, in fact, we see that, with a Canadian presence in the air as allied nations respond to ISIS insurgencies. When the Canadian military steps up to defend our peaceful way of life, soldiers make an immeasurable commitment that can be extreme in costs. The impact of this commitment can be felt by many, but most importantly by families and children.

That is when we, as educators, need to step up. We need to be sure that we are there to support the academic, emotional, and social needs of our students who are impacted in any way by family life in the military. It is a responsibility of all of us in the education system, and one that we cannot take lightly.

David McTimoney
Superintendent of Schools
Anglophone West School District
Fredericton, New Brunswick

Appendix 1: Interview Schedule

Introduction
Thank you for being here. We appreciate your help with our project.

Demographic Data
- So, tell me a bit about you. You're [age]? Grade _____?
- Do you live in PMQs [Permanent Married Quarters]? Have you lived in PMQs a lot?
- How long have you lived in this area? How long have you been at this school?
- [If graduated from AHS, ask what student is doing now, how does s/he like it, etc.]
- Could you tell me a bit about what your dad (or mom) does (or did) in the military?
- What is/was [if retired] his/her rank?

Filter Questions
- You said you'd been living around here for _____ years. Where have you lived before this?

[Proceed to *Geographical Transfers – Questions for Movers*]
Or, if no significant geographical transfers:
[Proceed to *Geographical Transfers – Questions for Everyone*]

Geographical Transfers
Questions for Movers
Think of a move that you remember a lot about.
- How old were you? Where did you move from? Where to?
- Were you living in PMQs at either place?
- Start at the beginning: How did you feel when your parents told you about this move?

- Tell me what you most remember about it.
  [Probe for school, friends, extended family issues, etc., if participant gets stuck]
- [If it represented a change from being in PMQs to being in civilian housing, or the reverse, ask how this made it different]
- Did the new school do anything to help you adjust to this move? Or not? What?
- Did the base do anything to help you adjust to this move? Or not? What?
- What was the hardest part of the move, and why?
- [Possible follow up: Were things ever really tough during this move? How? How did you get through it?]
- How did this move affect your CAF parent(s)?
- How did it affect your non-CAF parent (if applicable)? [Probe for work outside home, friendships, extended family, isolatedness]
- How did the move affect the relationship between your parents?
- How did it affect any of your own relationships? (e.g., with your mother, father, siblings, friends, teachers)
- What was the best part of the move, and why, if anything? [Probe for accomplishments and new experiences—this is where you may get something on resilience]
- Have you benefited from moving around? (If yes) How?
- How have moves affected your friendships? school life? extended family life? your relations with each of your parents? with your siblings?
- Have moves affected who your friends have been? Thinking in terms of "CAF" versus "non-CAF," how would you characterize most of your closest friends? Why do you think this is so?
  [Ask about living in PMQs and/or being in civilian housing]
- How do you think your life might have been different if you had not moved so much (if applicable)?

Questions for Everyone
- What has it been like for you living in a community where families are often leaving and arriving?

Deployments Questions
- Has your dad (or mom) gone on a lot of deployments? How does this relate to what his (her) job is in the CAF?

If no significant deployments:
[Proceed to **School Questions** and those that follow]

Questions for Deployers
- Which deployments really stand out for you?
- Think of a deployment you remember a lot about. Where was it to, and how old were you at the time?

Questions for Everyone
- Start at the beginning: How did you find out?
- How did you react?
- Tell me what you most remember about the preparation.
  [Probe for school, friends, extended family issues, if participant gets stuck]
- What was the hardest part of this deployment for you?
- Did the school do anything to help you adjust to this deployment? Or not? What?
- Did the base do anything to help you adjust to this deployment? Or not? What?
- Did other institutions—for example, a church?
- How did the deployment affect your parent who went away? your other parent?
- How did the deployment affect your parents' relationship?
- How did the deployment affect dynamics in the family?
- How did your life change during the deployment (extra responsibilities? less or more freedom?)?
- Were there any readjustment problems after your parent came back?
  [Pay special attention to injuries, including operational stress injuries (PTSD)]
- What was the best part of this deployment for you, if any?
  [Probe for accomplishments, school accomplishments, improved family relationships, relations with teachers, friends, siblings, etc.—this is where you may get something on resilience]

PTSD Questions
[if CAF parent has suffered from this during a particular deployment]
- How did you first notice this?
- Did it take a long time for your dad/mom to ask for help?

[If yes] Why do you think it might have been hard for him/her to do so?
- Was there a tipping point that finally caused him/her to reach out?
- What kind of help/support did s/he get from the CAF?
- How has your dad's/mom's PTSD affected you?
- How has it affected your other parent? your siblings?

- Has the CAF provided any support to your other parent? To you and your siblings? [If so, what?]
- What kind of support has AHS been providing? Has it been good enough?
- How has the experience of your dad/mom having PTSD changed you as a person? (if it has)

Deployments Summary Questions
[only for participants whose parent (or parents) has (have) had at least one significant deployment]
- Have you benefited from the fact that your dad (or mom) went away/goes away a lot? (If yes) How?
- How have your parent(s)' deployments affected your friendships? school life? relations with each of your parents? with your siblings?
- Have deployments affected who your friends have been (CAF vs. non-CAF)?
  [If yes] Why do you think this is so?
- How do you think your life might have been different if your parent(s) had not been deployed away?
- How do you think your dad's (or mom's) deployment(s) has/have affected who you are today?

School Questions
- How have you enjoyed life at AHS? [Ask for elaboration on good and bad features; probe for school subjects, relations with teachers, extracurricular activities]
- What makes (or made) AHS similar/different from your other school experiences? [Ask this only if participant has attended other high schools]
- Describe a typical civilian kid at AHS, and describe a typical kid from a CAF family at AHS (if you think there is a difference).
- Why are they so different from each other? (if they are)
- Have your own friends mainly been CAF or civilian? Why? [if this hasn't been answered in earlier sections]
- Having experienced what you've experienced, if you were a teacher at AHS what might you do for students from CAF families? (i.e., even if you have never moved, had a parent deployed, or had a parent with PTSD, has the school done everything it could have to support your friends who have been in these situations?)
- What is AHS already doing well for students from CAF families?

Military Family Resource Centre Questions

- What does the MFRC do to help kids from CAF families who are new here? Is there anything else it could be doing?
- How does it try to support families of members who are deployed? What else could it do?
- How have you and your family benefited from the MFRC?

Family Dynamics/Crises Questions

- How do you think being affiliated with the CAF has affected each of your parents' lives? Would either or both of them have been very different people without this affiliation?
- Have they both always benefited from being part of the CAF?
- Have there been any tough times for either of them? [If so, ask for chronological description]
- How did this tough time affect your dad (or mom—presumably, the CAF member)? You? Your siblings?

[N.B. If a parent was medically released from the CAF as a result of an accident or illness, explore the event and its impact on the parent, on family dynamics, on the participant, etc.]

- How has being part of the CAF affected your parents' relationship?
- How has all this affected you?
- How has your life been affected by your dad's (or mom's) particular job in the CAF? [This question will be more appropriate for some participants than for others.]

Gender Questions

- How would you rate your self-esteem?
- According to the survey you filled out in October 2008, girls at AHS have lower self-esteem than boys. Do you have any ideas why this might be so? [If the participant doesn't feel comfortable with this topic, move on.]

General Questions

- Do you feel connected with this community or with the Canadian Armed Forces? Or both? Why?
- Would you consider either becoming a CAF member or marrying one?
- Do a large proportion of AHS students seem to be joining the CAF after graduation?

[If yes] Are these mainly students from CAF families, or from civilian families as well?

- The media very much distort the information about military life received by ordinary Canadians. If there was one message *you* would want to send out about growing up in the CAF, what would it be?
- Is there anything else you wish to tell us about your experiences that we did not get to in the interview?

Wrap-up

Thank you very much for your time. Your answers will help us a great deal.

Appendix 2: Recommendations Made at the 2011 Project Symposium

1. The Armyville School District (ASD) should create a joint committee of representatives from the school district, the Military Family Resource Centre (MFRC), CFB Armyville, teachers, parents, and students. Purpose: to oversee and enhance the well-being of students from CAF families.
2. The MFRC should expand its "homework help" program to include high-school students.
3. CFB Armyville should add a "notify school" check box to the MFRC pre-deployment checklist that is distributed to CAF parents.
4. The ASD should appoint an employee from each willing school to liaise/share information with the MFRC.
5. The ASD should organize a booth at every CFB Armyville Departure Assistance Group (DAG) function, to solicit voluntary information sharing with schools and teachers about the deployment as part of each military member's pre-deployment checklist.
6. The ASD should request voluntary information about upcoming deployments from students and parents on annual intake registration forms.
7. The ASD should add more multimedia links to its websites—for example, links to the MFRC, pamphlets, videos, Sesame Street website, books, and US websites for military kids and parents.
8. The ASD should update its current deployment binder to include information on the post-deployment phase and PTSD, information on our team's research project, and deployment-related information from the MFRC.
9. The ASD should make deployments and other military adolescents' issues part of professional development (PD) days on a regular basis (e.g., with keynote speakers).
10. ASD teachers should send a personal note to parents known to be affected by a deployment, acknowledging their knowledge of the situation and offering support.

11. The ASD should explore the possibility of school-to-school collaborative support of multiple-child families during deployments.

12. The ASD should provide resources to Grade 10 Personal Development teachers on the topics of (a) Military Deployments; (b) PTSD Information; and (c) Stress, Juggling Responsibilities, and Mental Health (including women and domestic-labour issues), to help them incorporate these topics into their curricula, should they wish to do so.

13. The ASD should include the topic of deployments in transition meetings between schools (at which individual students are discussed by representatives from both schools).

14. The AHS Guidance Department should start a monthly pre-deployment and deployment peer support group for interested eligible students during the school day.

15. ASD principals should include education/information about all aspects of PTSD, including social stigma and support resources, in grade-specific assemblies.

16. ASD Guidance Departments should enhance "buddy programs" for new students by including face-to-face meetings between new students and their buddies.

17. The ASD should continue its monthly PTSD peer support groups during the school day for high-school students. Middle schools should initiate a monthly PTSD peer support group during the school day for middle-school students.

18. The new joint committee (Recommendation 1) should create a resource for parents on how to tell children about deployments (using, e.g., findings from this research project).

Notes

Introduction

1 The text of this survey was originally envisioned as the first appendix to this book; however, space considerations intervened. To find the text of the survey, please go to http://www2.unb.ca/youthwellbeing/documents/Quantitative Survey.pdf.

2 In 2016, the SCSN transferred the main body of its work to a larger UK charity that services vulnerable children.

Chapter 1

1 Government of Canada, 2008.

2 In 1993, after 30 years of peacekeeping, then Prime Minister Brian Mulroney withdrew Canadian troops from Cyprus. The UN mission continues.

3 Bill C-90, *An Act to Amend the National Defence Act*, was enacted on 1 August 1964; it integrated the headquarters structure under one CDS, in an effort to eliminate duplication, streamline the command structure, and create significant cost savings.

4 These 11 were reduced to six: Mobile Command (encompassing the army and tactical air support), Maritime Command (which included naval air resources), Air Defence Command, Air Transport Command, Training Command, and Material Command (Gosselin, 2009).

5 White Papers on Defence were produced in 1964, 1971, 1987, and 1994. More reorganization took place in the mid-1970s. Separate service uniforms were reintroduced in 1986, and the service chiefs were reinstated and returned to National Defence.

6 Kasurak's (2013) book outlines the tug-of-war between the Canadian Army and the state from the end of World War II until the end of the twentieth century. He argues that, during that period, although there was an army in Canada, there was no Canadian Army. In great detail, he presents the story of a troubled relationship in which the army appeared to be out of touch with domestic politics and unable to understand the limits of military spending (Kasurak, 2013, p. 292). On the flip side, civilians, and especially politicians, were neglectful of the Canadian Armed Forces and lacked an appreciation of what they were capable of doing (Kasurak, 2013, p. 292).

7 Canada's International Policy Statement (IPS) marked the beginning of a new, proactive government engagement in international security and foreign relations. Recognizing that Canada could not sustain its standard of living through isolation, international co-operation was viewed as the first line of defence for collective security. The IPS noted that only through global engagement could Canada expect to remain safe and prosperous. Four pillars of the IPS were diplomacy, defence, development, and commerce (Godefroy, 2010).

8 This Ottawa-based organization (which has charitable status) was created in 1987 to promote public debate on national security and defence issues, on behalf of the defence community. It participates in various research activities, events, and publications that are disseminated to various audiences including the general public, the media, policymakers, the military, the diplomatic corps, the business community, and academia.

9 In his memoir, Chrétien stated, "We were going to get our soldiers in a more secure place where their assignment was closer to traditional peacekeeping" (Chrétien 2007, p. 305).

10 For example, on January 10, 2014, CBC News reported that the Canadian military was dealing with the third case of suspected suicide in a single week. (Canadian Press, 2014). Only one month earlier, a similar headline reported that there had been four suicides in a matter of days (Canadian Press, 2013).

11 For example, Brown and Hollis (2013) note that despite occupational therapists having strong historical ties to the Canadian military, there are currently no uniformed occupational therapists and only a few permanent occupational therapists employed by the Canadian Armed Forces. Occupational therapy is provided, in the main, through civilian occupational therapists.

12 The Highway of Heroes began in the spring of 2002 as a "reportedly spontaneous gathering of around 30 people on a bridge in Port Hope, Ontario, to honour the first four fallen soldiers from the mission in Afghanistan" (Fletcher and Hove, 2012, p. 34).

13 In an article published in the *Canadian Army Journal*, Colonel Fred Lewis put it bluntly: "The almost daily media tally of US casualties in Iraq, or indeed, news of Canadian casualties in Afghanistan, provide the likely answer to our own operational centre of gravity. If too many body bags come home when the vital interests of a nation are not at stake, almost assuredly, the military as a whole will come home too.... Thus, the operational level commanders must understand that if the forces are not to return home prematurely, casualties must be minimized" (Chivers, 2009, p. 325).

14 Improvements in battlefield medicine and body armour mean that soldiers are more likely to survive attacks and injuries that might previously have killed them. *The Journal of the American Academy of Orthopedic Surgeons* reports that the rates of both single and double amputations have doubled for the recent actions in Iraq and Afghanistan, compared to earlier conflicts such as the Korean War, as a result of new body armour that protects vital organs (Chivers, 2009).

Chapter 2

1 *Family* is defined by the Vanier Institute of the Family as "any combination of two or more persons who are bound together over time by ties of mutual consent, birth and/or adoption or placement and who, together, assume responsibilities for variant combinations of some of the following: physical maintenance and care of group members; addition of new members through procreation or adoption; socialization of children; social control of members; production, consumption, distribution of goods and services; affective nurturance—love" (Vanier Institute of the Family, 2015, para. 2).

2 The researchers used multiple logistic regression of US national health data and controlled for a range of demographic variables.

3 To postpone a move, one option for families is to request an Imposed Restriction (IR) posting, where the family will stay behind as a short-term solution as the member moves to the next posting by himself/herself. Reasons for Imposed Restriction postings include relocations outside of the usual posting season, undue disruption to children's education, particular financial hardship associated with the posting, or medical requirements precluding the family from relocating. These are subject to approval—usually to do with the best interests of the CAF, posting history, duration of the posting, financial impact on the member, educational opportunities at the current and new places of duty, specialized or exceptional health requirements, and spousal employment opportunities at the current and new locations.

4 Daigle (2013) noted that common complaints included water leaks, mould, freezing of pipes, limited storage space, ungrounded electrical outlets, the presence of asbestos, dated kitchens, uneven flooring, bedrooms too small to be practical, narrow driveways, and unusable basements due to water infiltration.

5 Daigle's (2013) report revealed recent increases in the number of families requesting emergency loans, grocery vouchers, and hampers of household goods from military commanders and service providers.

6 The researchers controlled for such socio-demographic characteristics as age, education, employment status, first official language, and number of children in the home.

7 Gouliquer and Poulin (2005), Poulin and Gouliquer (2012) and Poulin, Gouliquer, and Moore (2009) provide interesting insight into lesbian experiences in the Canadian military, including the challenges that accompany a partner's posting if the women have not come out to their families.

8 Gilreath and colleagues analyzed a subsample of the 2011 California Healthy Kids Survey (N = 14,512), focusing on the survey items assessing victimization, which included physical acts (e.g., victims being pushed or shoved), nonphysical acts (e.g., victims having rumours spread about them), and weapon carrying.

9 The researchers' hypothesis—that a favourable school climate would be associated with adolescents' higher scores on mental health and well-being measures—was generally supported.

Chapter 3

This chapter was co-authored by Karen Robson and Chris Sanders.

1 These data are not available in the 2011 Census Community Profiles.

2 The text of this survey can be found at http://www2.unb.ca/youthwellbeing/ documents/QuantitativeSurvey.pdf.

3 In Cycle 8, collected in 2008–2009, there were 35,795 children and youths aged 0–25 years (Statistics Canada, 2014b).

4 According to Statistics Canada documents about the NLSCY (for example, http://data.library.utoronto.ca/microdata/national-longitudinal-survey -children-and-youth-cycle-5-2002-2003-synthetic-files), the target population ("the universe") for the NLSCY comprised the non-institutionalized civilian population aged 0–19 (aged 0–11 at the time of their selection) from across Canada's 10 provinces. The documents stated that the NLSCY "exclude[d] children living on Indian reserves or Crown lands, residents of institutions, full-time members of the Canadian Armed Forces, and residents of some remote regions." Information on how the sample for the NLSCY was selected provides further background. The Microdata User Guide for the NLSCY (http://www23.statcan.gc.ca/imdb/p2SV.pl?Function=getSurvey&SurvId= 1342&InstaId=3513#a1) explains that the NLSCY sample was selected from the Labour Force Survey (LFS) of Canadian households. The LFS is conducted on a monthly basis and collects basic demographic information about all household members of a representative sample of Canadian households (as well as labour market information about the adults living in these house-holds). Approximately 97 percent of the population 15 years of age and over is covered in the LFS; however, the LFS excludes populations in the three territo-ries, residents of Indian reserves, full-time members of the Canadian Armed Forces, and residents of institutions, such as chronic-care hospitals, prisons, and child residential treatment facilities.

5 The survey had been constructed mainly by Karen Robson. During the spring of 2008, we had pretested it on a variety of adolescents, based in two different provinces.

6 Five percent (52 respondents) were categorized as neither CAF nor civilian adolescents. Some of our survey findings have been discussed elsewhere (Har-rison, Robson, Albanese, Sanders, & Newburn-Cook, 2011; Robson, Albanese, Harrison, & Sanders, 2013).

7 The latter were located at the Statistics Canada Research Data Centre at York University, Toronto.

8 The three psychological indicators Karen and Chris focused on were depres-sion, self-esteem, and suicide ideation. The depression scale included 12 feel-ings or behaviours whose recent (past seven days) frequency the respondent was asked to identify, on a four-point scale ranging from "rarely or none of the time" to "most or all of the time." These included "I did not feel like eat-ing; my appetite was poor," "I felt I could not shake off the blues . . .," and "I had trouble keeping my mind on what I was doing." Since these items were administered only to 16- and 17-year-olds in the NLSCY, Karen and Chris

restricted their comparative analysis to 16- and 17-year-old Armyville adolescents. The self-esteem scale contained five items, including "In general, I like the way I am," "Overall I have a lot to be proud of," and "I like the way I look." The response categories were "false," "mostly false," "sometimes true/sometimes false," "mostly true," and "true." The suicide ideation scale contained one question: "During the past 12 months, did you seriously consider attempting suicide?" All respondents who answered "Yes" were given a score of 1.

9 In table 3.1, a higher number reflects a better score on the variable that is being measured. For example, in the School Attachment column—the second column from the left—the number 3.175 next to the box "None," as compared with the number 3.123 next to the box "More than once," means that AHS students who had never moved scored higher on school attachment than students who had moved more than once. In the bottom row of the table, the number of asterisks beside each "F" score tells us the extent to which the differences were "real differences" and the extent to which the outcomes were significantly different from one another, with a greater number of asterisks signifying a larger/more "real" difference between the outcomes.

10 In table 3.2, the number of asterisks beside each "T" score gives us an indication of the significance of the difference between the outcomes.

11 We employed the longitudinal weight provided in the data set for the NLSCY cohort to account for sampling and attrition, although it should be noted that unweighted results were quite similar.

12 The measures used in the CHKS were similar to those used in the NLSCY. The depressive scale included such items as "everything is an effort." The suicide ideation scale included the one item: "During the past 12 months, did you ever seriously consider attempting suicide?"

13 See De Pedro et al. (2015) for another analysis of CHKS data, which produced findings that were very similar.

14 A quota sample is a non-probability sample of self-selected individuals.

15 All participants' names, as reported in this book, are pseudonyms.

Chapter 4

1 The website of the Military Family Resource Centre at CFB Armyville contains a document titled *Preparing for Deployment Stress*. A section of this document, titled "Pre-Deployment Checklist," contains the subsections "Legal Issues" (e.g., wills, powers of attorney), "Financial Issues" (e.g., budgets, bank accounts, investments, income tax), "Health Issues" (e.g., insurance, medical records, phone numbers, emergency plan), "Homes Issues" (e.g., mortgage/rent, utilities, security, maintenance), "Car Issues," "Travel Issues," and "Information/Support" (e.g., Military Family Resource Centre, military chaplain, military social worker).

2 The principle of *universality of service* requires CAF members to be able to perform general defence and security duties, as well as the duties specific to their occupations. They consequently must be both physically fit and deployable (Daigle, 2012, p. 93).

Chapter 5

1 Research has also been carried out on adolescents' physical health. When they compared a group of adolescents with a parent deployed to Iraq with a group of their civilian peers, Barnes, Davis, and Treiber (2007) found that the former group reported significantly higher levels of post-traumatic stress and had significantly higher measured heart rates. Waasdorp, Caboot, Robinson, Abraham, and Adelman (2007), who compared a sample of adolescent children of recently deployed members with general population statistics, found a significantly higher rate of eating disorder behaviours among members of the former sample. Similarly, recently deployed mothers of adolescents reported to Ternus (2008) that their children engaged in a large array of risky health behaviours during the deployment, as compared with prior to the deployment, especially if the deployment was long and/or little support was being provided by the extended family.

2 We have so far found no research on how solo civilian fathers cope emotionally during the long deployments of their partners.

3 Personal communication from ASD superintendent.

Chapter 6

1 Anger as a PTSD symptom has been the object of numerous research investigations (e.g., Chemtob, Hamada, Roitblat, & Muraoka, 1994; Chemtob, Novaco, Hamada, Gross, & Smith, 1997; Frederikson, Chamberlain, & Long, 1996; Ray & Vanstone, 2009; Rosenheck, 1986; Shaler, Hathaway, Sells, & Youngstedt, 2013).

2 Brian O'Toole and colleagues (2010) have instead used the term *recurrent moderate depression*.

3 A significant body of research has also associated PTSD severity with afflicted members' dissatisfaction with their couple relationships (Carroll et al., 1985; Caselli & Motta, 1995; Gewirtz et al., 2010; Solomon, Mikulincer, Freid, & Wosner, 1987), with spouses' and partners' dissatisfaction with their couple relationships (e.g., Frederikson et al., 1996; MacDonald, Chamberlain, Long, & Flett, 1999; Verbosky & Ryan, 1988; Westerink & Giarratano, 1999), and with relationship dissatisfaction experienced by both partners (Allen, Rhoades, Stanley, & Markman, 2010; Ford et al., 1993; Gerlock et al., 2014; Hendrix et al., 1998; Jordan et al., 1992; Nelson Goff, Crow, Reisbig, & Hamilton, 2007; Riggs et al., 1998).

4 See also Allen et al., 2010, 2011; Caselli & Motta, 1995; Frederikson et al., 1996; Glenn et al., 2002; Jordan et al., 1992; Melvin, Gros, Hayat, Jennings, & Campbell, 2012; Sayer et al., 2010; Sayers et al., 2009; Solomon et al., 1987; Taft et al., 2008; Taft, Watkins, Stafford, Street, & Monson, 2011; Westerink & Giarratano, 1999.

5 See also Begic & Jokic-Begic, 2001; Byrne & Riggs, 1996; Carroll et al., 1985; Dekel & Solomon, 2006; Frederikson et al., 1996; Gerlock, 2004; Harkness,

1993; Jordan et al., 1992; Orcutt, King, & King, 2003; Savarese et al., 2001; Sayers et al., 2009; Taft, Street, et al., 2007; Taft, Vogt, et al., 2007.

6 Personal communication with the AHS guidance counsellor who facilitates the group.

Chapter 7

1 Personal communication from Joy O'Neill, Founder and Chair, Service Children's Support Network, United Kingdom.

References

Abraham, M., & Purkayastha, B. (2012). Making a difference: Linking research and action in practice, pedagogy and policy for social justice: Introduction. *Current Sociology, 60*(2), 123–141.

Abram, Z. (2012). In the service of peace: The symbolic power of peacekeeping in Canada. *Dalhousie Review, 92*(1/2), 193–199.

Achenbach, T. M., & Edelbrock, C. (1983). *Manual for the child behavior checklist and revised child behavior profile.* Burlington: Department of Psychiatry, University of Vermont.

Agaibi, C. E., & Wilson, J. P. (2005). Trauma, PTSD, and resilience: Review of the literature. *Trauma, Violence & Abuse, 6*(3), 195–216.

Ahmadzadeh, G., & Malekian, A. (2004). Aggression, anxiety, and social development in adolescent children of war veterans with PTSD versus those of non-veterans. *Journal of Research in Medical Sciences, 9*(5), 231–234.

Akin, D. (2007, August 26). Harper skips Afghanistan in Que. byelection speech. CTV News. Retrieved from http://www.ctvnews.ca/harper-skips-afghanistan -in-que-byelection-speech-1.253974

Albo, G. (2007). Canada and world order after the wreckage. *Canadian Dimension, 41*(2), 42–45.

Ali, M., Amialchuk, A., & Heiland, F. (2011). Weight-related behavior among adolescents: The role of peer effect. *PLOS One, 6*(6), 1–9.

Allen, E. S., Rhoades, G. K., Stanley, S. M., & Markman, H. J. (2010). Hitting home: Relationships between recent deployment, posttraumatic stress symptoms, and marital functioning for army couples. *Journal of Family Psychology, 24*(3), 280–288.

Allen, E. S., Rhoades, G. K., Stanley, S. M., & Markman, H. J. (2011). On the home front: Stress for recently deployed army couples. *Family Process, 50*(2), 235–247.

Allen, S. (2008). Finding home: Challenges faced by geographically mobile families. *Family Relations, 57*(1), 84–99.

Ambert, A. (2011). *Changing families: Relationships in context.* Toronto: Pearson Allyn & Bacon.

Amen, D. G., Jellen, L., Merves, E., & Lee, R. E. (1988). Minimizing the impact of deployment separation on military children: Stages, current preventive efforts, and system recommendations. *Military Medicine, 153*(9), 441–446.

American Psychiatric Association. (2000). *Diagnostic and statistical manual of mental disorders.* (4th ed.). Washington, DC: Author.

American Psychiatric Association. (2013). *Diagnostic and statistical manual of mental disorders* (5th ed.). Washington, DC: Author.

American Psychological Association Presidential Task Force on Military Deployment Services for Youth, Families, and Service Members. (2007). *The psychological needs of U.S. military service members and their families: A preliminary report.* American Psychological Association.

Andres, M., & Moelker, R. (2011). There and back again: How parental experiences affect children's adjustments in the course of military deployments. *Armed Forces & Society, 37*(3), 418–447.

Aranda, M. C., Middleton, L. S., Flake, E., & Davis, B. E. (2011). Psychosocial screening in children with wartime-deployed parents. *Military Medicine, 176*(4), 402–407.

Aronson, K., & Perkins, D. (2013). Challenges faced by military families: Perceptions of United States Marine Corps school liaisons. *Journal of Child & Family Studies, 22*(4), 516–525.

Arrabito, G. R., & Leung, A. S. (2014). Combating the impact of stigma on physically injured and mentally ill Canadian Armed Forces (CAF) members. *Canadian Military Journal, 14*(2), 25–35.

Astor, R., De Pedro, K., Gilreath, T., Esqueda, M., & Benbenishty, R. (2013). The promotional role of school and community contexts for military students. *Clinical Child and Family Psychology Review, 16*(3), 233–244.

Avison, W. R. (1999). The impact of mental illness on the family. In B. Howard, C. S. Aneshensel, & J. C. Phelan (Eds.), *Handbook of the sociology of mental health* (pp. 495–515). Secaucus, NJ: Springer.

Bacchini, D., & Magliulo, F. (2003). Self-image and perceived self-efficacy during adolescence. *Journal of Youth and Adolescence, 32*(5), 337–350.

Baker, S. P., & Norris, D. (2011). The experiences of female partners of Canadian Forces veterans diagnosed with post-traumatic stress disorder. In A. B. Aiken & S. A. H. Belanger (Eds.), *Shaping the future: Military and veteran health research* (pp. 175–185). Kingston, ON: Canadian Defence Academy Press.

Barnes, V., Davis, H., & Treiber, F. A. (2007). Perceived stress, heart rate, and blood pressure among adolescents with family members deployed in Operation Iraqi Freedom. *Military Medicine, 172*(1), 40–43.

Barnett, B., & Parker, G. (1998). The parentified child: Early competence or childhood deprivation? *Child Psychology & Psychiatry Review, 3*(4), 146–155.

Basham, K. (2009). Weaving a tapestry of resilience and challenges, commentary: Clinical assessment of Canadian military couples. *Clinical Social Work Journal, 37*(4), 340–345.

Battistelli, F. (1997). Organizational change and soldier subjectivity: Peacekeeping and the postmodern soldier. *Armed Forces & Society, 23*(3), 467–484.

Beckham, J., Braxton, L., Kudler, H., Feldman, M., Lytle, B., & Palmer, S. (1997). Minnesota Multiphasic Personality Inventory profiles of Vietnam combat veterans with posttraumatic stress disorder and their children. *Journal of Clinical Psychology, 53*(8), 847–852.

Begic, D., & Jokic-Begic, N. (2001). Aggressive behavior in combat veterans with post-traumatic stress disorder. *Military Medicine, 166*(8), 671–676.

Bell Canada. (2015). Bell true patriot love fund. Retrieved from http://true patriotlove.com/about-us/tpl-national-programs/

Bell, S. (2013, June 18). Memo to Stephen Harper in 2007 downplayed a Canadian casualty rate in Afghanistan up to 10 times higher than allies. *National Post.*

Besemann, M. (2011). Physical rehabilitation following polytrauma: The Canadian Forces physical rehabilitation program 2008–2011. *Canadian Journal of Surgery, 54*(6), S135–S141.

Black, W. G., Jr. (1993). Military-induced family separation: A stress reduction intervention. *Social Work, 38*(3), 273–280.

Blais, R. K., Renshaw, K. D., & Jakupcak, M. (2014). Posttraumatic stress and stigma in active-duty service members relate to lower likelihood of seeking support. *Journal of Traumatic Stress, 27*(1), 116–119.

Bland, D., & Maloney, S. (2004). *Campaigns for international security—Canada's defence policy at the turn of the century.* Kingston, ON: McGill-Queen's University Press.

Boss, P. (1999). *Ambiguous loss: Learning to live with unresolved grief.* Cambridge, MA: Harvard University Press.

Boucher, J. (2010). Evaluating the "Trenton effect": Canadian public opinion and military casualties in Afghanistan (2006–2010). *American Review of Canadian Studies, 40*(2), 237–258.

Bouldin, M. (2003). Keeper of the peace: Canada and security transition operations. *Defense & Security Analysis, 19*(3), 265–276.

Boulos, D., & Zamorski, M. A. (2013). Deployment-related mental disorders among Canadian Forces personnel deployed in support of the mission in Afghanistan, 2001–2008. *Canadian Medical Association Journal, 185*(11), 545–552.

Bradshaw, C. P., Sudhinaraset, M., Mmari, K., & Blum, R. W. (2010). School transitions among military adolescents: A qualitative study of stress and coping. *School Psychology Review, 39*(1), 84–105.

Bremner, J. D., Southwick, S. M., Darnell, A., & Charney, D. S. (1996). Chronic PTSD in Vietnam combat veterans: Course of illness and substance abuse. *American Journal of Psychiatry, 153*(3), 369–375.

Brett, J. M. (1982). Job transfer and well-being. *Journal of Applied Psychology, 67*(4), 450–463.

Brewster, M. (2011, September 14). Defence department scraps plans to honour Afghanistan veterans. *Globe and Mail.*

Broszormenyi-Nagy, I., & Spark, G. (1973). *Invisible loyalties: Reciprocity in intergenerational family therapy.* Hagerstown, MD: Harper & Row.

Brown, H., & Hollis, V. (2013). The meaning of occupation, occupational need, and occupational therapy in military context. *Physical Therapy, 93*(9), 1244–1253.

Byers, S., & Harrison, D. (2004). Building collaborative action-oriented research teams. In M. L. Stirling et al. (Eds.), *Understanding abuse: Partnering for change* (pp. 21–52). Toronto: University of Toronto Press.

Byrne, C. A., & Riggs, D. S. (1996). The cycle of trauma: Relationship aggression in male Vietnam veterans with symptoms of posttraumatic stress disorder. *Violence & Victims, 11*(3), 213–225.

Cambron, M. J., & Acitelli, L. K. (2009). Explaining gender differences in depression: An interpersonal contingent self-esteem perspective. *Sex Roles, 61*, 751–761.

Canadian Forces Military Family Services. (2013). *Supporting military families: 2013 annual report.* Ottawa: Department of National Defence Canada.

Canadian Press. (2013, December 3). *Canadian soldier's apparent suicide would be 4th in days.* CBC News. Retrieved from http://www.cbc.ca/news/canada/montreal/canadian-soldier-s-apparent-suicide-would-be-4th-in-days-1.2450095

Canadian Press. (2014, January 10). *Canada's soldier's death 3rd suspected suicide in a week: Tom Mulcair urges Stephen Harper to make the issue of military suicides a personal priority.* CBC News. Retrieved from http://www.cbc.ca/news/politics/canadian-soldier-s-death-3rd-suspected-suicide-in-a-week-1.2492125

Card, N. A., Bosch, L., Casper, D. M., Wiggs, C. B., Hawkins, S. A., Schlomer, G. L., & Borden, L. M. (2011). A meta-analytic review of internalizing, externalizing, and academic adjustment among children of deployed military service members. *Journal of Family Psychology, 25*(4), 508–520.

Carroll, E. M., Rueger, D. B., Foy, D. W., & Donahoe, C. P., Jr. (1985). Vietnam combat veterans with posttraumatic stress disorder: Analysis of marital and cohabitating adjustment. *Journal of Abnormal Psychology, 94*(3), 329–337.

Caselli, L. T., & Motta, R. W. (1995). The effect of PTSD and combat level on Vietnam veterans' perceptions of child behavior and marital adjustment. *Journal of Clinical Psychology, 51*(1), 4–12.

Cassidy, M., Lawrence, E., Vierbuchen, C., & Konold, T. (2013). Family inventory of resources and stressors: Further examination of the psychometric properties. *Information, 49*(3), 191–211.

Cederbaum, J., Gilreath, T., Benbenishty, R., Astor, R., Pineda, D., De Pedro, K.,... Atuel, H. (2014). Well-being and suicidal ideation of secondary school students from military families. *Journal of Adolescent Health, 54*(6), 672–677.

Chandra, A., Lara-Cinisomo, S., Jaycox, L. H., Tanielian, T., Burns, R. M., Ruder, T., & Han, B. (2009). Children on the homefront: The experience of children from military families. *Journal of the American Academy of Pediatrics, 125*(1), 13–22.

Chandra, A., Lara-Cinisomo, S., Jaycox, L. H., Tanielian, T., Han, B., Burns, R. M., & Ruder, T. (2011). *Views from the homefront: The experiences of youth and spouses from military families.* Arlington, VA: RAND Corporation and National Military Family Association.

Chandra, A., Martin, L. T., Hawkins, S. A., & Richardson, A. (2010). The impact of parental deployment on child social and emotional functioning: Perspectives of school staff. *Journal of Adolescent Health, 146*(3), 218–223.

Chapin, M. (2011). Family resilience and the fortunes of war. *Social Work in Health Care, 50*(7), 527–542.

Chapman, J. M. (1981). *Military and civilian relations: A study of sub-community maintenance and development in Oromocto* (Unpublished master's thesis). University of New Brunswick, Fredericton.

Chappel, A., Suldo, S., & Ogg, J. (2014). Associations between adolescents' family stressors and life satisfaction. *Journal of Child and Family Studies, 23*(1), 76–84.

Chapple, S. (2009). Child well-being and sole-parent family structure in the OECD: An analysis. *OECD Social, Employment, and Migration Working Papers, 82.*

Charles, G., Stainton, T., & Marshall, S. (2008). Young carers in Canada: An invisible population. *Relational Child and Youth Care Practice, 21*(4), 5–12.

Charles, G., Stainton, T., & Marshall, S. (2012). Young carers in Canada: The hidden costs and benefits of young caregiving. Retrieved from http://vanier institute.ca/wp-content/uploads/2015/12/CFT_2012-07-00_EN.pdf

Charmaz, K. (2004). Grounded theory. In S. N. Hesse-Biber & P. Leavy (Eds.), *Approaches to qualitative research* (pp. 496–521). New York: Oxford University Press.

Chemtob, C. M., Hamada, R. S., Roitblat, H. L., & Muraoka, M. Y. (1994). Anger, impulsivity, and anger control in combat-related posttraumatic stress disorder. *Journal of Consulting and Clinical Psychology, 62*(4), 827–832.

Chemtob, C. M., Novaco, R. W., Hamada, R. S., Gross, D. M., & Smith, G. (1997). Anger regulation deficits in combat-related posttraumatic stress disorder. *Journal of Traumatic Stress, 10*(1), 17–36.

Chivers, S. (2009). Disabled veterans in the Americas: Canadians "soldier on" after Afghanistan—Operation Enduring Freedom and the Canadian mission. *Canadian Review of American Studies, 39*(3), 321–342.

Chrétien, J. (2007). *My Years as Prime Minister.* Toronto: Alfred A. Knopf.

Clair, D. J., & Genest, M. (1992). The children of alcoholics screening test: Reliability and relationship to family environment, adjustment, and alcohol-related stressors of adolescent offspring of alcoholics. *Journal of Clinical Psychology, 48*(3), 414–420.

Coleman, N. (2013). Unlimited liability. *Encyclopedia of military ethics.* Retrieved from http://www.militaryethics.org/Unlimited-Liability/15/

Coser, L. (1974). *Greedy institutions: Patterns of undivided commitment.* New York: Free Press.

Cozza, S. J., Guimond, J. M., McKibben, J. B., Chun, R. S., Arata-Maiers, T. L., Schneider, B.,... Ursano, R.J. (2010). Combat-injured service members and their families: The relationship of child distress and spouse-perceived family distress and disruption. *Journal of Traumatic Stress, 23*(1), 112–115.

Cozza, S. J., Holmes, A. K., & Ost, S. (2013). Family-centered care for military and veteran families affected by combat injury. *Clinical Child and Family Psychology Review, 16*(3), 311–321.

Cripps, K., & McGlade, H. (2008). Indigenous family violence and sexual abuse: Considering pathways forward. *Journal of Family Studies, 14*, 240–253.

Crockett, L. J., Petersen, A. C., Graber, J. A., Schulenberg, J. E., & Ebata, A. (1989). School transitions and adjustment during early adolescence. *Journal of Early Adolescence, 9*(3), 181–210.

Cronin, C. (1995). Adolescent reports of parental spousal violence in military and civilian families. *Journal of Interpersonal Violence, 10*(1), 117–122.

Crum-Cianflone, N., Fairbank, J., Marmar, C., & Schlenger, W. (2014). The millennium cohort family study: A prospective evaluation of the health and well-being of military service members and their families. *International Journal of Methods in Psychiatric Research, 23*(3), 320–330.

Daigle, P. (2012). *Fortitude under fatigue: Assessing the delivery of care for operational stress injuries that Canadian Forces members need and deserve.* Special report to the Minister of National Defence. Ottawa: National Defence and Canadian Forces Ombudsman.

Daigle, P. (2013). *On the home front: Assessing the well-being of Canada's military families in the new millennium.* Special report to the Minister of National Defence. Ottawa: National Defence and Canadian Forces Ombudsman.

D'Aliesio, R. (2015, November 2). At least 59 Canadian soldiers died by suicide after Afghanistan war. *Globe and Mail.*

Davidson, A. C., & Mellor, D. J. (2001). The adjustment of children of Australian Vietnam veterans: Is there evidence for the transgenerational transmission of the effects of war-related trauma? *Australian & New Zealand Journal of Psychiatry, 35*, 345–351.

Davis, J., & Finke, E. (2015). The experience of military families with children with autism spectrum disorders during relocation and separation. *Journal of Autism & Developmental Disorders, 45*(7), 2019–2034.

De Burgh, H. T., White, C. J., Fear, N., & Iversen, A. (2011). The impact of deployment to Iraq or Afghanistan on partners and wives of military personnel. *International Review of Psychiatry, 23*(2): 192–200.

Dekel, R. (2007). Posttraumatic distress and growth among wives of prisoners of war: The contribution of husbands' posttraumatic stress disorder and wives' own attachment. *American Journal of Orthopsychiatry, 77*(3), 419–426.

Dekel, R., & Monson, C. (2010). Military-related post-traumatic stress disorder and family relations: Current knowledge and future directions. *Aggression and Violent Behavior, 15*, 303–309.

Dekel, R., & Solomon, Z. (2006). Secondary traumatization among wives of Israeli POWs: The role of POWs' distress. *Social Psychiatry and Psychiatric Epidemiology, 41*(1), 27–33.

Dekel, R., Solomon, Z., & Bleich, A. (2005). Emotional distress and marital adjustment of caregivers: Contribution of level of impairment and appraised burden. *Anxiety, Stress, and Coping, 18*(1), 71–82.

Department of National Defence Canada. (1994). *Special joint commission of the Senate and the House of Commons on Canada's defence policy: Security in a changing world.* Ottawa: Canada Communications Group.

Department of National Defence Canada. (1995). *Canadian Forces administrative order 19-42. Family violence and abuse.* Ottawa: Department of National Defence.

Department of National Defence Canada. (2014). *Current operations*. Retrieved from http://www.forces.gc.ca/en/operations/current.page

Department of National Defence Canada Military Police Criminal Intelligence Program—Strategic Criminal Intelligence Section. (2009). *2008 statistical overview of military police investigations involving domestic violence*. Ottawa: Department of National Defence.

De Pedro, K. T., Astor, R. A., Gilreath, T. D., Benbenishty, R., & Berkowitz, R. (2015). School climate, deployment, and mental health among students in military-connected schools. *Youth & Society*, 1–23.

Deployment Health and Family Readiness Library. (2006). *New emotional cycles of deployment for service members and their families*. US Department of Defense.

Dimiceli, E., Steinhardt, M., & Smith, S. (2010). Stressful experiences, coping strategies, and predictors of health-related outcomes among wives of deployed military servicemen. *Armed Forces & Society, 36*(2), 351–373.

Ditmars, H. (2015, September 6). Canada tries to discourage refugees and the results are deadly. *The Guardian*. Retrieved from http://www.theguardian.com/commentisfree/2015/sep/06/canada-discourage-refugees-results-are-deadly

Dobson, J., Henthorne, K., & Lynas, Z. (2000). *Pupil mobility in schools: Final report*. London: Migration Research Unit, University College London.

Doherty, D., & Hornosty, J. (2004). Abuse in a rural and farm context. In M. L. Stirling et al. (Eds.), *Understanding abuse: Partnering for change* (pp. 55–82). Toronto: University of Toronto Press.

Douglas, S. (2003). *Readiness and rights: Developments in Canadian military family politics and policy*. Paper presented at the Fifth Annual Society for Military and Strategic Studies Conference, Calgary, AB.

Drummet, A. R., Coleman, M., & Cable, S. (2003). Military families under stress: Implications for family life education. *Family Relations, 53*(3), 279–287.

Dunn, J., Urban, S., & Wang, Z. (2011). Spousal employment income of Canadian Forces personnel: A comparison of civilian spouses. Retrieved from https://www.cfmws.com/en/AboutUs/MFS/FamilyResearch/Documents/DGPRAM/Employment/Spousal%20Employment%20Income%20of%20Canadian%20Forces%20Personnel%20A%20Com.pdf

Dursun, S., & Sudom, K. (2009). *Impacts of military life on families: Results from the perstempo survey of Canadian Forces spouses*. Ottawa: Defence R&D Canada, Director General Military Personnel Research & Analysis, Department of National Defence.

Earley, L., & Cushway, D. J. (2002). The parentified child. *Clinical Child Psychology & Psychiatry, 7*(2), 163–178.

Easterbrooks, M. A., Ginsberg, K., & Lerner, R. M. (2013). Resilience among military youth. *The future of children: A collaboration of the Woodrow Wilson School of Public and International Affairs at Princeton University and the Brookings Institution, 23*(2), 99–120.

Eaton, K., Hoge, C., Messer, S., Whitt, A., Cabrora, O., McGurk, D., . . . Castro, C. (2008). Prevalence of mental health problems, treatment need, and barriers to care among primary care-seeking spouses of military service members involved in Iraq and Afghanistan deployments. *Military Medicine, 173*(11), 1051–1056.

Eccles, J. S., Barber, B. L., Stone, M., & Hunt, J. (2003). Extracurricular activities and adolescent development. *Journal of Social Issues, 59*(4), 865–889.

Emmen, R., Malda, M., Mesman, J., van Uzendoorn, M., Prev, M., & Yeniad, N. (2013). Socioeconomic status and parenting in ethnic minority families: Testing a minority family stress model. *Journal of Family Psychology, 27*(6), 896–904.

Enloe, C. (1983). *Does khaki become you? The militarization of women's lives.* Boston: South End Press.

Esposito-Smythers, C., Wolff, J., Lemmon, K., Bodzy, M., Swenson, R., & Spirito, A. (2011). Military youth and the deployment cycle: Emotional health consequences and recommendations for intervention. *Journal of Family Psychology, 25*(4), 497–507.

Esqueda, M. C., Astor, R. A., & De Pedro, K. (2012). A call to duty: Educational policy and school reform addressing the needs of children from military families. *Educational Researcher, 41*(2), 65–70.

Evans, L., McHugh, T., Hopwood, M., & Watt, C. (2003). Chronic posttraumatic stress disorder and family functioning of Vietnam veterans and their partners. *Australian & New Zealand Journal of Psychiatry, 37*, 765–772.

Everson, R. B., Darling, C. A., & Herzog, J. R. (2013). Parenting stress among U.S. army spouses during combat-related deployments: The role of sense of coherence. *Child and Family Social Work, 18*, 168–178.

Farrell, A. F., Bowen, G., & Swick, D. (2014). Network supports and resiliency among U.S. military spouses with children with special health care needs. *Family Relations, 63*(1), 55–70.

Fear, N. T., Iversen, A., Meltzer, H., Workman, L., Hull, L., Greenberg, N.,… Wessely, S. (2007). Patterns of drinking in the UK Armed Forces. *Addiction, 102*(11), 1749–1759.

Figley, C. R. (1995). Compassion fatigue as secondary traumatic stress disorder: An overview. In C.R. Figley (Ed.), *Compassion fatigue: Coping with secondary traumatic stress disorder in those who treat the traumatized* (pp. 1–20). New York: Brunner-Routledge.

Fikretoglu, D., Brunet, A., Guay, S., & Pedlar, D. (2007). Mental health treatment seeking by military members with posttraumatic stress disorder: Findings on rates, characteristics, and predictors from a nationally representative Canadian military sample. *Canadian Journal of Psychiatry, 52*(2), 103–110.

Finkelhor, D., Hamby, S., Ormrod, R., & Turner, H. (2005). The juvenile victimization questionnaire: Reliability, validity, and national norms. *Child Abuse & Neglect, 29*, 383–412.

Fitzgerald, A., Fitzgerald, N., & Aherne, C. (2012). Do peers matter? A review of peer and/or friends' influence on physical activity among American adolescents. *Journal of Adolescence, 35*(4), 941–958.

Fitzsimons, V. M., & Krause-Parello, C. A. (2009). Military children: When parents are deployed overseas. *Journal of School Nursing, 25*(1), 40–47.

Fletcher, J. F., & Hove, J. (2012). Emotional determinants of support for the Canadian mission in Afghanistan: A view from the bridge. *Canadian Journal of Political Science, 45*(1), 33–62.

Ford, J. D., Shaw, D., Sennhauser, S., Greaves, D., Thacker, B., Chandler, P., … McClain, V. (1993). Psychosocial debriefing after Operation Desert Storm: Marital and family assessment and intervention. *Journal of Social Issues, 49*(4), 73–102.

Foreign Affairs, Trade and Development Canada. (2014a). *Canada's response to the conflict in Syria.* Ottawa: Government of Canada. Retrieved from http://www.international.gc.ca/development-developpement/humanitarian_response-situations_crises/syria-syrie.aspx?lang=eng

Foreign Affairs, Trade and Development Canada. (2014b). *Canada's response to the situation in Iraq.* Ottawa: Government of Canada. Retrieved from http://www.international.gc.ca/development-developpement/humanitarian_response-situations_crises/index.aspx?lang=eng

Foreign Affairs, Trade and Development Canada. (2015). *Canada's response to the situation in Syria.* Ottawa: Government of Canada. Retrieved from http://www.international.gc.ca/development-developpement/humanitarian_response-situations_crises/syria-syrie.aspx?lang=eng

Frederikson, L., Chamberlain, K., & Long, N. (1996). Unacknowledged casualties of the Vietnam War: Experiences of partners of New Zealand veterans. *Qualitative Health Research, 6*(1), 49–70.

Fremeth, H. (2010). Searching for the militarization of Canadian culture: The rise of a military-cultural memory network. *Topia* (York University), 23/24. Retrieved from /z_ebsco_a9h/ database.

Gabany, E., & Shellenbarger, T. (2010). Caring for families with development stress: How nurses can make a difference in the lives of military families. *American Journal of Nursing, 110*(11), 36–41.

Gaylord-Harden, N. K., Taylor, J. J., Campbell, C. L., Kesselring, C. M., & Grant, K. E. (2009). Maternal attachment and depressive symptoms in urban adolescents: The influence of coping strategies and gender. *Journal of Clinical Child & Adolescent Psychology, 38*(5), 684–695.

Geddes, J. (2006, August 28). Bullets fly. *Maclean's* 19, 22–29.

Gentile, B., Grabe, S., Dolan-Pascoe, B., Twenge, J. T., Wells, B. E., & Maitino, A. (2009). Gender differences in domain-specific self-esteem: A meta-analysis. *Review of General Psychology, 13*(1), 34–45.

Gerlock, A. A. (2004). Domestic violence and post-traumatic stress disorder severity for participants of a domestic violence rehabilitation program. *Military Medicine, 169,* 470–473.

Gerlock, A. A., Grimesey, J. L., & Sayre, G. (2014). Military-related posttraumatic stress disorder and intimate relationship behaviors: A developing dyadic relationship model. *Journal of Marital and Family Therapy, 40*(3), 344–356.

Gewirtz, A. H., Polusny, M. A., DeGarno, D. S., Khaylis, A., & Erbes, C. R. (2010). Posttraumatic stress symptoms among National Guard soldiers deployed to Iraq: Associations with parenting behaviors and couple adjustment. *Journal of Consulting and Clinical Psychology, 78*(5), 599–610.

Gewirtz, A., Polusny, C. E., Erber, C., & Forgatch, M. (2011). Helping military families through the deployment process: Strategies to support parenting. *Professional Psychology: Research and Practice, 42*(1), 56–62.

Gibbs, D. A., Clinton-Sherrod, M., & Johnson, R. E. (2012). Interpersonal conflict and referrals to counseling among married soldiers following return from deployment. *Military Medicine, 177,* 1178–1183.

Gifford, S., Hutchinson, J., & Gibson, M. (2011). Lifespan considerations in the psychological treatment of CF veterans with post-traumatic stress disorder. In A. B. Aiken & S. A. H. Belanger (Eds.), *Shaping the future: Military and veteran health research* (pp. 204–215). Kingston, ON: Canadian Defence Academy Press.

Gilreath, T., Astor, R., Cederbaum, J., Atuel, H., & Benbenishty, R. (2013). Prevalence and correlates of victimization and weapon carrying among military- and nonmilitary-connected youth in southern California. *Preventative Medicine, 60,* 21–26.

Gilreath, T., Cederbaum, J., Astor, R., Benbenishty, R., Pineda, D., & Atuel, H. (2013). Substance use among military-connected youth: The California healthy kids survey. *American Journal of Preventative Medicine, 44*(2), 150–153.

Glenn, D., Beckham, J., Feldman, M., Kirby, A., Hertzberg, M., & Moore, S. (2002). Violence and hostility among families of Vietnam veterans with combat-related posttraumatic stress disorder. *Violence and Victims, 17*(4), 473–489.

Godefroy, A. (2010). *Canada's international policy statement five years later.* Calgary, AB: Canadian Defence & Foreign Affairs Institute.

Golan, M., Hagay, N., & Tamir, S. (2014). Gender related differences in response to "In favor of myself" wellness program to enhance positive self and body image among adolescents. *PLOS One, 9*(3), 1–9.

Gosselin, M. D. (2009). Hellyer's ghosts: Unification of the Canadian Forces is 40 years old—Part Two. *Canadian Military Journal, 9*(30), 6–16.

Gouliquer, L., & Poulin, C. (2005). For better and for worse: Psychological demands and structural impacts on gay servicewomen and their long-term partners. In D. Pawluch, W. Shaffir, & C. Miall (Eds.), *Doing ethnography: Studying everyday life* (pp. 323–335). Toronto: Canadian Scholars' Press.

Government of Canada. (2008). *Speech by the Prime Minister of Canada: PM unveils revised motion on the future of Canada's mission in Afghanistan.* Ottawa: Government of Canada. Retrieved from http://news.gc.ca/web/article-en.do?crtr .sjlD=&mthd=advSrch&crtr.mnthndVl=&nid=380649&crtr.dptlD=&crtr .tplD=&crtr.lclD=&crtr.yrStrtVl=2008&crtr.kw=&crtr.dyStrtVl=26&crtr .audlD=&crtr.mnthStrtVl=2&crtr.yrndVl=&crtr.dyndVl=

Government of Canada. (2011, June 1). Backgrounder—Operation ATTENTION. Ottawa. Retrieved from http://www.forces.gc.ca/en/operations-abroad-current/op-attention.page

Government of Canada. (2013). History of Canada's engagement in Afghanistan 2001–2012. Retrieved from http://www.afghanistan.gc.ca/canada-afghanistan/progress-progres/timeline-chrono.aspx?lang=eng

Government of Canada. (2014, March 18). *Speech by the Prime Minister of Canada: PM delivers remarks welcoming home members of the Canadian Armed Forces returning from Canada's mission in Afghanistan at a ceremony in Ottawa.* Ottawa: Government of Canada. Retrieved from http://news.gc.ca/web/article-en.do?nid=826979

Government of Canada. (2015). *The Canadian Armed Forces legacy in Afghanistan.* Ottawa: Government of Canada. Retrieved from http://www.forces.gc.ca/en/operations-abroad-past/cafla.page

Granatstein, J. L. (2012). The end of peacekeeping? *Canada's History, 92*(5), 44–51.

Griffin, W. A., & Morgan, A. R. (1988). Conflict in maritally distressed military couples. *American Journal of Family Therapy, 16*(1), 14–22.

Hall, G. S. (1904). *Adolescence: Its psychology and its relations to physiology, anthropology, sociology, sex, crime, religion and education* (Vols. 1–2). New York: Appleton.

Hamby, S. L., Finkelhor, D., Ormrod, R., & Turner, H. (2004). *The juvenile victimization questionnaire (JVQ): Administration and scoring manual.* Durham: Crimes Against Children Research Center, University of New Hampshire. Retrieved from http://www.unh.edu/ccrc/pdf/jvq/CV55newedition04.pdf

Hango, D. (2006). The long-term effect of childhood residential mobility on educational attainment. *Sociological Quarterly, 47*(4), 631–664.

Harkness, L. L. (1993). Transgenerational transmission of war-related trauma. In J. P. Wilson & B. Raphael (Eds.), *International handbook of traumatic stress syndromes* (pp. 635–643). New York: Plenum.

Harrison, D., with Laliberté, L., Bertrand, M., Blaney, E., Deveau, J., Ericson, P., Friars, G., and Koller, A. (2002). *The first casualty: Violence against women in Canadian military communities.* Toronto: James Lorimer & Company.

Harrison, D. (2004). The Canadian Forces' response to woman abuse in military families. In M.L. Stirling et al. (Eds.), *Understanding abuse: Partnering for change* (pp. 155–194). Toronto: University of Toronto Press.

Harrison, D. (2006). The role of military culture in military organizations' responses to woman abuse in military families. *Sociological Review, 54,* 546–574.

Harrison, D., & Albanese, P. (2012). The "parentification" phenomenon as applied to adolescents living through parental military deployments. *Canadian Journal of Family and Youth, 4*(1), 1–27.

Harrison, D., Albanese, P., & Berman, R. (2014). Parent-adolescent relationships in military families affected by post-traumatic stress disorder. *Canadian Social Work Review, 31*(1), 81–103.

Harrison, D., & Laliberté, L. (1994). *No life like it: Military wives in Canada.* Toronto: James Lorimer & Company.

Harrison, D., & Laliberte, L. (1997). Gender, the military, and military family support. In L. Weinstein & C. White (Eds.), *Wives and warriors: Women and the military in the United States and Canada* (pp. 35–53). Westport, CT: Greenwood.

Harrison, D., Robson, K., Albanese, P., Sanders, C., & Newburn-Cook, C. (2011). The impact of shared location on the mental health of military and civilian adolescents in a community affected by frequent deployments: A research note. *Armed Forces and Society, 37*(3), 550–560.

Hartfiel, R. M. (2010). Planning without guidance: Canadian defence policy and planning, 1993–2004. *Canadian Public Administration, 53*(3).

Härting, H., & Kamboureli, S. (2009). Introduction: Discourses of security, peacekeeping narratives and the cultural imagination in Canada. *University of Toronto Quarterly, 78*(2), 659–686.

Hendrix, C. C., Erdmann, M. A., & Briggs, K. (1998). Impact of Vietnam veterans' arousal and avoidance on spouses' perceptions of family life. *American Journal of Family Therapy, 26*, 115–128.

Heyman, R. E., & Neidig, P. H. (1999). A comparison of spousal aggression prevalence rates in U.S. army and civilian representative samples. *Journal of Consulting and Clinical Psychology, 67*(2), 239–242.

Holland, K., & Kirkey, C. (2010). Special issue introduction: Canada's commitment to Afghanistan. *American Review of Canadian Studies, 40*(2).

Holmes, A. K., Rauch, P. K., & Cozza, S. J. (2013). When a parent is injured or killed in combat. *The future of children: A collaboration of the Woodrow Wilson School of Public and International Affairs at Princeton University and the Brookings Institution, 23*(2), 143–162.

Hooper, L. (2007). Expanding the discussion regarding parentification and its varied outcomes: Implications for mental health research and practice. *Journal of Mental Health Counseling, 29*(4), 322–337.

Hooper, L. M., Moore, H. M., & Smith, A. K. (2014). Parentification in military families: Overlapping constructs and theoretical explorations in family, clinical, and military psychology. *Children and Youth Services Review, 39*, 123–134.

Houston, J. B., Pfefferbaum, B., Sherman, M. D., Melson, A., Jeon-Slaughter, H., Brand, M., & Jarman, Y. (2009). Children of deployed National Guard troops: Perceptions of parental deployment to Operation Iraqi Freedom. *Psychiatric Annals, 39*(8), 805–811.

Huebner, A., & Mancini, J. A. (2005). *Adjustments among adolescents in military families when a parent is deployed.* Lafayette, IN: Purdue University Military Family Research Institute.

Huebner, A., Mancini, J. A., Wilcox, R. M., Grass, S. R., & Grass, G. A. (2007). Parental deployment and youth in military families: Exploring uncertainty and ambiguous loss. *Family Relations, 56*, 112–122.

Janigan, M. (2003, February 10). Military myths. *Maclean's, 116*(6).

Jefferess, D. (2009). Responsibility, nostalgia, and the mythology of Canada as a peacekeeper. *University of Toronto Quarterly, 78*(2), 709–727.

Jelleyman, T., & Spencer, N. (2008). Residential mobility in childhood and health outcomes: A systematic review. *Journal of Epidemiology & Community Health*, *62*(7), 584–592.

Jensen, P. S., Martin, D., & Wantanabe, H. (1996). Children's response to parental separation during Operation Desert Storm. *Journal of the American Academy of Child and Adolescent Psychiatry*, *35*(4), 433–441.

Jiwani, Y. (2009). Helpless maidens and chivalrous knights: Afghan women in the Canadian press. *University of Toronto Quarterly*, *78*(2), 728–744.

Johnson, H. L., & Ling, C. G. (2013). Caring for military children in the 21st century. *Journal of the American Association of Nurse Practitioners*, *25*, 195–202.

Jones, J. W. (1983). *Children of alcoholics screening test*. Chicago: Camelot Unlimited.

Jordan, B. K., Marmar, C. R., Fairbank, J. A., Schlenger, W. E., Kulka, R. A., Hough, R. L., & Weiss, D. S. (1992). Problems in families of male Vietnam veterans with posttraumatic stress disorder. *Journal of Consulting and Clinical Psychology*, *60*(6), 916–926.

Kasurak, P. (2013). *A national force: The evolution of Canada's army, 1950–2000*. Vancouver: UBC Press.

Keating, T. (1993). *Canada and world order*. Toronto: McClelland & Stewart.

Kelley, M. L. (1994). Military-induced separation in relation to maternal adjustment and children's behaviors. *Military Psychology*, *6*(3), 163–176.

Kenny, C., Tkachuk, D., Banks, T., Day, J. A., Mitchell, G., Meighen, M. A., …Zimmer. R. A. A. (2008). *How are we doing in Afghanistan? Canadians need to know*. Report of the Standing Senate Committee on National Security and Defence. Ottawa.

Kenny, M. E., Gallagher, L. A., Alvarez-Salvat, R., & Silsby, J. (2002). Sources of support and psychological distress among academically successful inner-city youth. *Adolescence*, *37*(145), 161–182.

King, D., Taft, C., King, L., Hammond, C., & Stone, E. (2006). Directionality of the association between social support and posttraumatic stress disorder: A longitudinal investigation. *Journal of Applied Social Psychology*, *36*(12), 2980–2992.

Knobloch, L. K., Pusateri, K. B., Ebata, A. T., & McGlaughlin, P. C. (2015). Experiences of military youth during a family member's deployment: Changes, challenges, and opportunities. *Youth & Society*, *47*(3), 319–342.

Kohler, N. (2012). *Signs of operational stress injury (OSI) and the family*. Valcartier, QC: Valcartier Family Centre.

Krause-Parello, C. A. (2008). Loneliness in the school setting. *Journal of School Nursing*, *24*(2), 66–70.

Kudler, H., & Porter, R. (2013). Building communities of care for military children and families. *The future of children: A collaboration of the Woodrow Wilson School of Public and International Affairs at Princeton University and the Brookings Institution*, *23*(2), 163–185.

Kwan-Lafond, D., Harrison, D., & Albanese, P. (2011). Parental military deployments and adolescents' household work. *Studies in Political Economy*, *88*, 161–188.

Lambert, J. E., Engh, R., Hasbun, A., & Holzer, J. (2012). Impact of posttraumatic stress disorder on the relationship quality and psychological distress of intimate partners: A meta-analytic review. *Journal of Family Psychology, 26*(5), 729–737.

Lara-Cinisomo, S., Chandra, A., Burns, R., Jaycox, L. H., Tanielian, T., Ruder, T., & Han, B. (2012). A mixed-method approach to understanding the experiences of non-deployed military caregivers. *Maternal & Child Health Journal, 16*(2), 374–384.

Laser, J. A., & Stephens, P. M. (2011). Working with military families through deployment and beyond. *Clinical Social Work Journal, 39*, 28–38.

Lease, S., & Yanico, B. J. (1995). Evidence of validity for the children of alcoholics screening test. *Measurement and Evaluation in Counseling and Development, 27*, 200–210.

Leckie, G. (2008). Modelling the effects of pupil mobility and neighbourhood on school differences in educational achievement. *CMPO Working Paper Series, 08*(189).

Lemmon, K. M., & Chartrand, M. M. (2009). Caring for America's children: Military youth in time of war. *Pediatrics in Review, 30*(6), 42–48.

Lester, P., & Flake, E. (2013). How wartime military service affects children and families. *The future of children: A collaboration of the Woodrow Wilson School of Public and International Affairs at Princeton University and the Brookings Institution, 23*(2), 121–142.

Lewis, T. D. (1996). *Oromocto, New Brunswick, from village to model town: Rural community transformed* (Unpublished master's thesis). University of New Brunswick, Fredericton.

Lewis-Fleming, G. (2014). Reaching across boundaries: A military providers and public schools partnership on behalf of children with special needs. *Military Medicine, 179*(8), 920–925.

Lietz, C., Stromwall, L., & Carlson, B. (2013). Women service members and family reintegration. *Families in Society, 94*(3), 186–193.

Lincoln, A. J., & Sweeten, K. (2011). Considerations for the effects of military deployment on children and families. *Social Work in Health Care, 50*(1), 73–84.

Lincoln, A., Swift, E., & Shorteno-Frazer, M. (2008). Psychological adjustment and treatment of children and families with parents deployed in military combat. *Journal of Clinical Psychology, 64*(8), 984–992.

Lofland, J. (2006). *Analyzing social settings: A guide to qualitative observation and analysis.* Belmont, CA: Wadsworth.

Logan, K. V. (1987). The emotional cycle of deployment. *Proceedings, 113*, 43–47.

Lucier-Greer, M., Arnold, A. L., Mancini, J., Ford, J., & Bryant, C. (2015). Influences of cumulative risk and protective factors on the adjustment of adolescents in military families. *Family Relations, 64*(3), 363–377.

Lum, J., & Phares, V. (2005). Assessing the emotional availability of parents. *Journal of Psychopathology & Behavioral Assessment, 27*(3), 211–226.

Lytle, L., Hearst, M., Fulkerson, J., Murray, D., Martinson, B., Klein, E., . . . Samuelson, A. (2011). Examining the relationships between family meal practices, family stressors, and the weight of youth in the family. *Annals of Behavioral Medicine, 41*(3), 353-362.

Maccoby, E. (1992). Family structure and children's adjustment: Is quality of parenting the major mediator? *Monographs of the Society for Research in Child Development, 57*(2/3), 230–238.

MacDonald, C., Chamberlain, K., Long, N., & Flett, R. (1999). Posttraumatic stress disorder and interpersonal functioning in Vietnam War veterans: A mediational model. *Journal of Traumatic Stress, 12*(4), 701–707.

Managhan, T. (2012). Highways, heroes, and secular martyrs: The symbolics of power and sacrifice. *Review of International Studies, 38*(1), 97–118.

Manley, J., Burney, D., Epp, J., Tellier, P., & Wallin, P. (2008). *Independent panel on Canada's future role in Afghanistan.* Ottawa: Government of Canada.

Mansfield, A. J., Kaufman, J. S., Engel, C. C., & Gaynes, B. N. (2011). Deployment and mental health diagnoses among children of U.S. army personnel. *Archives of Pediatric and Adolescent Medicine, 165*(11), 999–1005.

Mansfield, A. J., Kaufman, J. S., Marshall, S. W., Gaynes, B. N., Morrissey, J. P., & Engel, C. C. (2010). Deployment and the use of mental health services among U.S. army wives. *New England Journal of Medicine, 362*(2), 101–109.

Marin, A. (2001). *Special report to the Minister of National Defence on the systemic treatment of CF members with PTSD.* Ottawa: Department of National Defence and Canadian Forces Ombudsman.

Marin, A. (2002). *Follow-up report: Review of DND/CF actions on operational stress injuries.* Ottawa: Department of National Defence and Canadian Forces Ombudsman.

Marin, A. (2003). *Off the rails—crazy train float mocks operational stress injury sufferers.* Ottawa: Department of National Defence and Canadian Forces Ombudsman.

McCarroll, J. E., Ursano, R. J., Liu, X., Thayer, L. E., Newby, J. H., Norwood, A. E., & Fullerton, C.S. (2000). Deployment and the probability of spousal aggression by U.S. army soldiers. *Military Medicine, 165*(1), 41–44.

McCubbin, H. I., & Figley, C. R. (1983). Bridging normative and catastrophic family stress. In H. I. McCubbin & C. R. Figley (Eds.), *Stress and the family: Vol. 1. Coping with normative transitions* (5th ed., pp. 218–229). New York: Brunner/Mazel.

McFadyen, M. (2008a). *A long road to recovery: Battling operational stress injuries. Second review of the Department of National Defence and Canadian Forces' action on operational stress injuries.* Ottawa: Department of National Defence and Canadian Forces Ombudsman.

McFadyen, M. (2008b). *Assessing the state of mental health services at CFB Petawawa.* Ottawa: Department of National Defence and Canadian Forces Ombudsman.

Medway, F. J., Davis, K. E., Cafferty, T. P., Chappell, K. D., & O'Hearn, R. E. (1995). Family disruption and adult attachment correlates of spouse and child reactions to separation and reunion due to Operation Desert Storm. *Journal of Social and Clinical Psychology, 14*(2), 97–118.

Melvin, K. C., Gros, D., Hayat, M. J., Jennings, B. M., & Campbell, J. C. (2012). Couple functioning and post-traumatic stress symptoms in U.S. army couples: The role of resilience. *Research in Nursing & Health, 35*(2), 164–177.

Middlemiss, D., & Stairs, D. (2002). Canadian Forces and the doctrine of interoperability: The issues. *Policy Matters, 3*(7), 3–4.

Miedema, B., & Wachholz, S. (1998). *A complex web: Access to justice for abused immigrant women in New Brunswick*. Ottawa: Research Directorate Status of Women Canada.

Milburn, N., & Lightfoot, M. (2013). Adolescents in wartime US military families: A developmental perspective on challenges and resources. *Clinical Child and Family Psychology Review, 16*(3), 266–277.

Mmari, K. N., Bradshaw, C. P., & Sudhinaraset, M. (2010). Exploring the role of social connectedness among military youth: Perceptions from youth, parents and school personnel. *Child Youth Care Forum, 39*(5), 351–366.

Mmari, K., Roche, K., Sudhinaraset, M., & Blum, R. (2009). When a parent goes off to war: Exploring the issues faced by adolescents and their families. *Youth & Society, 40*(4), 455–475.

Moksnes, U. K., & Espnes, G. A. (2013). Self-esteem and life satisfaction in adolescents—gender and age as potential markers. *Quality of Life Research, 22*(10), 2921–2928.

Moksnes, U. K., & Espnes, G. A. (2014). Stress, sense of coherence and emotional symptoms in adolescents. *Psychology & Health, 29*(1), 32–49.

Morris, A. S., & Age, T. R. (2009). Adjustment among youth in military families: The protective roles of effortful control and maternal social support. *Journal of Applied Developmental Psychology, 30*, 695–707.

Murray, R.W., & McCoy, M. J. (2010). From middle power to peacebuilder: The use of the Canadian Forces in modern Canadian foreign policy. *American Review of Canadian Studies, 40*(2), 171–188.

Nelson Goff, B. S., Crow, J. R., Reisbig, A. M. J., & Hamilton, S. (2007). The impact of individual trauma symptoms of deployed soldiers on relationship satisfaction. *Journal of Family Psychology, 21*(3), 344–353.

Norwood, A. E., Fullerton, C. S., & Hagen, K. P. (1996). Those left behind: Military families. In R. J. Ursano & A. E. Norwood (Eds.), *Emotional aftermath of the Persian Gulf War: Veterans, families, communities, and nations* (pp. 163–196). Washington, DC: American Psychiatric Association.

Orcutt, H., King, L., & King, D. (2003). Male-perpetrated violence among Vietnam veteran couples: Relationships with veteran's early life characteristics, trauma history, and PTSD symptomatology. *Journal of Traumatic Stress, 16*(4), 381–390.

O'Toole, B. I., Outram, S., Catts, S. V., & Pierse, K. R. (2010). The mental health of partners of Australian Vietnam veterans three decades after the war and its relation to veteran military service, combat, and PTSD. *Journal of Nervous and Mental Disease, 198*(11), 841–845.

Paley, B., Lester, P., & Mogil, C. (2013). Family systems and ecological perspectives on the impact of deployment on military families. *Clinical Child and Family Psychology Review, 16*(3), 245–265.

Paré, J., & Radford, M. (2013). *Current issues in mental health in Canada: Mental health in the Canadian Forces and among veterans.* Publication No. 2013-91-E. Ottawa: Library of Parliament.

Park, N. (2011). Military children and families: Strengths and challenges during peace and war. *American Psychologist, 66*(1), 65–72.

Parsons, J., Kehle, T., & Owen, S. V. (1990). Incidence of behavior problems among children of Vietnam War veterans. *School Psychology International, 11*(4), 253–259.

Pedersen, F. A. (1966). Relationships between father-absence and emotional disturbance in male military dependents. *Merrill-Palmer Quarterly, 12*, 321–331.

Peebles-Kleiger, M. J., & Kleiger, J. H. (1994). Re-integration stress for Desert Storm families: Wartime deployments and family trauma. *Journal of Traumatic Stress, 7*(2), 173–194.

Pincus, S. H., House, R., Christenson, J., & Adler, L. E. (2005). The emotional cycle of deployment: A military family perspective. *Journal of the Army Medical Department*, 615–623.

Pittman, J., Kerpelman, J., & McFadyen, J. (2004). Internal and external adaptation in Army families: Lessons from Operations Desert Shield and Desert Storm. *Family Relations, 53*(3), 249–260.

Poulin, C., & Gouliquer, L. (2012). Clandestine existences and secret research: Eliminating official discrimination in the Canadian military and going public in academia. *Journal of Lesbian Studies, 16*(1), 54–64.

Poulin, C., Gouliquer, L., & Moore, J. (2009). Discharged for homosexuality from the Canadian military: Health implications for lesbians. *Feminism & Psychology, 19*(4), 496–516.

Price, J., Monson, C., Callahan, K., & Rodriguez, B. (2006). The role of emotional functioning in military-related PTSD and its treatment. *Journal of Anxiety Disorders, 20*(5), 661–674.

Ray, S. L., & Vanstone, M. (2009). The impact of PTSD on veterans' family relationships: An interpretative phenomenological inquiry. *International Journal of Nursing Studies, 46*, 838–847.

Reed, S. C., Bell, J. F., & Edwards, T. C. (2011). Adolescent well-being in Washington state military families. *American Journal of Public Health, 101*(9), 1676–1682.

Renshaw, K. D., Allen, E. S., Rhoades, G. K., Blais, R. K., Markman, H. J., & Stanley, S. M. (2011). Distress in spouses of service members with symptoms of combat-related PTSD: Secondary traumatic stress or general psychological distress? *Journal of Family Psychology, 25*(4), 461–469.

Rentz, E. D., Martin, S. L., Gibbs, D. A., Clinton-Sherrod, M., Hardison, J., & Marshall, S. W. (2006). Family violence in the military: A review of the literature. *Trauma, Violence & Abuse, 7*(2), 93–108.

Repetti, R., Wang, S., & Saxbe, D. (2009). Bringing it all back home: How outside stressors shape families' everyday lives. *Current Directions in Psychological Science, 18*(2), 106–111.

Richardson, A., Chandra, A., Martin, L.T., Setodji, C.M., Hallmark, B.W., Campbell, N.F., …Grady, P. (2011). *Effects of soldiers' deployment on children's academic performance and behavioral health.* Santa Monica, CA: Rand Corporation.

Riggs, D. S., Byrne, C. A., Weathers, F. W., & Litz, B. T. (1998). The quality of the intimate relationships of male Vietnam veterans: Problems associated with posttraumatic stress disorder. *Journal of Traumatic Stress, 11*(1), 87–101.

Riggs, S. A., & Riggs, D. S. (2011). Risk and resilience in military families experiencing deployment: The role of the family attachment network. *Journal of Family Psychology, 25*(5), 675–687.

Robson, K., Albanese, P., Harrison, D., & Sanders, C. (2013). School engagement among youth in Canadian Forces families: A comparative analysis. *Alberta Journal of Educational Research, 59*(3), 363–381.

Roeher Institute. (1995). *In harm's way: The many faces of violence and abuse against persons with disabilities.* Toronto: Author.

Rolland-Harris, E., Whitehead, J., Matheson, H., & Zamorski, M. (2015). *2015 Report on suicide mortality in the Canadian Armed Forces (1995 to 2014).* Surgeon General Report. Ottawa: National Defence/Canadian Armed Forces.

Rosen, L. N., & Teitelbaum, J. M. (1993). Children's reactions to the Desert Storm deployment: Initial findings from a survey of Army families. *Military Medicine, 158*(7), 465–469.

Rosenheck, R. (1986). Impact of posttraumatic stress disorder of World War II on the next generation. *Journal of Nervous and Mental Disease, 174*(6), 319–327.

Rosenheck, R., & Nathan, P. (1985). Secondary traumatization in children of Vietnam veterans. *Hospital and Community Psychiatry, 36*(5), 538–539.

Rossetto, K. (2015). Developing conceptual definitions and theoretical models of coping in military families during deployment. *Journal of Family Communication, 15*(3), 249–268.

Ruscio, A. M., Weathers, F. W., King, L. A., & King, D. W. (2002). Male war-zone veterans' perceived relationships with their children: The importance of emotional numbing. *Journal of Traumatic Stress, 15*(5), 351–357.

Saltzman, W., Pynoos, R., Lester, P., Layne, C., & Beardslee, W. (2013). Enhancing family resilience through family narrative co-construction. *Clinical Child and Family Psychology Review, 16*(3), 294–310.

Samper, R. E., Taft, C. T., King, D. W., & King, L. A. (2004). Posttraumatic stress disorder symptoms and parenting satisfaction among a national sample of male Vietnam veterans. *Journal of Traumatic Stress, 17*(4), 311–315.

Sanchez, Y., Lambert, S., & Colley-Stickland, M. (2013). Adverse life events, coping and internalizing and externalizing behaviors in urban African American youth. *Journal of Child and Family Studies, 22*(1), 38–47.

Savarese, V. W., Suvak, M. K., King, L. A., & King, D. W. (2001). Relationships among alcohol use, hyperarousal, and marital abuse and violence in Vietnam veterans. *Journal of Traumatic Stress, 14*(4), 717–732.

Sayer, N. A., Noorbaloochi, S., Frazier, P., Carlson, K., Gravely, A., & Murdoch, M. (2010). Reintegration problems and treatment interests among Iraq and Afghanistan combat veterans receiving VA medical care. *Psychiatric Services, 61*(6), 589–597.

Sayers, S. L., Farrow, V. A., Ross, J., & Oslin, D. W. (2009). Family problems among recently returned military veterans referred for a mental health evaluation. *Journal of Clinical Psychiatry, 70*(2), 163–170.

Schoenfeld, A. J., Nelson, J. H., Burks, R., Belmont, P. J., Jr. (2013). Temporal changes in combat casualties from Afghanistan by nationality: 2006–2010. *Military Medicine, 178*(4), 389–393.

Segal, D., Segal, M., & Eyre, D. (1992). The social construction of peacekeeping in America. *Sociological Forum, 7*(1), 121–136.

Segal, M. W. (1986). The military and the family as greedy institutions. *Armed Forces & Society, 13*(1), 9–38.

Seiffge-Krenke, I. (2004). Adaptive and maladaptive coping styles: Does intervention change anything? *European Journal of Developmental Psychology, 1*(4), 367–382.

Shaler, L., Hathaway, W., Sells, J., & Youngstedt, S. (2013). Correlates of anger among Operation Enduring Freedom and Operation Iraqi Freedom veterans. *Journal of Military and Government Counseling, 1*(3), 136–151.

Sheppard, S., Malatras, J. W., & Israel, A. (2010). The impact of deployment on U.S. military families. *American Psychologist, 65*(6), 599–609.

Siegel, B. S., Davis, B. E., & and the Committee on Psychological Aspects of Child and Family Health and Section on Uniformed Services. (2013). Health and mental health needs of children in US military families. *Pediatrics, 131*(6), e2002–e2015.

Simpson, G. A., & Fowler, M. G. (1994). Geographical mobility and children's emotional/behavioral adjustment and school functioning. *Pediatrics, 93*(2), 303–309.

Simpson, J. (2014, January 16). *Afghanistan Taliban 'confident of victory' over NATO.* BBC News. Retrieved from http://www.bbc.com/news/world-asia -25765603

Skomorovsky, A. (2014). Deployment stress and well-being among military spouses: The role of social support. *Military Psychology, 26*(1), 44–54.

Small, S. A. (1995). Action-oriented research: Models and methods. *Journal of Marriage and Family, 57*(4), 941–955.

Smith, G. (2013). *The dogs are eating them now: Our war in Afghanistan.* Toronto: Alfred A. Knopf.

Snyder, V. (2013). Caring for each other, together and apart: Military families in Canada. *Transition, 43*(1), 5–7.

Solomon, Z., Mikulincer, M., Freid, B., & Wosner, Y. (1987). Family characteristics and posttraumatic stress disorder: A follow-up of Israeli combat stress reaction casualties. *Family Process, 26*, 383–394.

Solomon, Z., Waysman, M., Levy, G., Fried, B., Mikulincer, M., Benbenishty,... Bleich, A. (1992). From front line to home front: A study of secondary traumatization. *Family Process, 31*, 289–302.

South, S., & Haynie, D. (2004). Friendship networks of mobile adolescents. *Social Forces, 83*(1), 315–350.

Statistics Canada. (1997). *National longitudinal survey of children and youth 1994–1995: Public use microdata files user's documentation.* Ottawa: Statistics Canada.

Statistics Canada. (2006). *Census profiles.* Ottawa: Statistics Canada.

Statistics Canada. (2014a). *Census profiles.* Ottawa: Statistics Canada.

Statistics Canada. (2014b). *National longitudinal survey of children and youth (NLSCY).* Ottawa: Statistics Canada. Retrieved from http://www23.statcan.gc.ca/imdb/p2SV.pl?Function=getSurvey&SDDS=4450

Statistics Canada. (Undated). *Microdata user guide. National longitudinal survey of children and youth: Cycle 7 (September 2006–June 2007).* Retrieved from http://www23.statcan.gc.ca/imdb-bmdi/document/4450_D4_T9_V7-eng.pdf

Steelfisher, G. K., Zaslavsky, A. M., & Blendon, R. J. (2008). Health-related impact of deployment extensions on spouses of active duty army personnel. *Military Medicine, 173*(3), 221–229.

Stein, J. G., & Lang, E. (2007). *The unexpected war: Canada in Kandahar.* Toronto: Penguin.

Steinberg, S. J., & Davila, J. (2008). Romantic functioning and depressive symptoms among early adolescent girls: The moderating role of parental emotional availability. *Journal of Clinical Child & Adolescent Psychology, 37*(2), 350–362.

Strauss, A., & Corbin, J. (1990). *Basics of qualitative research: Grounded theory procedures and techniques.* Newbury Park, CA: Sage Publications.

Sudom, K. (2009). *Family violence in the Canadian Forces.* Ottawa: Department of National Defence Canada, Director General Military Personnel Research & Analysis.

Sudom, K. (2010). *Quality of life among military families: Results from the 2008–2009 survey of Canadian Forces spouses.* Ottawa: Department of National Defence Canada.

Sudom, K., & Dursun, S. (2006). *The relationship study: Qualitative findings.* Ottawa: Department of National Defence Canada, Centre for Operational Research and Analysis.

Sudom, K., Zamorski, M., & Garber, B. (2012). Stigma and barriers to mental health care in deployed Canadian Forces personnel. *Military Psychology, 24*(4), 414–431.

Sullivan, T. A. (2014). Greedy institutions, overwork, and work–life balance. *Sociological Inquiry, 84*(1), 1–15.

Swenson, R., & Wolff, J. (2011). Deployment for military families carries emotional and behavioural consequences. *Brown University Child and Adolescent Behavior Letter, 27*(10), 5–7.

Taber, N. (2013). A composite life history of a mother in the military: Storying gendered experiences. *Women's Studies International Forum, 36*(2), 16–25.

Taft, C. T., Schumm, J. A., Panuzio, J., & Proctor, S. P. (2008). An examination of family adjustment among Operation Desert Storm veterans. *Journal of Consulting and Clinical Psychology, 76*(4), 648–656.

Taft, C. T., Street, A. E., Marshall, A. D., & Dowdall, D. J. (2007). Posttraumatic stress disorder, anger, and partner abuse among Vietnam combat veterans. *Journal of Family Psychology, 21*(2), 270–277.

Taft, C. T., Vogt, D. S., Marshall, A. D., Panuzio, J., & Niles, B. L. (2007). Aggression among combat veterans: Relationships with combat exposure and symptoms of posttraumatic stress disorder, dysphoria, and anxiety. *Journal of Traumatic Stress, 20*(2), 135–145.

Taft, C. T., Watkins, L. E., Stafford, J., Street, A. E., & Monson, C. M. (2011). Posttraumatic stress disorder and intimate relationship problems: A meta-analysis. *Journal of Consulting and Clinical Psychology, 79*(1), 22–33.

Ternus, M. (2008). *Military women's perceptions of the effect of deployment on their role as mothers and on adolescents' health.* Paper presented at the 114th Annual Meeting of the Association of Military Surgeons of the United States, San Antonio, TX.

Teten, A. L., Schumacher, J. A., Taft, C. T., Stanley, M. A., Kent, T. A., Bailey, S. D.,... White, D. L. (2010). Intimate partner aggression perpetrated and sustained by male Afghanistan, Iraq, and Vietnam veterans with and without posttraumatic stress disorder. *Journal of Interpersonal Violence, 25*(9), 1612–1630.

Theiss, J., & Knobloch, L. (2014). Relational turbulence and the post-deployment transition: Self, partner, and relationship focused turbulence. *Communication Research, 41*(1), 27–51.

Thompson, D. E., Baptist, J., Miller, B., & Henry, U. (2015, February 24). Children of the U.S. National Guard: Making meaning and responding to parental deployment. *Youth & Society,* 1–17. doi: 10.1177/0044118X15570883

TorStar News Service. (2010, November 5). Tories' secret Afghan casualty list revealed. *Hamilton Spectator.* Retrieved from http://www.thespec.com/news-story/2130516-tories-secret-afghan-casualty-list-revealed/

Travis, W., Collins, P., McCarthy, R., Rabenhorst, M., & Milner, J. (2014). Characteristics associated with incidents of family maltreatment among United States Air Force families. *Military Medicine, 179*(11), 1244–1249.

Treasury Board of Canada. (2007). *Expenditure review of federal public sector: Vol. 2. Compensation snapshot and historical perspective, 1990 to 2003.* Ottawa: Author.

Ungar, M., Theron, L., & Didkowsky, N. (2011). Adolescents' precocious and developmentally appropriate contributions to their families' well-being and resilience in five countries. *Family Relations, 60*(2), 231–246.

United Nations High Commissioner for Refugees. (2015). Syrian Arab Republic. Geneva: Author. Retrieved from http://www.unhcr.org/pages/49e486a76.html

Urban, S., Wang, Z. & Dunn, J. (2011). *The employment status and experiences of CF spouses.* Retrieved from https://www.cfmws.com/en/AboutUs/MFS/FamilyResearch/Documents/DGPRAM/Employment/The%20Employment%20Status%20and%20Experience%20of%20CF%20Spouses.pdf

Valdez, C., Chavez, T., & Woulfe, J. (2013). Emerging adults' lived experience of formative family stress: The family's lasting influence. *Qualitative Health Research, 23*(8), 1089–1102.

Van Winkle, E. P., & Lipari, R. N. (2015). The impact of multiple deployments and social support on stress levels of women married to active duty servicemen. *Armed Forces & Society, 41*(3), 395–412.

Vanier Institute of the Family. (2012). *Military families: By the numbers.* Ottawa: Author.

Vanier Institute of the Family. (2015). *Definition of family.* Ottawa: Vanier Institute of the Family. Retrieved from http://vanierinstitute.ca/definition-family

Verbosky, S. J., & Ryan, D. A. (1988). Female partners of Vietnam veterans: Stress by proximity. *Issues in Mental Health Nursing, 9,* 95–104.

Verdeli, H., Baily, C., Vousoura, E., Belser, A., Singla, D., & Manos, G. (2011). The case for treating depression in military spouses. *Journal of Family Psychology, 25*(4), 488–496.

Vernberg, E., Greenhoot, A., & Biggs, B. (2006). Intercommunity relocation and adolescent friendships: Who struggles and why? *Journal of Consulting and Clinical Psychology, 74*(3), 511–523.

Veterans Affairs Canada. (2015). *Understanding mental health.* Ottawa. Retrieved from http://www.veterans.gc.ca/eng/services/health/mental-health/understanding-mental-health

Visser-Meily, A., Post, M., Meijer, A. M., Maas, C., Ketelaar, M., & Lindeman, E. (2005). Children's adjustment to a parent's stroke: Determinants of status and psychological problems, and the role of support from the rehabilitation team. *Journal of Rehabilitation Medicine, 37,* 236–241.

Vuga, J., & Juvan, J. (2013). Work-family conflict between two greedy institutions—the family and the military. *Current Sociology, 61*(7), 1058–1077.

Waasdorp, C. E., Caboot, J. B., Robinson, C. A., Abraham, A. A., & Adelman, W. P. (2007). Screening military dependent adolescent females for disordered eating. *Military Medicine, 172*(9), 962–967.

Watkins, D., Pittman, C., & Walsh, M. (2013). The effects of psychological distress, work, and family stressors on child behavior problems. *Journal of Comparative Family Studies, 44*(1), 1–16.

Waysman, M., Mikulincer, M., Solomon, Z., & Weisenberg, M. (1993). Secondary traumatization among wives of posttraumatic combat veterans: A family typology. *Journal of Family Psychology, 7*(1), 104–118.

Weathers, F. W., Litz, B. T., Herman, D. S., Huska, J. A., & Keane, T. M. (1993). *The PTSD checklist (PCL): Reliability, validity, and diagnostic utility.* San Antonio, TX: International Society for Traumatic Stress Studies.

Weber, E. G., & Weber, D. K. (2005). Geographic relocation frequency, resilience, and military adolescent behavior. *Military Medicine, 170*(7), 638–642.

Weiner, G. (2004). Critical action research and third wave feminism: A meeting of paradigms. *Educational Action Research, 12*(4), 631–644.

Werner, E. E., & Smith, R. S. (1992). *Overcoming the odds: High-risk children from birth to adulthood.* Ithaca, NY: Cornell University Press.

Wertsch, M. E. (1991). *Military brats: Legacies of childhood inside the fortress.* New York: Random House.

West, L., Mercer, S. O., & Altheimer, E. (1993). Operation Desert Storm: The response of a social work outreach team. *Social Work in Health Care, 19,* 81–98.

Westerink, J., & Giarratano, L. (1999). The impact of posttraumatic stress disorder on partners and children of Australian Vietnam veterans. *Australian & New Zealand Journal of Psychiatry, 33,* 841–847.

Wheaton, B., & Montazer, S. (2010). Stressors, stress, and distress. In T. L. Scheid & T. N. Brown (Eds.), *A handbook for the study of mental health: Social contexts, theories, and systems* (2nd ed., pp. 171–199). Cambridge: Cambridge University Press.

White, C. J., de Burgh, H. T., Fear, N. T., & Iversen, A. C. (2011). The impact of deployment to Iraq or Afghanistan on military children: A review of the literature. *International Review of Psychiatry, 23*(2), 210–217.

Wiens, T. W., & Boss, P. (2006). Maintaining family resiliency before, during, and after military separation. In C. A. Castro, A. B. Adler, & C. A. Britt (Eds.), *Military life: The psychology of serving in peace and combat* (pp. 13–39). Bridgeport, CT: Praeger Security International.

Williams, B. (2013). Supporting middle school students whose parents are deployed: Challenges and strategies for schools. *Clearing House, 86*(4), 128–135.

Wong, L., & Gerras, S. (2010). *The effects of multiple deployments on Army adolescents.* Carlisle, PA: Strategic Studies Institute, US War College.

Wuest, J., & Merritt-Gray, M. (2008). A theoretical understanding of abusive intimate partner relationships that become non-violent: Shifting the pattern of abusive control. *Journal of Family Violence, 23,* 281–293.

Zamorski, M. A., & Wiens-Kincaid, M. E. (2013). Cross-sectional prevalence survey of intimate partner violence perpetration and victimization in Canadian military personnel. *BMC Public Health, 13*(1019). doi: 10.1186/1471-2458-13-1019

Index

acting out, 71, 77, 115, 123, 132

Afghanistan mission: AHS initial response to, 1, 2; cost of, 19; end of, 180; overview, 17–21; as peace-building, 9–11, 17. *See also* Kanda-har combat mission

alcohol: abuse of, 39, 146, 152; use by adolescents, 34, 93, 142

ambiguous loss, 163, 186

anger: as adolescent reaction, 146, 159, 162, 168, 174; and family dy-namics, 152, 164; and the media, 89; over lack of school support, 128–29; over parental deployment, 70, 85; as PTSD symptom, 77, 146, 150–52, 160, 164, 210n1

anticipation, as pre-deployment phase. *See* pre-deployment

anxiety: in CAF adolescents, 190; in children of PTSD veterans, 162; in girls, 66, 67, 91–93; media reports as cause of, 90; in military families, 34, 69–70, 71, 115; over dangerous deployment, 75–78; parental de-parture and, 70, 79, 81, 84; parental deployment and, 72–73, 75, 77–79, 81, 84–85; parental safety and, 75, 85, 96, 115; during pre-deployment phase, 70–72, 75; and quality-of-life loss, 85; responsibility and, 115; self-reassurance and, 75–77; vari-ables in amount experienced, 70, 78. *See also* worry, coping with

Armyville: demographics, 43–44; as military community, 116, 118–19, 124; relative isolation of, 51–52, 188; as supportive environment, 124

Armyville High School (AHS): de-mographics, 44; participation in project, 3–5, 45, 173, 188; relation-ship with military, 1, 44–45; stu-dent feedback summary, 133–34. *See also* Armyville School District (ASD); deployment support, Ar-myville High School (AHS); guid-ance counsellors, AHS; teachers (AHS)

Armyville project: interview findings, gender and self-esteem, 54–62, 66, 67; interview findings, geo-graphical transfers and self-esteem, 62–65, 66–67; interview methodol-ogy, 52–54; interview schedule, 5, 54, 197–202; post-project, 180–83, 189–90; project methodology, 4–5; project origin, 1–4; quantitative survey methodology, 45–48; survey interpretation, 51–52, 66; survey results, 49–50; survey sample comparison, 50–51; symposium, 173–77; symposium follow-up, 177–80; symposium recommenda-tions, 203–4

Armyville School District (ASD), 4, 75, 124; collaboration with project,

Books in the Studies in Childhood and Family in Canada Series
Published by Wilfrid Laurier University Press

Making Do: Women, Family, and Home in Montreal during the Great Depression | Denyse Baillargeon; Yvonne Klein, translator | 1999 | ISBN 978-0-88920-326-6

Children in English-Canadian Society: Framing the Twentieth-Century Consensus | Neil Sutherland; with a new foreword by Cynthia Comacchio | 2000 | ISBN 978-0-88920-351-8

The Challenge of Children's Rights for Canada | Katherine Covell and R. Brian Howe | 2001 | ISBN 978-0-88920-380-8

Love Strong as Death: Lucy Peel's Canadian Journal, 1833–1836 | J.I. Little, editor | 2001 | ISBN 978-0-88920-389-230-X

Something to Cry About: An Argument against Corporal Punishment of Children in Canada | Susan M. Turner | 2002 | ISBN 978-0-88920-382-2

NFB Kids: Portrayals of Children by the National Film Board of Canada, 1939–1989 | Brian J. Low | 2002 | ISBN 978-0-88920-386-0

Freedom to Play: We Made Our Own Fun | Norah L. Lewis, editor | 2002 | ISBN 978-0-88920-406-5

Evangelical Balance Sheet: Character, Family, and Business in Mid-Victorian Nova Scotia | B. Anne Wood | 2006 | ISBN 978-0-88920-500-0

The Social Origins of the Welfare State: Quebec Families, Compulsory Education, and Family Allowances, 1940–1955 | Dominique Marshall; Nicola Doone Danby, translator | 2006 | ISBN 978-088920-452-2

A Question of Commitment: Children's Rights in Canada | R. Brian Howe and Katherine Covell, editors | 2007 | ISBN 978-1-55458-003-3

Taking Responsibility for Children | Samantha Brennan and Robert Noggle, editors | 2007 | ISBN 978-1-55458-015-6

Home Words: Discourses of Children's Literature in Canada | Mavis Reimer, editor | 2008 | ISBN 978-1-55458-016-3

The Dominion of Youth: Adolescence and the Making of Modern Canada, 1920–1950 | Cynthia Comacchio | 2006 | ISBN 978-0-88920-488-1

Depicting Canada's Children | Loren Lerner, editor | 2009 | ISBN 978-1-55458-050-7

Babies for the Nation: The Medicalization of Motherhood in Quebec, 1910–1970 | Denyse Baillargeon; W. Donald Wilson, translator | 2009 | ISBN 978-1-5548-058-3

The One Best Way? Breastfeeding History, Politics, and Policy in Canada | Tasnim Nathoo and Aleck Ostry | 2009 | ISBN 978-1-55458-147-4

Fostering Nation? Canada Confronts Its History of Childhood Disadvantage | Veronica Strong-Boag | 2011 | ISBN 978-1-55458-337-9

Cold War Comforts: Maternalism, Child Safety, and Global Insecurity, 1945–1975 | Tarah Brookfield | 2012 | ISBN 978-1-55458-623-3

Ontario Boys: Masculinity and the Idea of Boyhood in Postwar Ontario, 1945–1960 | Christopher Greig | 2014 | ISBN 978-1-55458-900-5

A Brief History of Women in Quebec | Denyse Baillargeon; W. Donald Wilson, translator | 2014 | ISBN 978-1-55458-950-0

With Children and Youth: Emerging Theories and Practices in Child and Youth Care Work | Kiaras Gharabaghi, Hans A. Skott-Myhre, and Mark Krueger, editors | 2014 | ISBN 978-1-55458-966-1

Abuse or Punishment? Violence Towards Children in Quebec Families, 1850–1969 | Marie-Aimée Cliche; W. Donald Wilson, translator | 2014 | ISBN 978-1-77712-063-0

Engendering Transnational Voices: Studies in Families, Work and Identities | Guida Man and Rina Cohen, editors | 2015 | ISBN 978-1-77112-112-5

Girls, Texts, Cultures | Clare Bradford and Mavis Reimer, editors | 2015 | ISBN 978-1-77112-020-3

Growing Up in Armyville: Canada's Military Families during the Afghanistan Mission | Deborah Harrison and Patrizia Albanese | 2016 | ISBN 978-1-77112-234-4